For your convenience, the code examples found in Advanced Quick C are available on disk. Save yourself the time and trouble of typing in the many useful examples in this book. Just fill out the order form below and send it, along with payment of $25.00, to:

> LawCom Co.
> Quick C Disk Order
> 593 S. 4th Ave.
> Yuma, AZ 85364
> No telephone orders please!

Order Form

Name _____

Address _____

City _____ State _____ Zip _____

Date _____

Please send me _____ disks to accompany Advanced Quick C, at **$25.00** each.

Disk Size (check one): _____ 5.25" _____ 3.5"

Method of payment:

_____ Check _____ Money Order _____ Visa _____ Master Card

Credit Card Number: _____

Expiration Date: _____

Signature: _____

Amount enclosed: $ _____

Advanced Quick C

Advanced Quick C

Ken Knecht

Scott, Foresman and Company
Glenview, Illinois   London

Cover photo: The Image Bank

Trademarks

IBM is a registered trademark of International Business Machines Corporation.

Data For Windows is a trademark of Vermont Creative Software.

Quick C is a registered trademark of Microsoft Corporation.

Microsoft is a registered trademark of Microsoft Corporation.

Qmodem is a trademark of the Forbin Project and John Friel III.

Library of Congress Cataloging-in-Publication Data

Knecht, Ken
    Advanced Quick C / Ken Knecht.
      p. cm.
    Includes index.
    1. C (Computer program language)   2. Quick C (Computer program)
    I. Title.
    QA76.73.C15K538   1989
    005.13'3--dc19   88-35975
                                                       CIP

1 2 3 4 5 6 RRC 94 93 92 91 90 89

ISBN 0-673-38396-2

Notice of Liability

The information in this book is distributed on an "As Is" basis, without warranty. Neither the author nor Scott, Foresman and Company shall have any liability to customer or any other person or entity with respect to any liability, loss, or damage caused or alleged to be caused directly or indirectly by the programs contained herein. This includes, but is not limited to, interruption of service, loss of data, loss of business or anticipatory profits, or consequential damages from the use of the programs.

Scott, Foresman professional books are available for bulk sales at quantity discounts. For information, please contact Marketing Manager, Professional Books Group, Scott, Foresman and Company, 1900 East Lake Avenue, Glenview, IL 60025.

CONTENTS

APPENDIX **A**

PROGRAMS WHERE FUNCTIONS APPEAR   508

INDEX

INTRODUCTION

This book was designed to help you learn how to program in C. You are expected to already know the basics of programming in the language; if not, you can probably use the useful programs included, but you probably won't learn too much. The version of Quick C used was 1.0.

Once you reach the point where you have an idea of what functions there are in the library and how to use them, you are ready for this book. In it you will be shown how to use the common C functions to put together your own useful applications. I firmly believe that the way to learn to program in C is to examine other programs that accomplish the same thing you are trying to do and that use the library functions you are trying to use. To that end, I have included a number of very useful functions that you might wish to use in your applications; as is or with your modifications. These include menus, windows, formatted data entry, sorts, merges, and much more. I do not recommend just blindly copying parts of various programs; you should understand how the pieces work and how to modify them for your specific purposes.

Frequently, you know what you want to accomplish but don't exactly know how to convert that wish into compilable, linkable C code. The examples in this book should give you a lot of ideas.

Techniques covered include:

- Changing character attributes
- Using the cursor keys in your programs
- Using the printer
- Using arrays
- Using structures
- Allocating memory for your buffers, etc.
- Using sequential files
- Using random access files
- Creating a database with indexing

1

- Sorting arrays, structures, and files
- Graphics
- Word wrap in windows
- Exploding and imploding windows
- Designing hash tables
- Merging sorted sequential files and arrays
- Merging unsorted sequential files and arrays

and many others.

The book does not contain a tutorial on using the Quick C environment or separate compilation and linking. Debugging will not be discussed.

The standard Quick C environment was used, with all the defaults set as they were when the compiler was received. All errors and warnings were enabled and all the programs compiled with no errors or warnings. The only exception is an occasional warning that a dummy variable was declared and set to some value but never used or that the stack overflowed.

The programs were written with the idea of providing easy-to-understand code with lots of annotations. No recursion was used. No effort was made to write space-efficient or fast programs. Thus, I would recommend some "tuning" if you are going to use these programs for serious computing. You will see that you can write useful C programs with the simplest instructions and functions and a minimum of hard-to-understand code. If you look at the source code for most commercial libraries (Data for Windows by Vermont Software comes immediately to mind), you'll see that their code is as simple as can be. The only difficulty in understanding it is the large number of constants used and defined elsewhere (usually in header files).

A disk containing the source code of all the examples is available.

All the programs ran quickly on my 286 clone, as well as my IBM 80.

The programs are almost all complete. I tried to avoid dividing a program into several functions, and then spreading the functions throughout the book. It annoys me no end to have to leaf here and there to find all the correct versions of the functions required to make the program go.

I have included a sort of functions index. In it I list all the functions used in the book examples, and with each a list of the program examples in which they appear.

You may not like the way I designed some of these programs; for example, where I used multidimensional character arrays you might prefer to use structures or arrays of pointers. (Of course, you can modify them as you wish.) I frequently chose the program designs I did because I think that many of the new C programmers are proficient in BASIC. Therefore, I tried to do things in the early programs the familiar way you would do them in BASIC. Later on I use structures and pointers more.

1

Menus

This chapter includes several programs that permit you to design your own pull-down, pop-up, "Lotus" style, or plain old vertical menus. If you use these routines, you need only supply the contents of the menu and a few other details. The menu windows position and size automatically.

All the programs are complete. A driver program is included with each of them to demonstrate the way to use the subroutines and to permit you to test the programs. This will hold true for almost all the programs in this book.

In almost all cases, I chose to keep all the program material together even if it is repeated several times in different programs in the book. I felt this was better than making you search through the book to find the appropriate functions.

In this and the other programs, you will often find long lines extended to the next line. The usual indentation is three spaces, and these are indented far more. Also, the previous line usually ends in a non-normal manner.

I chose to use multidimensional arrays to avoid confusion. You might wish to change these to arrays of pointers to strings—the headings and menu choices. You can put the headings and choices in separate menus. This modification will require quite a bit of rewriting, but it will teach you about pointers. Another possibility is to set up each menu as a structure in an array of structures. I simply chose the easiest way. You'll be seeing plenty of pointers and structures in other chapters' examples.

SIMPLE POP-UP MENU

The first program shows how to create a simple pop-up menu. "Pop-up" means that the menu choices under the selected menu heading are always visible. The menu heading is selected with the left- and right-arrow keys; the menu choice with the up- and down-arrow keys. The active choice is highlighted. The carriage return sends the selection back to the calling program.

```
/* Chapter 1, Example 1, QuickC, 03/13/88
   Pop-up menu */



#include <dos.h>
#include <stdio.h>
```

```
#include <string.h>
#include <conio.h>
#include <bios.h>



#define MAX_1       4        /* size of names array first
                                dimension */
#define MAX_2       4        /* size of names array second
                                dimension */
#define MAX_3       40       /* maximum length of menu
                                selection or header */
#define MAX_menu    3        /* maximum number of menus */
#define MAX_choice 4         /* maximum number of menu
                                choices */



/* function prototypes */
void get_key(int key []);
void p_menu(char names [] [MAX_2] [MAX_3],int *vpos,
            int *hpos);
int print_menu(char names [] [MAX_2] [MAX_3],
               int position [],int hpos,int vpos,int flag);
void outline(int position [],int hpos,int depth,int across);
void bioskey(int key []);
void gotoxy(int x,int y);
void main(void);
void hilite(int bright_char);
void clrscr(void);



void main(void)
{
   /* zero element included in dimension values */
   char names [MAX_1] [MAX_2] [MAX_3];
   int vpos,   /* vertical position (menu choice) */
       hpos;   /* horizontal position (menu heading
                  choice) */
   strcpy(&names [0] [0] [0],"Menu 1");
   strcpy(&names [0] [1] [0],"Menu 1, Choice 1");
   strcpy(&names [1] [1] [0],"Menu 1, Choice 2");
   strcpy(&names [2] [1] [0],""); /* indicate end of first
                                     menu */
```

```
strcpy(&names [1] [0] [0],"Menu 2");
strcpy(&names [0] [2] [0],"Menu 2, Choice 1");
strcpy(&names [1] [2] [0],"Menu 2, Choice 2");
strcpy(&names [2] [2] [0],"Menu 2, Choice 3");
strcpy(&names [3] [2] [0],"Menu 2, Choice 4");
strcpy(&names [2] [0] [0],"Menu 3");
strcpy(&names [0] [3] [0],"Menu 3, Choice 1");
strcpy(&names [1] [3] [0],"Menu 3, Choice 2");
strcpy(&names [2] [3] [0],"Menu 3, Choice 3");
strcpy(&names [3] [3] [0],"");  /* indicate end of third
                                   menu */

strcpy(&names [3] [0] [0],"");  /* indicate end of menu
                                   headings */

vpos = 0;  /* default */
hpos = 0;  /* default */

printf("\n");   /* required for following clscr() to work
                   properly in environment */

clrscr();

/* do it */
p_menu(names,&vpos,&hpos);

/* verify choice */
clrscr();
gotoxy(1,1);
printf("Heading choice was %s\n",names [hpos] [0]);
printf("Menu selection was %s\n",names [vpos] [hpos +
                                                 1]);

} /* end function main */



void get_key(int key [])
/* to get ASCII and scan codes */
{

   bioskey(key);

} /* end function get_key */
```

```
void p_menu(char names [] [MAX_2] [MAX_3],int *vpos,
            int *hpos)
{
    /* This function is used to initialize various variables
       and arrays in preparation for using the menu. It also
       gets the keystrokes provided by the operator to
       indicate the heading and menu choice. */

    char header [80]; /* composite first line of menu */
    int true = 1, /* for boolean type responses */
        false = 0,
        x = 0, /* menu position counter */
        flag = true, /* redisplay outline or not */
        y = MAX_menu, /* maximum number of menus */
        position [MAX_menu], /* horizontal position of
                                 beginning of each heading */
        key [2], /* keypress */
        depth = 0; /* number of menu selections */

    /* for get_key function */
    key [0] = 0;
    key [1] = 0;

    /* create menu header */
    header [0] = '\0';
    while (x <= y) {
        if (names [x] [0] [0] != '\0') { /* no more headers */
            /* keep track of header positions for positioning
               each menu */
            position [x] = strlen(header) + 1;

            /* add next header name */
            strcat(header,names [x] [0]);

            /* space between header names */
            strcat(header," ");
        }
        x++; /* next header */
    }
```

```
/* display header line */
gotoxy(1,1);
printf("%s",header);

/* print the menu */
depth = print_menu(names,position,*hpos,*vpos,flag);

/* use the menu */
/* get operator's commands */
while (key [0] != 13) {
    get_key(key);
    if (key [0] == 0) {
        switch (key [1]) {

            case 77: /* right-arrow */
                /* go right one heading */
                *hpos = *hpos + 1;
                if (*hpos > MAX_menu - 1) {
                    /* no heading to the right so start
                        over */
                    *hpos = 0;
                }
                clrscr();
                gotoxy(1,1);
                / *display header */
                printf("%s",header);
                *vpos = 0; /* default menu selection */
                flag = true; /* redisplay the outline */
                /* display the menu */
                depth = print_menu(names,position,*hpos,
                            *vpos,flag);
                break;

            case 75: /* left-arrow */
                /* go left one heading */
                *hpos = *hpos - 1;
                if (*hpos < 0) {
                    /* no heading to the left so start over */
                    *hpos = MAX_menu - 1;
                }
                clrscr();
                gotoxy(1,1);
```

```
         /* display the header */
         printf("%s",header);
         *vpos = 0; /* default menu choice */
         flag = true; /* redisplay the outline */
         /* display the menu */
         depth = print_menu(names,position,*hpos,
                            *vpos,flag);
         break;

  case 72: /* up-arrow */
      /* move up one menu selection */
      *vpos = *vpos - 1;
      if (*vpos < 0) {
         /* no more selections in that direction so
            start over */
         *vpos = depth - 1;
      }
      /* don't redisplay the outline */
      flag = false;
      /* display the menu */
      depth = print_menu(names,position,*hpos,
                         *vpos,flag);
      break;

  case 80: /* down-arrow */
      /* move down one menu selection */
      *vpos = *vpos + 1;
      if (*vpos > depth - 1) {
         /* no more selections that way so start
            over */
         *vpos = 0;
      }
      /* don't redisplay the outline */
      flag = false;
      /* display the menu */
      depth = print_menu(names,position,*hpos,
                         *vpos,flag);
      break;

default: /* not an arrow key */
   /* beep */
   putch(7);
```

```
                    break;
             } /* end switch */
        }

      else {
         /* if not a carriage return it's an invalid key */
         if (key [0] != 13)
             putch(7); /* beep */
      } /* end if */
   } /* end while */
} /* end pmenu function */


int print_menu(char names [] [MAX_2] [MAX_3],
               int position [],int hpos,int vpos,int flag)
/* display the menu */
{
    int x = 0, /* menu position counter */
        y = MAX_choice, /* maximum number of menu choices */
        across = strlen(names [hpos] [0]), /* menu column
                                         width default */
        true = 1, /* for boolean type responses */
        depth = 0, /* number of menu selections */
        counter,
        bright_char;

    while (x < y && names [x] [hpos + 1] [0] != '\0') {
       gotoxy(position [hpos] + 1,x + 3);
       if (x == vpos) {    /* highlight selected choice */
          bright_char = 32; /* space */
          hilite(bright_char); /* spaces before choice */
          hilite(bright_char);

          /* step through menu choice */
          for (counter = 0; counter < strlen(names [x]
                              [hpos + 1]); counter++) {
             gotoxy(position [hpos] + counter + 1,x + 3);
             bright_char = names [x] [hpos + 1] [counter];
             hilite(bright_char);
          }
       }
```

```
          else
             /* display without highlight */
             printf("%s",names [x] [hpos + 1]);

          /* find longest menu line and put value in across */
          if (strlen(names [x] [hpos + 1]) > across)
             across = strlen(names [x] [hpos + 1]);
          depth++;
          x++;
      }

      if (flag == true)
          outline(position,hpos,depth,across);
      return depth;
} /* end print_menu function */



void outline(int position [],int hpos,int depth,int across)
{
      /* this function provides the double-line outline around
         the menu */
      int x; /* counter */

      /* draw top */
      gotoxy(position [hpos],2);
      putch(201); /* upper-left corner character */
      for (x - 2;x <= across | 1;x++)
          putch(205); /* horizontal double-line character */
      putch(187); /* upper-right corner character */

      /* draw sides */
      gotoxy(position [hpos],2);
      for (x = 1;x <= depth;x++) {
          /* left side of outline */
          gotoxy(position [hpos],x + 2);
          putch(186); /* vertical double-line character */
          /* right edge */
          gotoxy(position [hpos] + across + 1,x + 2);
          putch(186);
      }
```

```
      /* draw bottom */
      gotoxy(position [hpos],depth + 3);
      putch(200); /* lower-left corner character */
      gotoxy(position [hpos] + across + 1,depth + 3);
      putch(188); /* lower-right corner character */
      gotoxy(position [hpos] + 1,depth + 3);
      for (x = 2;x <= across + 1;x++)
         putch(205); /* horizontal double-line character */
} /* end outline function */


void clrscr(void)
/* clear screen */
{
   union REGS regs;

   regs.h.ah = 6;                         /* bios function */
   regs.h.al = 0;                         /* clear entire screen */
   regs.h.bh = 7;                         /* normal attribute */
   regs.h.ch = 0;                         /* upper row position */
   regs.h.cl = 0;                         /* upper-left column
                                             position */
   regs.h.dh = 24;                        /* lowest row */
   regs.h.dl = 79;                        /* rightmost column */
   int86(0x10,&regs,&regs);               /* bios interrupt
                                             number */

} /* end function clear screen */

void bioskey(int key [])
/* get key press via bios */
{
   union REGS inregs, outregs;

   inregs.h.ah = 0;
   int86(0x16,&inregs,&outregs);

   key [0] = (int) outregs.h.al; /* ASCII value */
   key [1] = (int) outregs.h.ah; /* scan code */
} /* end function bioskey */

void gotoxy(int x,int y)
/* position cursor */
{
```

```
    union REGS regs;


    regs.h.ah = 2;                   /* bios function */
    regs.h.dh = (char) y;            /* row */
    regs.h.dl = (char) x;            /* column */
    regs.h.bh = 0;                   /* video page */
    int86(0x10,&regs,&regs);         /* bios interrupt number */
} /* end function gotoxy */



void hilite(int bright_char)
/* highlight the character at the cursor */
{
    union REGS regs;

    regs.h.ah = 9;                       /* bios function */
    regs.h.al = (char) bright_char;      /* ASCII value of
                                            character */
    regs.h.bh = 0;                       /* display page */
    regs.h.bl = 0x0f;                    /* bold */
    regs.h.cl = 1;                       /* number of
                                            characters */
    regs.h.ch = 0;
    int86(0x10,&regs,&regs);             /* bios interrupt
                                            number */
} /* end function hilite */
```

The program is fairly simple. I will skip all the obvious parts, since the book assumes you know the basics of programming in C.

The get_key function returns a 2-byte array. The 0 byte contains the ASCII value of the key pressed, the second the key's scan code. If the ASCII value is 0, the scan code is required to distinguish between the various cursor keys—in this case the arrow keys.

In the p_menu function we first create the header bar and store in the position array the positions of the beginning of each header name. Next the default menu is displayed with print_menu, which returns the number of choices in that menu.

The next step is to watch the keyboard for operator input. The horizontal arrows change menu headings and show the new menu; the values in the position array tell just where the next heading is located. Also, each time we change headings we must erase the screen and redraw the menu. The vertical arrows move the highlight among the available menu choices. If the heading is changed, a new outline is drawn around the menu.

When print_menu is used, the menu is displayed with the highlight on the correct choice. Also, each menu choice is tested to find the longest. This information is stored in the across variable to help calculate the horizontal size of the outline. The depth variable indicates the vertical size of the outline.

The outline function draws a double-line border around the menu. See Figure 1-1.

FIGURE 1-1   Pop-up menu

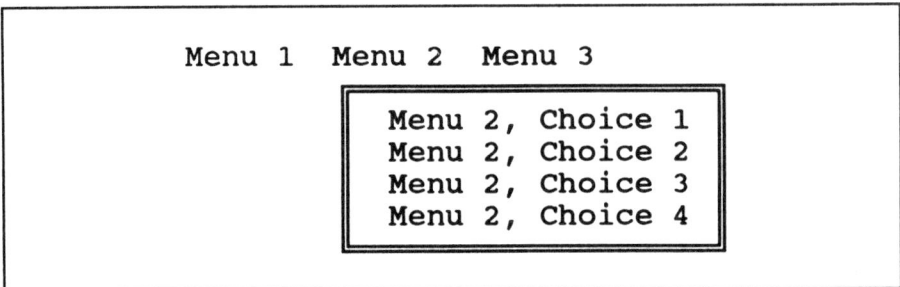

Remember, you don't have to key in these programs; a disk is available that contains the source code for all the program examples in this book.

If you use this program or any of the others in this book in your application, be sure to make the appropriate changes in the #define statements and, of course, in the names and prompts arrays.

Note that the program does not require the programmer to calculate any screen positions, outline dimensions, etc.

POP-UP MENU WITH CHOOSE BY LETTER

The following program is almost the same as the previous, with the additions that menu choices (not headings) can be chosen by entering their initial character and a prompt line is displayed for each menu selection.

```
/* Chapter 1, Example 2, QuickC, 03/13/88
   Pop up menu with prompts and choose by letter


   set stack to 3072 for this program */

#include <dos.h>
#include <stdio.h>
#include <string.h>
#include <conio.h>
#include <bios.h>
#include <ctype.h>

#define MAX_1       4   /* size of names array first
                           dimension */
#define MAX_2       4   /* size of names array second
                           dimension */
#define MAX_3      40   /* maximum length of menu selection
                           or header */
#define MAX_menu    3   /* maximum number of menus */
#define MAX_choice 4    /* maximum number of menu choices */
#define PROMPT_row 23   /* row where prompt appears */
#define PROMPT_len 79   /* maximum prompt length */

/* function prototypes */
void get_key(int key []);
void p_menu(char names [] [MAX_2] [MAX_3],
            char prompts [] [MAX_2] [PROMPT_len],
            int *vpos,int *hpos);
int print_menu(char names [] [MAX_2] [MAX_3],
               char prompts [] [MAX_2] [PROMPT_len],
                            int position [],int hpos,
                            int vpos,int flag);
void outline(int position [],int hpos,int depth,int across);
void clrscr(void);
void bioskey(int key []);
void gotoxy(int x,int y);
void main(void);
void hilite(int bright_char);
void delline(void);
```

```c
void main(void)
{
    /* zero element included in dimension values */
    char names [MAX_1] [MAX_2] [MAX_3],
            /* menu prompt messages */
            prompts [MAX_1] [MAX_2] [PROMPT_len];
    int vpos,  /* vertical position (menu choice) */
        hpos;  /* horizontal position (menu head choice) */

    strcpy(&names [0] [0] [0],"Compiler");
    strcpy(&names [0] [1] [0],"Object file");
    strcpy(&names [1] [1] [0],"Executable file");
     /* indicate end of first menu */
    strcpy(&names [2] [1] [0],"");
    strcpy(&names [1] [0] [0],"Database");
    strcpy(&names [0] [2] [0],"Add");
    strcpy(&names [1] [2] [0],"Change");
    strcpy(&names [2] [2] [0],"Delete");
    strcpy(&names [3] [2] [0],"Merge");
    strcpy(&names [2] [0] [0],"Reports");
    strcpy(&names [0] [3] [0],"Names");
    strcpy(&names [1] [3] [0],"City and state");
    strcpy(&names [2] [3] [0],"Zip code");
    /* indicate end of third menu */
    strcpy(&names [3] [3] [0],"");
    /* indicate end of menu headings */
    strcpy(&names [3] [0] [0],"");
    strcpy(&prompts [0] [1] [0],"Create an .obj file");
    strcpy(&prompts [1] [1] [0],"Create an .exe file");
    strcpy(&prompts [0] [2] [0],"Add a new record");
    strcpy(&prompts [1] [2] [0],"Change a record");
    strcpy(&prompts [2] [2] [0],"Delete a record");
    strcpy(&prompts [3] [2] [0],"Merge records");
    strcpy(&prompts [0] [3] [0],"Report by name");
    strcpy(&prompts [1] [3] [0],"Report by city and state");
    strcpy(&prompts [2] [3] [0],"Report by zip code");

    printf("\n");  /* required for following clrscr() to work
                       properly in environment */
    clrscr(); /* clear screen */
```

```
   /* first menu choice is default */
   vpos = 0;
   /* first menu heading is the default */
   hpos = 0;

   /* do it */
   p_menu(names,prompts,&vpos,&hpos);

   /* verify choice */
   clrscr();
   gotoxy(1,1);
   printf("Heading choice %s\n",names [hpos] [0]);
   printf("Menu selection %s\n",names [vpos] [hpos + 1]);
} /* end function main */


void get_key(int key [])
/* to get ASCII and scan codes */
{
   bioskey(key);

}

void p_menu(char names [] [MAX_2] [MAX_3],
            char prompts [] [MAX_2] [PROMPT_len],
            int *vpos,int *hpos)
{
   /* This function is used to initialize various variables
      and arrays in preparation for using the menu. It also
      gets the keystrokes provided by the operator to
      indicate the heading and menu choice. */

   char header [80], /* composite first line of menu */
        ch; /* used for first letter comparison */
   int true = 1, /* for boolean type responses */
       false = 0,
       x = 0, /* menu position counter */
       flag = true, /* redisplay outline or not */
       y = MAX_menu, /* maximum number of menus */
       /* horizontal position of each heading beginning */
```

```
            position [MAX_menu],
            depth = 0, /* number of menu selections */
            key [2], /* keypress */
            found, /* used for first letter comparison */
            counter = 0; /* loop counter */

       key [0] = 0; /* for get_key function */
       key [1] = 0;

   /* create menu header */
   header [0] = '\0'; /* clear string */
   while (x <= y) {
      if (names [x] [0] [0] != '\0') { /* done */
         /* keep track of heading positions */
         position [x] = strlen(header) + 1;
         /* add to header line */
         strcat(header,names [x] [0]);
         /* blank between headings */
         strcat(header," ");
      }
      x++; /* next header */
   }

   /* display header */
   gotoxy(1,1);
   printf("%s",header);

   /* print the menu */
   depth = print_menu(names,prompts,position,*hpos,*vpos,
                      flag);

   /* use the menu */
   /* get commands from operator */
   while (key [0] != 13) {
      get_key(key); /* get key */
      if (key [0] == 0) { /* extended key */
         switch (key [1]) {

            case 77: /* right arrow */
               /* go right one heading */
               *hpos = *hpos + 1;
```

```
      if (*hpos > MAX_menu - 1) {
         /* no heading to the right, start over */
         *hpos = 0;
      }
      /* display header */
      clrscr();
      gotoxy(1,1);
      printf("%s",header);
      *vpos = 0; /* default menu selection */
      flag = true; /* redisplay the outline */
      /* display menu */
      depth = print_menu(names,prompts,position,
                          *hpos,*vpos,flag);

      break;

case 75: /* left-arrow */
      /* go left one heading */
      *hpos = *hpos - 1;
      if (*hpos < 0) {
         /* no heading to the left so start over */
         *hpos = MAX_menu - 1;
      }
      /* display header */
      clrscr();
      gotoxy(1,1);
      printf("%s",header);
      *vpos = 0; /* default menu choice */
      flag = true; /* redisplay the outline */
      /* display menu */
      depth = print_menu(names,prompts,position,
                          *hpos,*vpos,flag);

      break;

case 72: /* up-arrow */
      /* move up one menu selection */
      *vpos = *vpos - 1;
      if (*vpos < 0) {
         /* no more selections in that direction
            so start over */
         *vpos = depth - 1;
      }
```

```
                     flag = false; /* don't redisplay outline */
                     /* display menu */
                     depth = print_menu(names,prompts,position,
                             *hpos,*vpos,flag);
                     break;

                 case 80: /* down-arrow */
                     /* move down one menu selection */
                     *vpos = *vpos + 1;
                     if (*vpos > depth - 1) {
                         /* no more selections that way so start
                             over */
                         *vpos = 0;
                     }
                     flag = false; /* don't redisplay outline */
                     /* display menu */
                     depth = print_menu(names,prompts,position,
                             *hpos,*vpos,flag);
                     break;

                 default: /* not an arrow key */
                     /* beep */
                     putch(7);
                     break;
             } /* end switch */
         }

         else { /* look for first letter match */
             counter = 0;
             found = false; /* no match is default */
             do {
                 /* first character */
                 ch = names [counter] [*hpos + 1] [0];
                 /* does it match? */
                 if (key [0] == toascii(ch) ||
                     key [0] == toascii(ch) + 32) { /* matched */
                     /* move to new menu selection */
                   *vpos = counter;
                     flag = false; /* don't redraw outline */
                     depth = print_menu(names,prompts,position,
                                     *hpos,*vpos,flag);
```

```
                    found = true; /* found a matching letter */
                    break;
                }
                counter++; /* test next menu name */
            }
            while (counter < depth);

            /* not a carriage return and no matching letter */
            if (key [0] != 13 && found == false)
                putch(7); /* beep */
        } /* end if */
    } /* end while */
} /* end pmenu function */


int print_menu(char names [] [MAX_2] [MAX_3],
                char prompts [] [MAX_2] [PROMPT_len],
                int position [],int hpos,int vpos,int flag)
/* display the menu */
{
    int x = 0, /* menu position counter */
        y = MAX_choice, /* maximum number of menu choices */
        /* menu column width default */
        across = strlen(names [hpos] [0]),
        true = 1, /* for boolean type responses */
        depth = 0, /* number of menu selections */
        bright_char, /* character to highlight */
        counter;

    /* display menu choices */
    while (x < y && names [x] [hpos + 1] [0] != '\0') {
        gotoxy(position [hpos] + 1,x + 3);
        if (x == vpos) {  /* highlight selected choice */
            bright_char = 32;
            hilite(bright_char); /* two leading spaces */
            hilite(bright_char);
            /* highlight each character in menu choice */
            for (counter = 0; counter < strlen(names [x]
                                    [hpos + 1]); counter++) {
                gotoxy(position [hpos] + counter + 1,x + 3);
                bright_char = names [x] [hpos + 1] [counter];
                hilite(bright_char);
            }
```

```
         }
         else
            /* no highlight */
            printf("%s",names [x] [hpos + 1]);


         /* find longest menu line & put in across */
         if (strlen(names [x] [hpos + 1]) > across)
            across = strlen(names [x] [hpos + 1]);
         depth++;
         x++;
      }

   /* print prompt */
   gotoxy(1,PROMPT_row + 1);
   delline(); /* delete old prompt */

   /* center prompt line */
   gotoxy((PROMPT_len - strlen(prompts [vpos] [hpos + 1]))
         / 2,PROMPT_row + 1);
   printf("%s",prompts [vpos] [hpos + 1]);

   if (flag == true)
      outline(position,hpos,depth,across);
   return depth;
} /* end print_menu function */


void outline(int position [],int hpos,int depth,int across)
{
   /* this function provides the double-line outline around
      the menu */
   int x; /* counter */
   /* draw top */
   gotoxy(position [hpos],2);
   putch(201); /* upper-left corner character */
   for (x = 2;x <= across + 1;x++)
      putch(205); /* horizontal double-line character */
   putch(187); /* upper-right corner character */

   /* draw sides */
   gotoxy(position [hpos],2);
```

```
    for (x = 1;x <= depth;x++)
    {
        /* left side of outline */
        gotoxy(position [hpos],x + 2);
        putch(186); /* vertical double-line character */
        /* right edge */
        gotoxy(position [hpos] + across + 1,x + 2);
        putch(186);
    }

    /* draw bottom */
    gotoxy(position [hpos],depth + 3);
    putch(200); /* lower-left corner character */
    gotoxy(position [hpos] + across + 1,depth + 3);
    putch(188); /* lower-right corner character */
    gotoxy(position [hpos] + 1,depth + 3);
    for (x = 2;x <= across + 1;x++)
        putch(205); /* horizontal double-line character */
} /* end outline function */



void clrscr(void)
/* clear screen */
{
    union REGS regs;

    regs.h.ah = 6;                        /* bios function */
    regs.h.al = 0;                        /* clear entire screen */
    regs.h.bh = 7;                        /* normal attribute */
    regs.h.ch = 0;                        /* upper row position */
    regs.h.cl = 0;                        /* upper-left column
                                             position */
    regs.h.dh = 24;                       /* lowest row */
    regs.h.dl = 79;                       /* rightmost column */
    int86(0x10,&regs,&regs);              /* bios interrupt
                                             number */

} /* end function clear screen */



void bioskey(int key [])
/* get key press via bios */
{
    union REGS inregs, outregs;
```

```
    inregs.h.ah = 0;
    int86(0x16,&inregs,&outregs);

    key [0] = (int) outregs.h.al; /* ASCII value */
    key [1] = (int) outregs.h.ah; /* scan code */
} /* end function bioskey */



void gotoxy(int x,int y)
/* position cursor */
{

    union REGS regs;


    regs.h.ah = 2;              /* bios function */
    regs.h.dh = (char) y;       /* row */
    regs.h.dl = (char) x;       /* column */
    regs.h.bh = 0;              /* video page number */
    int86(0x10,&regs,&regs);    /* bios interrupt number */
} /* end function gotoxy */



void hilite(int bright_char)
/* highlight the character at the cursor */
{
    union REGS regs;

    regs.h.ah = 9;                      /* bios function */
    regs.h.al = (char) bright_char;     /* ASCII value of
                                           character */
    regs.h.bh = 0;                      /* display page */
    regs.h.bl = 0x0f;                   /* bold */
    regs.h.cl = 1;                      /* number of
                                           characters */
    regs.h.ch = 0;
    int86(0x10,&regs,&regs);            /* bios interrupt
                                           number */

} /* end function hilite */
```

```
void delline(void)
/* deletes whole line starting at cursor position */
{
    int space;

    for (space = 1; space < 79; space++)
        printf(" ");

} /* end function delline */
```

PULL-DOWN MENU

The next program modifies the previous example to give you pull-down menus and the ability to turn the prompt line on and off. The screen is saved and restored at appropriate times so that the menu does not destroy the screen over which it is superimposed. This is done in print_menu with gettext( ) and puttext( ).

The pull-down menu works in two steps. The first carriage return selects the menu heading. The second displays the menu. When you press a horizontal arrow key the menu disappears and the heading highlight moves. If you press the escape key or carriage return while a menu is displayed, the highlighted choice will be returned to the calling program. These are the ways to exit the program.

Because the menu is superimposed over an existing screen, the program must fill the spaces before and after each menu choice within the outline to cover any underlying text.

The gettext and puttext functions contain

```
#if 0
    /* check retrace */
    while (((inp(0x3DA) & 0x08) >> 3) == 0);
#endif
```

If you are using a CGA card that snows (and the snow in this program annoys you), you will need to get rid of the "#if 0" and "#endif" lines and create a Quick Library that contains the inp( )

function. See your manual for more information about Quick Libraries.

These functions use iscolor( ) (provided) to test for color video. If they find color they assume it is a snowy CGA module. A while loop (mentioned in the previous paragraph) is used to loop until vertical retrace time. Then the movedata( ) routine moves 800 bytes to or from the video buffer. Only 800 bytes are moved because only that many can be moved during vertical retrace with a 4.77 MHz PC or clone. The while loop then waits for the next vertical retrace. This repeats five times until all 4000 bytes have been moved.

If you do not have snowy CGA color and you know the programs using this function won't be used on such a machine, you can get rid of all of this and just use the line after the else

```
movedata(0xB000,0,FP_SEG(screen_buffer),
        FP_OFF(screen_buffer),4000);
```

to replace the entire gettext( ) function and

```
movedata(FP_SEG(screen_buffer),FP_OFF(screen_buffer),
        0xB000,0,4000);
```

to replace puttext( ). You could also just leave the program as is and it will work just fine.

```
/* Chapter 1, Example 3, QuickC, 04/12/88
   Pull-down menu with prompts, choose by letter, save and
   restore screen, pull down, ability to turn prompt line on
   and off */

#include <stdio.h>
#include <dos.h>
#include <string.h>
#include <conio.h>
#include <bios.h>
#include <ctype.h>
#include <stdlib.h>
#include <process.h>
#include <memory.h>
#include <malloc.h>
```

```
#define MAX_1       4    /* size of names array first
                             dimension */
#define MAX_2       4    /* size of names array second
                             dimension */
#define MAX_3      40    /* maximum length of menu selection
                             or header */
#define MAX_menu    3    /* maximum number of menus */
#define MAX_choice  4    /* maximum number of menu choices */
#define PROMPT_row 24    /* row where prompt appears */
#define PROMPT_len 79    /* maximum prompt length */
#define PROMPTS     1    /* no prompts if zero */


void get_key(int key []);
int p_menu(char names [] [MAX_2] [MAX_3],
           char prompts [] [MAX_2] [PROMPT_len],
           int *vpos,int *hpos);
int print_menu(char names [] [MAX_2] [MAX_3],
               char prompts [] [MAX_2] [PROMPT_len],
               int position [],int hpos,
               int vpos,int flag);
void outline(int position [],int hpos,int depth,int across);
void lite_header(int hpos,int position [],char header []);
void clrscr(void);
void bioskey(int key []);
void gotoxy(int x,int y);
void hilite(int bright_char);
void main(void);
void gettext(char far *screen_buffer);
void puttext(char far *screen_buffer);
int iscolor(void);


void main()
{
    /* zero element included in dimension values */
    char names [MAX_1] [MAX_2] [MAX_3],
        /* menu prompt messages */
        prompts [MAX_1] [MAX_2] [PROMPT_len];
    int exit_key, /* returns key used to exit menu */
```

```
            vpos,   /* vertical position (menu choice) */
            hpos;   /* horizontal position (menu head choice) */

    strcpy(&names [0] [0] [0],"Compiler");
    strcpy(&names [0] [1] [0],"Object file");
    strcpy(&names [1] [1] [0],"Executable file");
     /* indicate end of first menu */
    strcpy(&names [2] [1] [0],"");
    strcpy(&names [1] [0] [0],"Database");
    strcpy(&names [0] [2] [0],"Add");
    strcpy(&names [1] [2] [0],"Change");
    strcpy(&names [2] [2] [0],"Delete");
    strcpy(&names [3] [2] [0],"Merge");
    strcpy(&names [2] [0] [0],"Reports");
    strcpy(&names [0] [3] [0],"Names");
    strcpy(&names [1] [3] [0],"City and state");
    strcpy(&names [2] [3] [0],"Zip code");
    /* indicate end of third menu */
    strcpy(&names [3] [3] [0],"");
    /* indicate end of menu headings */
    strcpy(&names [3] [0] [0],"");

    /* menu prompts */
    strcpy(&prompts [0] [1] [0],"Create an .obj file");
    strcpy(&prompts [1] [1] [0],"Create an .exe file");
    strcpy(&prompts [0] [2] [0],"Add a new record");
    strcpy(&prompts [1] [2] [0],"Change a record");
    strcpy(&prompts [2] [2] [0],"Delete a record");
    strcpy(&prompts [3] [2] [0],"Merge records");
    strcpy(&prompts [0] [3] [0],"Report by name");
    strcpy(&prompts [1] [3] [0],"Report by city and state");
    strcpy(&prompts [2] [3] [0],"Report by zip code");

    printf("\n");  /* required for following clscr() to work
                      properly in environment */
    clrscr(); /* clear screen */

    /* first menu choice is the default */
    vpos = 0;
    /* first heading is the default */
    hpos = 0;
```

```
   /* do it */
   exit_key = p_menu(names,prompts,&vpos,&hpos);

   clrscr();
   gotoxy(1,1);
   if (exit_key == 13) {
      /* verify choice */
      printf("Heading choice %s\n",names [hpos] [0]);
      printf("Menu selection %s\n",names [vpos] [hpos + 1]);
   }
   else
      printf("Escape key was used to exit menu.");
}  /* end function main */


void get_key(int key [])
/* to get ASCII and scan codes */
{

   bioskey(key);

}/* end function get_key*/


void lite_header(int hpos,int position [],char header [])
/* highlight the menu choice */
{
   int counter;

   gotoxy(1,1);
   printf("%s",header);
   /* highlight each character */
   for (counter = position [hpos];counter < position
                              [hpos + 1] - 1;counter++) {
      gotoxy(counter,1);
      hilite(header [counter - 1]);
   }
}


int p_menu(char names [] [MAX_2] [MAX_3],
           char prompts [] [MAX_2] [PROMPT_len],
           int *vpos,int *hpos)
```

```
{
    /* This function is used to initialize various variables
       and arrays in preparation for using the menu. It also
       gets the keystrokes provided by the operator to
       indicate the heading and menu choice. */

    char header [80], /* composite first line of menu */
         ch; /* used for first letter comparison */
    int true = 1, /* for boolean type responses */
        false = 0,
        x = 0, /* menu position counter */
        flag = true, /* redisplay outline or not */
        y = MAX_menu, /* maximum number of menus */
        /* horizontal position of each heading beginning */
        position [MAX_menu + 1],
        depth = 0, /* number of menu selections */
        key [2], /* keypress */
        found, /* used for first letter comparison */
        counter = 0, /* loop counter */
        menu_on = false; /* is menu displayed? */
    char far *screen_buffer;

    key [0] = 0; /* used by get_key() */
    key [1] = 0;

    /* create buffer to save screen */
    if ((screen_buffer = _fmalloc(4000)) == NULL ) {
        clrscr();
        printf("Not enough memory.\n");
        exit(1);
    }

    /* put something on the screen to demonstrate save and
       restore */
    gotoxy(1,3);
    printf("This is a line to put something on the screen");
    gettext(screen_buffer); /* save screen */

    /* create the header line and save position of each
       heading in the line */
    header [0] = '\0';
    x = 0;
```

```
while (x <= y) {
    if (names [x] [0] [0] != '\0') { /* not blank */
        /* position of header in line used for menu
            display */
        position [x] = strlen(header) + 1;
        /* append new heading */
        strcat(header,names [x] [0]);
        /* put a space between headings */
        strcat(header," ");
    }
    x++;
}


/* position of last header character */
position [MAX_menu] = strlen(header) + 1;

/* highlight first heading */
lite_header(*hpos,position,header);

/* return to calling program if carriage return or
    escape */

while (true) {
    get_key(key);
    if (key [0] == 0) { /* check for arrow keys */
        switch (key [1]) {

            case 77: /* right-arrow */
                /* go right one heading */
                *hpos = *hpos + 1;
                if (*hpos > MAX_menu - 1) {
                    /* no heading to the right, start over */
                    *hpos = 0; ·
                }
                if (menu_on == true) /* erase old menu */
                    /* replace original screen and write menu
                        over it */
                    puttext(screen_buffer);
                /* no menu, just header */
                menu_on = false;
                /* indicate new heading */
                lite_header(*hpos,position,header);
```

```
         *vpos = 0; /* default menu selection */
         break;

case 75: /* left-arrow */
   /* go left one heading */
   *hpos = *hpos - 1;
   if (*hpos < 0) {
      /* no heading to the left so start over */
      *hpos = MAX_menu - 1;
   }
   if (menu_on == true) /* erase old menu */
      /* replace original screen then write menu
         over it */
      puttext(screen_buffer);
   /* no menu, just header */
   menu_on = false;
   /* indicate new heading */
   lite_header(*hpos,position,header);
   *vpos = 0; /* default menu choice */
   break;

case 72: /* up-arrow */
   if (menu_on == false)
      putch(7); /* no menu showing so beep */
   else {
      /* move up one menu selection */
      *vpos = *vpos - 1;
      if (*vpos < 0) {
         /* no more selections in that direction
            so start over */
         *vpos = depth - 1;
      }
      /* don't redisplay outline */
      flag = false;
      /* display menu */
      depth = print_menu(names,prompts,position,
                     *hpos,*vpos,flag);
   }
   break;

case 80: /* down-arrow */
   if (menu_on == false)
      putch(7); /* no menu showing so beep */
```

```
                else {
                    /* move down one menu selection */
                    *vpos = *vpos + 1;
                    if (*vpos > depth - 1) {
                        /* no more selections that way so start
                            over */
                        *vpos = 0;
                    }
                    /* don't redisplay outline */
                    flag = false;
                    /* display menu */
                    depth = print_menu(names,prompts,position,
                                        *hpos,*vpos,flag);
                }
                break;

            default: /* not an arrow key */
                /* beep */
                putch(7);
                break;
        } /* end switch */
    }

    else { /* not an arrow */
        counter = 0;
        found = false;
        /* see if letter indicates a menu choice */
        if (menu_on == true) {
            do {
                /* first letter of menu choice */
                ch = names [counter] [*hpos + 1] [0];
                /* does it match key? */
                if (key [0] == toascii(ch) ||
                    key [0] == toascii(ch) + 32) {
                    /* move to new menu selection */
                    *vpos = counter;
                    flag = false; /* don't redraw outline */
                    /* display menu */
                    depth = print_menu(names,prompts,position,
                                        *hpos,*vpos,flag);
                    /* found a matching letter */
                    found = true;
                    break;
```

```
            }
            counter++;
        }
        while (counter < depth);
    }

    else {
        do {
            /* first letter of headings */
            ch = names [counter] [0] [0];
            /* does it match key? */
            if (key [0] == toascii(ch) ||
                key [0] == toascii(ch) + 32) {
                /* move to new header selection */
                *hpos = counter;
                /* found a matching letter */
                found = true;
                /* erase old menu */
                puttext(screen_buffer);
                /* indicate new heading */
                lite_header(*hpos,position,header);
                *vpos = 0; /* default menu choice */
                break;
            }
            counter++;
        }
        while (counter < MAX_menu);
    }
    /* not a carriage return and no matching letter */
    if (key [0] != 13 && found == false)
        putch(7); /* beep */
} /* end if key [0] == 0 */

/* escape or (carriage return and menu showing)? */
if (key [0] == 27 || (key [0] == 13 &&
                                menu_on == true))
    break; /* choice has been confirmed */
else {
    /* carriage return without menu showing? */
    if (key [0] == 13) { /* show menu */
        flag = true; /* display outline */
        /* display menu */
```

```
            depth = print_menu(names,prompts,position,
                               *hpos,*vpos,flag);
            /* header and menu showing */
            menu_on = true;
          }
        }
    } /* end while */

    /* we're done so give back original screen */
    puttext(screen_buffer);

    /* return screen_buffer memory to program */
    _ffree(screen_buffer);

    /* tell the calling program whether menu choice or
       escape */
    return key [0];
} /* end p_menu function */


int print_menu(char names [] [MAX_2] [MAX_3],char prompts []
          [MAX_2] [PROMPT_len],int position [],int hpos,
          int vpos,int flag)
/* display the menu */
{
    int x = 0, /* menu position counter */
        y = MAX_choice, /* maximum number of menu choices */
        /* menu column width default */
        across = strlen(names [hpos] [0]),
        true = 1, /* for boolean type responses */
        depth = 0, /* number of menu selections */
        counter,
        bright_char;

    while (x < y && names [x] [hpos + 1] [0] != '\0') {
       gotoxy(position [hpos] + 1,x + 3);
       if (x == vpos) {   /* highlight selected choice */
            bright_char = 32; /* space */
            hilite(bright_char); /* two spaces before menu */
            hilite(bright_char); /* choice to cover
                                     background */
```

```
                    /* step through menu choice and highlight each
                       character */
                    for (counter = 0; counter < strlen(names [x]
                                            [hpos + 1]); counter++) {
                        gotoxy(position [hpos] + counter + 1,x + 3);
                        bright_char = names [x] [hpos + 1] [counter];
                        hilite(bright_char);
                    }
            }
            else
                /* not selected so print normally */
                printf("%s",names [x] [hpos + 1]);
            depth++;
            x++;
        }

    /* find longest menu line for outline size */
    for (x = 0;x < depth;x++) {
        if (strlen(names [x] [hpos + 1]) + 1 > across)
            across = strlen(names [x] [hpos + 1]);
    }

    /* outline menu */
    if (flag == true)
        outline(position,hpos,depth,across);

    /* fill in area after menu selections within outline to
       cover background */
    for (x = 0;x < depth;x++) {
        counter = strlen(names [x] [hpos + 1]);
        gotoxy(position [hpos] + counter + 1,x + 3);
        while (counter < across) {
            putch(' ');
            counter++;
            gotoxy(position [hpos] + counter + 1,x + 3);
        }
    }

    if (PROMPTS == true) {
        /* print prompt */
        for (counter = PROMPT_row + 1;counter < 80;
                                            counter++) {
```

```
            gotoxy(1,counter);
            putch(' ');
        }

        /* center prompt line */
        gotoxy((PROMPT_len - strlen(prompts [vpos]
                [hpos + 1])) / 2,PROMPT_row + 1);
        printf("%s",prompts [vpos] [hpos + 1]);
    }

    return depth;
} /* end print_menu function */


void outline(int position [],int hpos,int depth,int across)
{
    /* this function provides the double-line outline around
       the menu */
    int x; /* counter */

    /* draw top */
    gotoxy(position [hpos],2);
    putch(201); /* upper-left corner character */
    for (x = 2;x <= across + 1;x++)
        putch(205); /* horizontal double-line character */
    putch(187); /* upper-right corner character */

    /* draw sides */
    gotoxy(position [hpos],2);
    for (x = 1;x <= depth;x++) {
        /* left side of outline */
        gotoxy(position [hpos],x + 2);
        putch(186); /* vertical double-line character */
        /* right edge */
        gotoxy(position [hpos] + across + 1,x + 2);
        putch(186);
    }

    /* draw bottom */
    gotoxy(position [hpos],depth + 3);
    putch(200); /* lower-left corner character */
    gotoxy(position [hpos] + across + 1,depth + 3);
    putch(188); /* lower-right corner character */
```

```c
      gotoxy(position [hpos] + 1,depth + 3);
      for (x = 2;x <= across + 1;x++)
          putch(205); /* horizontal double-line character */
} /* end outline function */

void clrscr(void)
/* clear screen */

{
   union REGS regs;

   regs.h.ah = 6;                    /* bios function */
   regs.h.al = 0;                    /* clear entire screen */
   regs.h.bh = 7;                    /* normal attribute */
   regs.h.ch = 0;                    /* upper row position */
   regs.h.cl = 0;                    /* upper-left column
                                        position */

   regs.h.dh = 24;                   /* lowest row */
   regs.h.dl = 79;                   /* rightmost column */
   int86(0x10,&regs,&regs);          /* bios interrupt number */
} /* end function clear screen */


void bioskey(int key [])
/* get key press via bios */
{
   union REGS inregs, outregs;

   inregs.h.ah = 0;
   int86(0x16,&inregs,&outregs);

   key [0] = (int) outregs.h.al; /* ASCII code */
   key [1] = (int) outregs.h.ah; /* scan code */
} /* end function bioskey */

void gotoxy(int x,int y)
/* position cursor */
{

   union REGS regs;
```

```
    regs.h.ah = 2;                /* bios function */
    regs.h.dh = (char) y;         /* row */
    regs.h.dl = (char) x;         /* column */
    regs.h.bh = 0;                /* video page  */
    int86(0x10,&regs,&regs);      /* bios interrupt number */
} /* end function gotoxy */


void hilite(int bright_char)
/* highlight the character at the cursor */
{
    union REGS regs;

    regs.h.ah = 9;                     /* bios function */
    regs.h.al = (char) bright_char;    /* ASCII code of
                                          character */
    regs.h.bh = 0;                     /* display page */
    regs.h.bl = 0x0f;                  /* bold */
    regs.h.cl = 1;                     /* number of
                                          characters */
    regs.h.ch = 0;
    int86(0x10,&regs,&regs);           /* bios interrupt
                                          number */
} /* end function hilite */

void gettext(char far *screen_buffer)
{
    register short i;
    register short delta;

    delta = 0;

    if (iscolor() == 1) {  /* iscolor() is a function that
                              tests for color video module */
       for (i = 0; i < 5; i++) {
#if 0
           /* This line is only required if you have a CGA
              that snows. See text. */
           /* the inp() function is not included in the
```

```
                   standard library */
            /* check for retrace */
            while (((inp(0x3DA) & 0x08) >> 3) == 0);
#endif

            /* Save 1/5 of data to screen_buffer. Note that
               data is moved in 800-byte chunks because this is
               all that can be moved during retrace, and
               therefore snow free. */
            movedata(0xB800,0 + delta,FP_SEG(screen_buffer),
                    FP_OFF(screen_buffer) + delta,800);
            delta += 800;
        }
    }
    else
       /* non_color can be moved all at once */
       /* (as can non_snow CGA, EGA, VGA, PGA, etc. but
          this routine does not provide for telling color
          modules apart) */
       movedata(0xB000,0,FP_SEG(screen_buffer),
                FP_OFF(screen_buffer),4000);
}  /* end function gettext() */


void puttext(char far *screen_buffer)
{
    register short i;
    register short delta;

    delta = 0;
    if (iscolor() == 1) {  /* iscolor() is a function that
                               tests for color video module */
        for (i = 0; i < 5; i++)  {

#if 0
            /* This line is only required if you have a CGA
               that snows. See text. */
            /* the inp() function is not included in the
               standard library */
            /* check for retrace */
```

```
                while (((inp(0x3DA) & 0x08) >> 3) == 0);
#endif

                /* Save 1/5 of data to screen_buffer. Note that
                   data is moved in 800-byte chunks because this is
                   all that can be moved during retrace, and
                   therefore snow free. */
                movedata(FP_SEG(screen_buffer),
                        FP_OFF(screen_buffer) + delta,0xB800,
                        0 + delta, 800);
                delta += 800;
            }
        }
        else
            /* non_color can be moved all at once */
            /* (as can non_snow CGA, EGA, VGA, PGA, etc. but
               this routine does not provide for telling color
               modules apart) */
            movedata(FP_SEG(screen_buffer),
                    FP_OFF(screen_buffer),0xB000,0,4000);
    }


int iscolor()
/* see if a color video module is present */
{
    int crt = 0;
    union REGS inregs,outregs;


    inregs.h.ah = 15;               /* bios function */
    int86(0x10,&inregs,&outregs);   /* bios interrupt
                                        number */

    crt = (int) outregs.h.al;
    if (crt == 7) /* monochrome */
        crt = 0;
    else
        crt = 1;
    return(crt);
} /* end function iscolor */
```

HORIZONTAL MENU

This next program shows how to program a "Lotus" style menu. See Figure 1-2. The current menu choice in the first line is highlighted and an explanation of the menu choice (or prompt) appears on the second line. Use the horizontal arrows or the first character to make your selection and the carriage return or escape key to confirm the selection.

The previous screen is saved and then restored after the menu selection has been made.

FIGURE 1-2   "Lotus" style menu

```
Compiler Database Reports
Compile the program
```

```
/* Chapter 1, Example 4, QuickC, 03/20/88
   Horizontal menu with prompts, choose by letter,
   save, and restore screen. The program also blanks
   the cursor. */

#include <dos.h>
#include <stdio.h>
#include <string.h>
#include <conio.h>
#include <bios.h>
#include <ctype.h>
#include <process.h>
#include <stdlib.h>
#include <memory.h>
#include <malloc.h>

#define MAX_len     20   /* maximum length of menu item */
#define MAX_menu    3    /* maximum number of menu items */
#define PROMPT_len 79    /* maximum prompt length */

/* function prototypes */
void get_key(int key []);
```

```
int h_menu(char names [] [MAX_len],
           char prompts [] [PROMPT_len],int *hpos);
void print_prompt(char prompts [] [PROMPT_len],int hpos);
void display_type(int *crt);
void lite_header(int hpos,int position [],char header []);
void clrscr(void);
void bioskey(int key []);
void gotoxy(int x,int y);
void hilite(int bright_char);
void main(void);
void gettext(char far *screen_buffer);
void puttext(char far *screen_buffer);
int iscolor(void);


void main(void)
{
   /* zero element included in dimension values */
   char names [MAX_menu] [MAX_len],
        /* menu prompt messages */
        prompts [MAX_menu] [PROMPT_len];
   int exit_key, /* returns key used to exit menu */
       hpos;  /* horizontal position (Menu choice) */

   strcpy(&names [0] [0],"Compiler");
   strcpy(&names [1] [0],"Database");
   strcpy(&names [2] [0],"Reports");

   /* menu prompts */
   strcpy(&prompts [0] [0],"Compile the program");
   strcpy(&prompts [1] [0],"Load the database");
   strcpy(&prompts [2] [0],"Print the reports");

   printf("\n");   /* required for following clscr() to work
                      properly in environment */
   clrscr(); /* clear screen */

   /* first menu choice is default */
   hpos = 0;

   /* do it */
   exit_key = h_menu(names,prompts,&hpos);
```

```
       clrscr();
       gotoxy(1,1);
       if (exit_key == 13) {
          /* verify choice */
          printf("Heading choice %s\n",names [hpos]);
       }
       else
          printf("Escape key was used to exit menu.");
} /*end function main*/



void get_key(int key [])
/* to get ASCII and scan codes */
{

    bioskey(key);

}/* end function get_key*/



void lite_header(int hpos,int position [],char header [])
/* highlight the menu choice */
{
    int counter,
        bright_char;

    gotoxy(1,1);
    printf("%s",header);
    for (counter = position [hpos];
            counter < position [hpos + 1] - 1;counter++) {
       gotoxy(counter,1);
       bright_char = header [counter - 1];
       hilite(bright_char);
    }
}

int h_menu(char names [] [MAX_len],
           char prompts [] [PROMPT_len],int *hpos)
{
    /* This function is used to initialize various variables
       and arrays in preparation for using the menu. It also
```

```
    gets the keystrokes provided by the operator to
    indicate the menu choice. */

char header [80], /* composite line of menu */
     ch; /* used for first letter comparison */
int true = 1, /* for boolean type responses */
    false = 0,
    x = 0, /* menu position counter */
    y = MAX_menu, /* maximum number of menus */
    /* horizontal position of each heading beginning */
    position [MAX_menu + 1],
    key [2], /* keypress */
    found, /* used for first letter comparison */
    counter = 0; /* loop counter */
 char far *screen_buffer;

 key [0] = 0; /* for get_key() */
 key [1] = 0;

/* create buffer to save screen */
if ((screen_buffer = _fmalloc(4000)) == NULL) {
    clrscr();
    printf("Not enough memory.\n");
    exit(1);
}

gettext(screen_buffer); /* save the screen */

/* create the menu line and save position of each item in
    the line */
header [0] = '\0';
x = 0;
while (x < y) {
    if (names [x] [0] != '\0') { /* not blank */
        /* position of header in line used for menu
            display */
        position [x] = strlen(header) + 1;
        /* append new heading */
        strcat(header,names [x]);
        /* put a space between headings */
        strcat(header," ");
```

```
        }
    x++;
}

/* position of last menu character */
position [MAX_menu] = strlen(header) + 1;

/* highlight first heading */
lite_header(*hpos,position,header);

/* print prompt line */
print_prompt(prompts,*hpos);

/* return to calling program if carriage return or
   escape */
while (true) {
    get_key(key);
    if (key [0] == 0) { /* check for arrow keys */
        switch (key [1]) {

            case 77: /* right-arrow */
                /* go right one heading */
                *hpos = *hpos + 1;
                if (*hpos > MAX_menu - 1) {
                    /* no heading to the right, start over */
                    *hpos = 0;
                }
                /* indicate new heading */
                lite_header(*hpos,position,header);
                /* display prompt */
                print_prompt(prompts,*hpos);
                break;

            case 75: /* left-arrow */
                /* go left one heading */
                *hpos = *hpos - 1;
                if (*hpos < 0) {
                    /* no heading to the left so start over */
                    *hpos = MAX_menu - 1;
                }
                /* indicate new heading */
                lite_header(*hpos,position,header);
```

```
                    /* display prompt */
                    print_prompt(prompts,*hpos);
                    break;

                default:
                    /* not an arrow key */
                    putch(7); /* beep */
                    break;
            } /* end switch */
        }

        else { /* not an arrow */
            counter = 0;
            found = false;
            do {
                /* first letter of choices */
                ch = names [counter] [0];
                /* does it match key? */
                if (key [0] == toascii(ch) ||
                    key [0] == toascii(ch) + 32) {
                    /* move to new menu selection */
                    *hpos = counter;
                    found = true; /* found a matching letter */
                    /* indicate new heading */
                    lite_header(*hpos,position,header);
                    /* display prompt */
                    print_prompt(prompts,*hpos);
                    break;
                }
                counter++;
            }
            while (counter < MAX_menu);

            /* not a carriage return and no matching letter */
            if (key [0] != 13 && found == false)
                putch(7); /* beep */
        } /* end if key [0] == 0 */

        /* if escape or carriage return */
        if (key [0] == 27 || key [0] == 13)
            break; /* choice has been confirmed */
} /* end while */
```

```
    /* we're done so give back original screen */
    puttext(screen_buffer);

    /* give memory back to program */
    _ffree(screen_buffer);

    /* tell the calling program whether menu choice or
       escape */
    return key [0]; /* contains last keypress */

} /* end p_menu function */


void print_prompt(char prompts [] [PROMPT_len],int hpos)
{
    /* print prompt */
    int counter;

    gotoxy(1,2);
    /* erase old prompt */
    for (counter = 2;counter < 80;counter++)
       putch(' ');
    gotoxy(1,2);
    /* display new prompt */
    printf("%s",prompts [hpos]);
    /* put cursor off-screen so it doesn't show */
    gotoxy(1,26);
} /* end print_prompt function */

void clrscr(void)
/* clear screen */

{
    union REGS regs;

    regs.h.ah = 6;                   /* bios function */
    regs.h.al = 0;                   /* clear entire screen */
    regs.h.bh = 7;                   /* normal attribute */
    regs.h.ch = 0;                   /* upper row position */
    regs.h.cl = 0;                   /* upper left column
                                        position */

    regs.h.dh = 24;                  /* lowest row */
```

```
      regs.h.dl = 79;                /* rightmost column */
      int86(0x10,&regs,&regs);       /* bios interrupt number *
} /* end function clear screen */


void bioskey(int key [])
/* get key press via bios */
{
   union REGS inregs, outregs;

   inregs.h.ah = 0;
   int86(0x16,&inregs,&outregs);

   key [0] = (int) outregs.h.al; /* ASCII value */
   key [1] = (int) outregs.h.ah; /* scan code */
} /* end function bioskey */


void gotoxy(int x,int y)
/* position cursor */
{

   union REGS regs;


   regs.h.ah = 2;                 /* bios function */
   regs.h.dh = (char) y;          /* row */
   regs.h.dl = (char) x;          /* column */
   regs.h.bh = 0;                 /* video page number */
   int86(0x10,&regs,&regs);       /* bios interrupt number */
} /* end function gotoxy */


void hilite(int bright_char)
/* highlight the character at the cursor */
{
   union REGS regs;

   regs.h.ah = 9;                      /* bios function */
   regs.h.al = (char) bright_char;     /* ASCII value of
                                          character */
   regs.h.bh = 0;                      /* display page */
```

```
      regs.h.bl = 0x0f;                    /* bold */
      regs.h.cl = 1;                       /* number of
                                              characters */

      regs.h.ch = 0;
      int86(0x10,&regs,&regs);             /* bios interrupt
                                              number */
} /* end function hilite */


void gettext(char far *screen_buffer)
/* see text and this function in example 3 for more
   information */
{
   register short i;
   register short delta;

   delta = 0;

   if (iscolor() == 1) {  /* iscolor() is a function that
                              tests for color */
      for (i = 0; i < 5; i++) {

#if 0
         while (((inp(0x3DA) & 0x08) >> 3) == 0);  /* check
                                                      retrace */
#endif

            movedata(0xB800, 0 + delta,
                FP_SEG(screen_buffer),
                FP_OFF(screen_buffer) + delta, 800);
            delta += 800;
         }
      }
   else
         movedata(0xB000, 0, FP_SEG(screen_buffer),
               FP_OFF(screen_buffer), 4000);
}  /* end function gettext() */



void puttext(char far *screen_buffer)
/* see text and this function in Example 3 for more
   information */
```

```
{
    register short i;
    register short delta;

    delta = 0;
    if (iscolor() == 1)  {
        for (i = 0; i < 5; i++)  {
#if 0
        while (((inp(0x3DA) & 0x08) >> 3) == 0);   /* check
                                                        retrace */
#endif

            movedata(FP_SEG(screen_buffer),
                    FP_OFF(screen_buffer) + delta,
                    0xB800,0 + delta, 800);
            delta += 800;
        }
    }
    else
        movedata(FP_SEG(screen_buffer), FP_OFF(screen_buffer),
                0xB000, 0, 4000);
 }


int iscolor()

{
    int crt = 0;
    union REGS inregs,outregs;

    inregs.h.ah = 15;                /* bios function */
    int86(0x10,&inregs,&outregs);   /* bios interrupt number */

    crt = (int) outregs.h.al;
    if (crt == 7) /* monochrome */
        crt =0;
    else
        crt = 1;
    return(crt);
} /* end function iscolor */
```

VERTICAL MENU

This is the ordinary type of menu: the one we write when we're in a hurry. See Figure 1-3. This version uses the vertical arrow keys to highlight the choice or the operator can select with the first character of the menu choice. The carriage return or escape key leaves the menu. The previous screen is saved and then restored after the menu selection has been made.

A prompt is shown if prompts are enabled (#define PROMPT) and there is sufficient room on the screen (display_prompt variable).

FIGURE 1-3   Vertical menu

```
     Main Menu

     Compiler
     Database
     Reports

     Use up or down arrows or first letter to
     make your selection.




                  Compile the file
```

```
/* Chapter 1, Example 5, QuickC, 04/14/88
   Vertical menu with prompts, choose by letter,
   save and restore screen, ability to turn prompt
   line on and off */

#include <dos.h>
#include <stdio.h>
```

```
#include <string.h>
#include <conio.h>
#include <bios.h>
#include <ctype.h>
#include <process.h>
#include <stdlib.h>
#include <memory.h>
#include <malloc.h>

#define MENU_len    40   /* maximum length of menu
                               selection */
#define MENU_size   3    /* maximum number of menu choices */
#define PROMPT_row  24   /* row where prompt appears */
#define PROMPT_len  79   /* maximum prompt length */
#define PROMPTS     1    /* no prompts if zero */
#define COLUMN      20   /* column where menu lines begin */
#define MENU_name   "Main Menu"
#define START_row   2    /* first row of menu */

void get_key(int key []);
int v_menu(char names [] [MENU_len],
           char prompts [] [PROMPT_len],int *vpos);
void print_prompt(char prompts [] [PROMPT_len], int vpos);
void lite_menu(int vpos,char names [] [MENU_len]);
void clrscr(void);
void bioskey(int key []);
void gotoxy(int x,int y);
void hilite(int bright_char);
void main(void);
void gettext(char far *screen_buffer);
void puttext(char far *screen_buffer);
int iscolor(void);


void main()
{
   /* zero element included in dimension values */
   char names [MENU_size] [MENU_len],
        /* menu prompt messages */
        prompts [MENU_size] [PROMPT_len];
   int exit_key, /* returns key used to exit menu */
       vpos;  /* vertical position (menu choice) */
```

```
   /* menu items */
   strcpy(&names [0] [0],"Compiler");
   strcpy(&names [1] [0],"Database");
   strcpy(&names [2] [0],"Reports");

   /* menu prompts */
   strcpy(&prompts [0] [0],"Compile the file");
   strcpy(&prompts [1] [0],"Access the database");
   strcpy(&prompts [2] [0],"Print a report");

   printf("\n");   /* required for following clscr() to work
                      properly in the environment */
   clrscr(); /* clear screen */

   /* first menu choice is default */
   hpos = 0;

   /* do it */
   exit_key = h_menu(names,prompts,&hpos);

   clrscr();
   gotoxy(1,1);
   if (exit_key == 13) {
      /* verify choice */
      printf("Menu selection %s\n",names [vpos]);
   }
   else
      printf("Escape key was used to exit menu.");
} /* end function main */


void get_key(int key [])
/* to get ASCII and scan codes */
{

   bioskey(key);

}/* end function get_key*/


int v_menu(char names [] [MENU_len],
           char prompts [] [PROMPT_len],int *vpos)
```

```
{
    /* This function is used to initialize various variables
       and arrays in preparation for using the menu. It also
       gets the keystrokes provided by the operator to
       indicate the menu choice. */

    char ch; /* used for first letter comparison */
    int true = 1, /* for boolean type responses */
        false = 0,
        key [2], /* keypress */
        found, /* used for first letter comparison */
        counter = 0, /* loop counter */
        display_prompt = true; /* room to display prompt? */
     char far *screen_buffer;

     key [0] = 0; /* for get_key() */
     key [1] = 0;

    /* create buffer to save screen */
    if ((screen_buffer = _fmalloc(4000)) == NULL) {
        clrscr();
        printf("Not enough memory.\n");
        exit(1);
    }

    /* put something on the screen to test save and
       restore */
    gotoxy(1,3);
    printf("This is a line to put something on the screen.");
    gettext(screen_buffer); /* save the screen */
    clrscr();

    /* create the menu */
    gotoxy(COLUMN + 1,START_row + 1);

    /* display name of menu */
    printf("%s",MENU_name);

    /* display menu choices */
    for (counter = START_row + 2,*vpos = 0;
         counter < START_row + 2 + MENU_size;
         counter++,*vpos += 1) {
```

```
      gotoxy(COLUMN + 1,counter + 1);
      printf("%s",names [*vpos]);
}

/* display instructions */
gotoxy(COLUMN + 1,counter + 3);
printf("Use up or down arrows or first letter to\n");
gotoxy(COLUMN + 1,counter + 4);
printf("make your selection.\n");

/* see if room for prompt */
if (counter + 4 > PROMPT_row)
   /* if not, disable prompts */
   display_prompt = false;

*vpos = 0;
lite_menu(*vpos,names); /* highlight first menu choice */

/* display prompt if enabled */
if (display_prompt == true && PROMPTS == true)
   print_prompt(prompts,*vpos);

/* return to calling program if carriage return or
   escape */
while (true) {
   get_key(key);
   if (key [0] == 0) { /* check for arrow keys */
      switch (key [1]) {

          case 72: /* up-arrow */
             /* move up one menu selection */
             gotoxy(COLUMN + 1,START_row + 3 + *vpos);
             /* replace highlighted entry */
             printf("%s",names [*vpos]);
             *vpos = *vpos - 1;
             if (*vpos < 0) {
                /* no more selections in that direction
                   so start over */
                *vpos = MENU_size - 1;
             }
             lite_menu(*vpos,names);
             /* display prompt if enabled */
```

```
                        if (display_prompt == true &&
                                            PROMPTS == true)
                            print_prompt(prompts,*vpos);
                        break;

                    case 80: /* down-arrow */
                        /* move down one menu selection */
                        gotoxy(COLUMN + 1,START_row + 3 + *vpos);
                        /* replace highlighted entry */
                        printf("%s",names [*vpos]);
                        *vpos = *vpos + 1;
                        if (*vpos > MENU_size - 1) {
                            /* no more selections that way so start
                                over */
                            *vpos = 0;
                        }
                        lite_menu(*vpos,names);
                        /* display prompt if enabled */
                        if (display_prompt == true &&
                                            PROMPTS == true)
                            print_prompt(prompts,*vpos);
                        break;

                    default: /* not an arrow key */
                        /* beep */
                        putch(7); /* beep */
                        break;
                } /* end switch */
            }

            else { /* not an arrow */
                counter = 0;
                found = false; /* no match */
                do {
                    /* first letter of menu choice */
                    ch = names [counter] [0];
                    /* does it match key? */
                    if (key [0] == toascii(ch) ||
                        key [0] == toascii(ch) + 32) {
                        /* move to new menu selection */
                        gotoxy(COLUMN + 1,START_row + 3 + *vpos);
                        /* replace highlighted entry */
```

```
                    printf("%s",names [*vpos]);
                    *vpos = counter;
                    /* highlight choice */
                    lite_menu(*vpos,names);
                    /* display prompt if enabled */
                    if (display_prompt == true &&
                                         PROMPTS == true)
                       print_prompt(prompts,*vpos);
                    found = true; /* found a matching letter */
                    break;
                }
                counter++;
             }
          while (counter < MENU_size);

          /* not a carriage return and no matching letter */
          if (key [0] != 13 && found == false)
             putch(7); /* beep */
       } /* end if key [0] == 0 */

       /* escape or carriage return? */
       if (key [0] == 27 || key [0] == 13)
          break; /* choice has been confirmed */
    } /* end while */

    /* we're done so give back original screen */
    puttext(screen_buffer);

    /* give screen memory back to program */
    _ffree(screen_buffer);

    /* tell the calling program whether menu choice or
       escape */
    return key [0];

} /* end v_menu function */


void print_prompt(char prompts [] [PROMPT_len],int vpos)
/* display the prompt */
{
    int counter;
```

```
      /* print prompt */
      gotoxy(1,PROMPT_row);
      for (counter = PROMPT_row + 1; counter < 80; counter++)
         putch(' ');
      /* center prompt line */
      gotoxy((PROMPT_len - strlen(prompts [vpos])) / 2,
             PROMPT_row);
      printf("%s",prompts [vpos]);
} /* end print_prompt function */



void lite_menu(int vpos,char names [] [MENU_len])
/* highlight the menu choice */
{
   int counter,
       bright_char; /* for character to highlight */

   /* highlight each character */
   for (counter = 0;counter < strlen(names [vpos]);
                                       counter++) {
      gotoxy(COLUMN + counter + 1,START_row + 3 + vpos);
      bright_char = names [vpos] [counter];
      hilite(bright_char);
   }
}



void clrscr(void)
/* clear screen */

{
   union REGS regs;

   regs.h.ah = 6;                    /* bios function */
   regs.h.al = 0;                    /* clear entire screen */
   regs.h.bh = 7;                    /* normal attribute */
   regs.h.ch = 0;                    /* upper row position */
   regs.h.cl = 0;                    /* upper-left column
                                        position */
   regs.h.dh = 24;                   /* lowest row */
   regs.h.dl = 79;                   /* rightmost column */
```

```
        int86(0x10,&regs,&regs);          /* bios interrupt
                                              number */

} /* end function clear screen */



void bioskey(int key [])
/* get key press via bios */
{
    union REGS inregs, outregs;

    inregs.h.ah = 0;
    int86(0x16,&inregs,&outregs);

    key [0] = (int) outregs.h.al;
    key [1] = (int) outregs.h.ah;
} /* end function bioskey */

void gotoxy(int x,int y)
/* position cursor */
{

    union REGS regs;


    regs.h.ah = 2;                 /* bios function */
    regs.h.dh = (char) y;          /* row */
    regs.h.dl = (char) x;          /* column */
    regs.h.bh = 0;                 /* video page number */
    int86(0x10,&regs,&regs);       /* bios interrupt number */
} /* end function gotoxy */



void highlite(int bright_char)
/* highlight the character at the cursor */
{
    union REGS regs;

    regs.h.ah = 9;                 /* bios function */
    regs.h.al = (char) bright_char;  /* ASCII value of
                                          character */
    regs.h.bh = 0;                 /* display page */
    regs.h.bl = 0x0f;              /* bold */
```

```
    regs.h.cl = 1;                      /* number of
                                            characters */

    regs.h.ch = 0;
    int86(0x10,&regs,&regs);           /* bios interrupt
                                            number */
} /* end function hilite */



void gettext(char far *screen_buffer)
/* see text and this function in Example 3 for more info */
{
    register short i;
    register short delta;

    delta = 0;
    if (iscolor() == 1) {  /* iscolor() is a function that
                                tests for color */
        for (i = 0; i < 5; i++) {

#if 0
        while (((inp(0x3DA) & 0x08) >> 3) == 0); /* check
                                                    retrace */
#endif

            movedata(0xB800,0 + delta,FP_SEG(screen_buffer),
                FP_OFF(screen_buffer) + delta,800);
            delta += 800;
            }
        }
        else
            movedata(0xB000,0,FP_SEG(screen_buffer),
                FP_OFF(screen_buffer),4000);
} /* end function gettext() */

void puttext(char far *screen_buffer)
/* see text and this function in Example 3 for more info */
{
    register short i;
    register short delta;

    delta = 0;
    if (iscolor() == 1) {
        for (i = 0; i < 5; i++) {
```

```
#if 0
    while (((inp(0x3DA) & 0x08) >> 3) == 0);   /* check
                                                    retrace */
#endif

    movedata(FP_SEG(screen_buffer),
            FP_OFF(screen_buffer) + delta,
                0xB800,0 + delta, 800);
    delta += 800;
    }
  }
  else
    movedata(FP_SEG(screen_buffer),FP_OFF(screen_buffer),
            0xB000,0,4000);
 }


int iscolor()
/* test for color video or monochrome */
{
   int crt = 0;
   union REGS inregs,outregs;


   inregs.h.ah = 15;                /* bios function */
   int86(0x10,&inregs,&outregs);    /* bios interrupt
                                        number */

   crt = (int) outregs.h.al;
   if (crt == 7) /* monochrome */
      crt = 0;
   else
      crt = 1;
   return(crt);
} /* end function iscolor */
```

Note again that there is a lot of code used in this program that was also used in previous programs. Essentially, menus are very similar.

2

Formatted Data Entry and Window Techniques

This chapter will show how to use formatted data entry and how to create text windows and send information to them. You'll also see examples of reading input from the key pad and positioning characters on the screen.

These programs, as did those in Chapter 1, use multidimensional character arrays. You may wish to change these to structures or arrays of pointers to the text. I felt the arrays made the programs easier to understand.

SIMPLEST FORMATTED DATA ENTRY

This first example fixes the position of the prompts and data entry fields on the screen. Only text, numeric, telephone, and data fields are specifically accommodated. The date is not checked for validity. Only a single page (screen) of entries can be used. Protected (just look, don't touch) fields are provided. As simple as this program is, it will work effectively in many applications.

```
/* Chapter 2, Example 1, Quick C, 4/14/88
 Simplest formatted data entry */

#include <stdio.h>
#include <string.h>
#include <dos.h>
#include <conio.h>
#include <bios.h>
#include <ctype.h>
#include <stdlib.h>

#define INPUT_data 5   /* number of prompts and data
                          including 0 */
#define INPUT_size 4   /* number of dimensions */
#define PROMPT_len 38  /* length of prompt and data
                          including 0 */
#define INDENT     2   /* indent prompt from left */
#define DATA_start 40  /* column entry starts in */
#define HELP_LEN   51  /* length of help instruction
                          string */
#define DATE 1         /* date data */
#define NUMERIC 2      /* numeric data */
```

```
#define PHONE 3        /* telephone number data */
#define ALPHA 4        /* alphanumeric data */
#define CHANGE 1       /* ok to change data */
#define NOCHANGE 0     /* not ok to change data */

struct date {
        int    da_year;
        char   da_day;
        char   da_mon;
};

/* function prototypes */
void get_key(int key []);
int data_entry(char prompts [] [2] [PROMPT_len],
                int data [] [INPUT_size]);
void lite_prompt(int vpos,char prompts [] [2] [PROMPT_len]);
void convert_date(struct date *today,char system_date []);
void put_char(int vpos,int *line_pointer,char ch,char
   prompts [] [2] [PROMPT_len],int data [] [INPUT_size]);
void clrscr(void);
void bioskey(int key []);
void gotoxy(int x,int y);
void hilite(int bright_char);
void main(void);
void getdate(struct date *today);


void main()
{
   /* zero element included in dimension values */
   int data [INPUT_data] [INPUT_size],
       return_key; /* key used to exit data entry */
   char prompts [INPUT_data] [2] [PROMPT_len],
       system_date [9];
   struct date today; /* for system date */

   /* get system date */
   convert_date(&today,system_date);

   /* prompts */
   strcpy(&prompts [0] [0] [0],"Name");
   strcpy(&prompts [1] [0] [0],"Date");
```

```
strcpy(&prompts [2] [0] [0],"Protected data");
strcpy(&prompts [3] [0] [0],"Telephone number");
strcpy(&prompts [4] [0] [0],"Enter a number");

/* default responses */
strcpy(&prompts [0] [1] [0],"");
strcpy(&prompts [1] [1] [0],system_date);
strcpy(&prompts [2] [1] [0],"You can't change this!");
strcpy(&prompts [3] [1] [0],"");
strcpy(&prompts [4] [1] [0],"0");

/* name data */
data [0] [0] = 2;          /* display on second line */
data [0] [1] = CHANGE;     /* ok to change */
data [0] [2] = 25;         /* length of string expected */
data [0] [3] = ALPHA;      /* alphanumeric */

/* date data */
data [1] [0] = 3;          /* display on third line */
data [1] [1] = CHANGE;     /* ok to change */
data [1] [2] = 8;          /* length of string expected */
data [1] [3] = DATE;       /* date */

/* protected data */
data [2] [0] = 4;          /* display on fourth line */
data [2] [1] = NOCHANGE;   /* not ok to change */
data [2] [2] = 21;         /* length of string expected */
data [2] [3] = ALPHA;      /* alphanumeric */

/* telephone data */
data [3] [0] = 5;          /* display on fifth line */
data [3] [1] = CHANGE;     /* ok to change */
data [3] [2] = 13;         /* length of string expected */
data [3] [3] = PHONE;      /* phone number */

/* number data */
data [4] [0] = 6;          /* display on sixth line */
data [4] [1] = CHANGE;     /* ok to change */
data [4] [2] = 10;         /* length of string expected */
data [4] [3] = NUMERIC;    /* numeric */
```

```
      printf("\n");  /* required for following clrscr() to work
                     properly in environment */
      clrscr(); /* clear screen */
      return_key = data_entry(prompts,data);

      /* verify choice */
      clrscr();
      gotoxy(1,1);
      if (return_key == 27)
         printf("Return key was escape\n");
      else {
         printf("Return key was F2\n\n");
         printf("%s %s\n",prompts [0] [0],prompts [0] [1]);
         printf("%s %s\n",prompts [1] [0],prompts [1] [1]);
         printf("%s %s\n",prompts [2] [0],prompts [2] [1]);
         printf("%s %s\n",prompts [3] [0],prompts [3] [1]);
         printf("%s %s\n",prompts [4] [0],prompts [4] [1]);
      }
}


int data_entry(char prompts [] [2] [PROMPT_len],
               int data [] [INPUT_size])
/* display the screen and get the data entered */
{
    int true = 1, /* for boolean type responses */
        down = 1, /* cursor movement direction */
        up = 0,
        direction = down,
        vpos = 0, /* default first entry line */
        counter,
        line_pointer = 0, */ character position in data line
                            including 0 */
        key [2]; /* keypress */
    char help [HELP_LEN],
         underlines [PROMPT_len]; /* for underlined data
                                     line */

    key [0] = 0;
    key [1] = 0;
    strcpy(help, "Use F2 to save data, escape to leave entry
screen");
```

```
clrscr();
/* print border */
for (counter = 0;counter < 79;counter++) {
   gotoxy(counter + 1,1);
   putch('=');
   gotoxy(counter + 1,INPUT_data + 3);
   putch('=');
}

/* print prompts and defaults */
for (counter = 0;counter < INPUT_data;counter++) {
   gotoxy(INDENT,data [counter] [0]);
   printf("%s",prompts [counter] [0]);
   gotoxy(DATA_start,data [counter] [0]);
   printf("%s",prompts [counter] [1]);
}

/* center and print help line */
gotoxy((80 - strlen(help)) / 2,INPUT_data + 2);
printf("%s",help);

/* highlight prompt line where data is being accepted */
vpos = 0;
lite_prompt(vpos,prompts);

while (true) {
   if (vpos < 0)
      vpos = INPUT_data - 1;
   if (vpos > INPUT_data - 1) /* past last prompt */
      vpos = 0;
   if (data [vpos] [1] == 0) {
      if (direction == down)
         vpos++;
      else
         vpos--;
      continue;
   }

   /* highlight new position */
   lite_prompt(vpos,prompts);
   gotoxy(DATA_start + line_pointer,data [vpos] [0]);
   get_key(key); /* get keypress */
```

```
if (key [0] == 0 && key [1] == 72) { /* up-arrow */
    gotoxy(INDENT,data [vpos] [0]);
    /* replace highlighted prompt */
    printf("%s",prompts [vpos] [0]);
    vpos--; /* up one line */
    direction = up; /* cursor movement direction */
    line_pointer = 0; /* set pointer to beginning of
                            line */
    continue;
}

if (key [0] == 13) { /* carriage return */
    gotoxy(INDENT,data [vpos] [0]);
    /* replace highlighted prompt */
    printf("%s",prompts [vpos] [0]);
    /* replace data with that stored */
    gotoxy(DATA_start,data [vpos] [0]);
    printf("%s",prompts [vpos] [1]);
    vpos++; /* down one line */
    direction = down; /* cursor movement direction */
    line_pointer = 0; /* set pointer to beginning of
                            line */
    continue;
}

if (key [0] == 0 && key [1] == 60) /* F2 key */
    break;

if (key [0] == 27) /* escape key */
    break;

if (key [0] == 0) { /* unused extended key */
    putch(7); /* beep */
    continue;
}

/* out of room (8 is backspace) */
if (line_pointer == data [vpos] [2] && key [0] != 8) {
    putch(7); /* beep */
    continue;
}
```

```
/* create empty prompt line */
if (line_pointer == 0) { /* no data entered yet */
   underlines [0] = '\0'; /* clear variable */
   for (counter = 1;counter <= data [vpos] [2];
                                      counter++)
      strcat(underlines,"_"); /* supply underlines */

   gotoxy(DATA_start,data [vpos] [0]);
   /* print underlined data line */
   printf("%s",underlines);
   /* set cursor to beginning of line */
   gotoxy(DATA_start,data [vpos] [0]);

   /* invalid key */
   if (key [0] == 0 || key [0] == 27 || key [0] == 9){
      putch(7); /* beep */
      continue;
   }

   /* clear variable */
   (prompts [vpos] [1][0]='\0';
}

if (key [0] == 8) { /* backspace */
   if (line_pointer == 0) { /* no place to back up */
      putch(7); /* beep */
      continue;
   }
   else { /* ok to back up */
      line_pointer--; /* move to deleted character */
      gotoxy(DATA_start + line_pointer,
             data [vpos] [0]);
      /* erase character */
      /* replace character with underline */
      putch('_');
      prompts [vpos] [1] [line_pointer] = '\0';
      continue;
   }
}

switch (data [vpos] [3]) {
```

```
case DATE: /* data is a date */
    if (isdigit(key [0])) { /* digits only */
        /* just past month or day */
        if (line_pointer == 2 || line_pointer == 5) {
            put_char(vpos,&line_pointer,'/',
                    prompts,data);
            put_char(vpos,&line_pointer,
                    (char) key [0],prompts,data);
            continue;
        }
        else {
            put_char(vpos,&line_pointer,
                    (char) key [0],prompts,data);
            continue;
        }
    }
    else {
        putch(7); /* beep */
        continue;
    }

case NUMERIC: /* data is a number */
    /* test character to see if digit */
    if (strchr("0123456789-.",key [0])) {
        put_char(vpos,&line_pointer,
                (char) key [0],prompts,data);
        continue;
    }
    else {
        putch(7); /* beep */
        continue;
    }

case PHONE: /* data is a telephone number */
    if (isdigit(key [0])) { /* test character */
        /* character position */
        switch (line_pointer) {

            case 0:
                put_char(vpos,&line_pointer,'(',
                        prompts,data);
```

```
                        put_char(vpos,&line_pointer,
                                    (char) key [0],prompts,data);
                        continue;

                case 4:
                    /* positioned just after area code */
                    put_char(vpos,&line_pointer,')',
                                prompts,data);
                    put_char(vpos,&line_pointer,
                                (char) key [0],prompts,data);
                    continue;

                case 8:
                    /* positioned just past exchange */
                    put_char(vpos,&line_pointer,'-',
                                prompts,data);
                    put_char(vpos,&line_pointer,
                                (char) key [0],prompts,data);
                    continue;

                default:
                    /* positioned anywhere else in
                        number */
                    put_char(vpos,&line_pointer,
                                (char) key [0],prompts,data);
                    continue;
            } /* end of second switch */
        } /* end of if */

        else {
            putch(7); /* beep */
            continue;
        }

    case ALPHA: /* alphanumeric */
        put_char(vpos,&line_pointer,
                    (char) key [0],prompts,data);
        continue;

    } /* end of first switch */

} /* end of while (true) */
return (key [0]);
```

```
} /* end of data_entry function */


void put_char(int vpos,int *line_pointer,char ch,
              char prompts [] [2] [PROMPT_len],
              int data [] [INPUT_size])
/* place new character */
{
   char new_char [2];

   /* convert character ch to string for strcat() */
   new_char [0] = ch;
   new_char [1] = '\0';

   /* add new character */
   strcat(prompts [vpos] [1],new_char);
   gotoxy(DATA_start + *line_pointer,data [vpos] [0]);
   putch(ch); /* place character on screen */
   if (*line_pointer < data [vpos] [2]) {
      *line_pointer += 1;
   }
}

void convert_date(struct date *now,char system_date [])
/* convert system date to MM/DD/YY format */
{
   char temp_date [3]; /* for date variables */

   getdate(now);

   /* convert the month */
   system_date [0] = '\0';
   itoa(now -> da_mon,temp_date,10);
   /* add a leading 0 if necessary */
   if (strlen(temp_date) == 1) {
      strcat(system_date,"0");
      strcat(system_date,temp_date);
   }
   else
      strcat(system_date,temp_date);

   /* convert days */
   strcat(system_date,"/");
```

```
      itoa(now -> da_day,temp_date,10);
      /* add a leading 0 if required */
      if (strlen(temp_date) == 1) {
         strcat(system_date,"0");
         strcat(system_date,temp_date);
      }
      else
         strcat(system_date,temp_date);

      /* convert year and truncate it */
      strcat(system_date,"/");
      itoa(now -> da_year - 1900,temp_date,10);
      strcat(system_date,temp_date);
   }


void lite_prompt(int vpos,char prompts [] [2] [PROMPT_len])
/* highlight the prompt for data to be entered */
{
   int counter,
       bright_char;

   for (counter = 0;counter < strlen(prompts [vpos]
                                      [0]);counter++) {
      gotoxy(INDENT + counter,vpos + 2);
      bright_char = prompts [vpos] [0] [counter];
      hilite(bright_char);
   }
}


void get_key(int key [])
/* to get ASCII and scan codes */
{

   bioskey(key);

}/* end function get_key*/


void clrscr(void)
/* clear screen */
```

```
{
   union REGS regs;

   regs.h.ah = 6;                 /* bios function */
   regs.h.al = 0;                 /* clear entire screen */
   regs.h.bh = 7;                 /* normal attribute */
   regs.h.ch = 0;                 /* upper row position */
   regs.h.cl = 0;                 /* upper-left column
                                     position */
   regs.h.dh = 24;                /* lowest row */
   regs.h.dl = 79;                /* rightmost column */
   int86(0x10,&regs,&regs);       /* bios interrupt number */
} /* end function clear screen */


void bioskey(int key [])
/* get key press via bios */
{
   union REGS inregs, outregs;

   inregs.h.ah = 0;
   int86(0x16,&inregs,&outregs);

   key [0] = (int) outregs.h.al; /* ASCII code */
   key [1] = (int) outregs.h.ah; /* scan code */
} /* end function bioskey */


void gotoxy(int x,int y)
/* position cursor */
{

   union REGS regs;


   regs.h.ah = 2;                 /* bios function */
   regs.h.dh = (char) y;          /* row */
   regs.h.dl = (char) x;          /* column */
   regs.h.bh = 0;                 /* video page number */
   int86(0x10,&regs,&regs);       /* bios interrupt number */
} /* end function gotoxy */
```

```
void hilite(int bright_char)
/* highlight the character at the cursor */
{
    union REGS regs;

    regs.h.ah = 9;                      /* bios function */
    regs.h.al = (char) bright_char;     /* ASCII code of
                                           character */

    regs.h.bh = 0;                      /* display page */
    regs.h.bl = 0x0f;                   /* bold */
    regs.h.cl = 1;                      /* number of
                                           characters */

    regs.h.ch = 0;
    int86(0x10,&regs,&regs);            /* bios interrupt
                                           number */

} /* end function hilite */


void getdate(struct date *today)
/* get date via bios */
{
    union REGS inregs, outregs;

    inregs.h.ah = 0x2A;
    int86(0x21,&inregs,&outregs);

    today->da_year = (int) outregs.h.cl + 256 *
                     (int) outregs.h.ch;
    today->da_day = outregs.h.dl;
    today->da_mon = outregs.h.dh;

} /* end function getdate */
```

The convert_date function illustrates a method of working with the date structure returned by the bios interrupt 21h, function 2Ah.

The prompts and data arrays are loaded with the information required by the program. The prompt array is simple: It includes the prompt asking for the data and the result returned by the operator. Note that numeric values are stored as characters and must be converted later on by your calling program.

The data array has four fields. The first value provides the row on the screen where the prompt will be displayed and the data entered. The horizontal positions of both the prompt and data fields are the same for all entries and are set with the #define INDENT and DATA_start constants. As mentioned earlier, you could easily convert these to structures.

The second data array value denotes whether the data is protected or not. A 0 (NOCHANGE) means protected, a 1 (CHANGE) means entry is permitted.

The third data value provides the length of data expected in characters.

The last data value can be one of four:

1. Date in XX/XX/XX format
2. Numeric
3. Telephone number
4. Character

When a date is entered the /s are supplied automatically; the phone entry expects an area code and supplies the (,), and - as the digits are entered. The date entry defaults to the system date using convert_date( ); the telephone number is blank. Dates are not validated.

Date and telephone entries only accept digits. Numeric entries accept the minus sign and period as well.

The Return key moves down to the next data entry; the up-arrow moves the highlight towards the top of the list. When entering data, a carriage return completes the entry. Automatic movement to the next field when the previous one is filled is not provided; however, you could easily add it if you wished. The code that tests for that condition is already present to provide a beep when the operator runs out of room.

When you begin entering data to a field, the available length of the field is underlined so the operator can see how much room remains. In this version, any previous data in a field is erased when you re-enter data.

The Backspace key works, but not the Insert and Delete keys. However, see the later versions in this chapter.

The F2 or Escape key will return you to the calling program. These can easily be changed.

A couple of switch loops to get and test the operator's input and a bunch of IF statements to test other conditions comprise the main program loop.

MULTIPLE PAGE DATA ENTRY

The next example adds multiple page entry to the first example. The program uses the #define PAGESIZE constant to determine which prompts and data fields go on which page.

```
/* Chapter 2, Example 2, QuickC, 4/14/88
 Simplest formatted data entry including multiple pages */

#include <stdio.h>
#include <string.h>
#include <dos.h>
#include <conio.h>
#include <bios.h>
#include <ctype.h>
#include <stdlib.h>

#define INPUT_data 7  /* number of prompts and data
                             including 0 */
#define INPUT_size 4  /* number of dimensions */
#define PROMPT_len 38 /* length of prompt and data
                             including 0 */
#define INDENT     2  /* indent prompt from left */
#define DATA_start 40 /* column entry starts in */
#define PAGESIZE   4  /* maximum number of lines per page
                             including 0 */
#define DATE 1          /* date data */
#define NUMERIC 2       /* numeric data */
#define PHONE 3         /* telephone number data */
#define ALPHA 4         /* alphanumeric data */
#define CHANGE 1        /* ok to change data */
#define NOCHANGE 0      /* not ok to change data */

struct date {
      int   da_year;
      char  da_day;
      char  da_mon;
};

/* function prototypes */
void get_key(int key []);
```

```
int data_entry(char prompts [] [2] [PROMPT_len],
               int data [] [INPUT_size]);
void lite_prompt(int vpos,char prompts [] [2] [PROMPT_len],
               int data [] [INPUT_size]);
void convert_date(struct date *today,char system_date []);
void put_char(int vpos,int *line_pointer,char ch,
               char prompts [] [2] [PROMPT_len],
               int data [] [INPUT_size]);
void start_screen(int form,int *maxlines,int *vpos,
               char prompts [] [2] [PROMPT_len],
               int data [] [INPUT_size]);
void getdate(struct date *today);
void main(void);
void clrscr(void);
void gotoxy(int x,int y);
void bioskey(int key []);
void hilite(int bright_char);


void main()
{
   /* zero element included in dimension values */
   int data [INPUT_data] [INPUT_size],
       return_key; /* key used to exit data entry */
   char prompts [INPUT_data] [2] [PROMPT_len],
       system_date [9];
   struct date today; /* for system date */

   /* get system date */
   convert_date(&today,system_date);

   /* prompts */
   strcpy(&prompts [0] [0] [0],"Name");
   strcpy(&prompts [1] [0] [0],"Date");
   strcpy(&prompts [2] [0] [0],"Protected data");
   strcpy(&prompts [3] [0] [0],"Telephone number");
   strcpy(&prompts [4] [0] [0],"Enter a number");
   strcpy(&prompts [5] [0] [0],"Testing second page, first
line");
   strcpy(&prompts [6] [0] [0],"Testing second page, second
line");
```

```
/* default responses */
strcpy(&prompts [0] [1] [0],"");
strcpy(&prompts [1] [1] [0],system_date);
strcpy(&prompts [2] [1] [0],"You can't change this!");
strcpy(&prompts [3] [1] [0],"");
strcpy(&prompts [4] [1] [0],"0");
strcpy(&prompts [5] [1] [0],"");
strcpy(&prompts [6] [1] [0],"");

/* name data */
data [0] [0] = 2;          /* display on second line */
data [0] [1] = CHANGE;     /* ok to change */
data [0] [2] = 25;         /* length of string expected */
data [0] [3] = ALPHA;      /* alphanumeric */

/* date data */
data [1] [0] = 3;          /* display on third line */
data [1] [1] = CHANGE;     /* ok to change */
data [1] [2] = 8;          /* length of string expected */
data [1] [3] = DATE;       /* date */

/* protected data */
data [2] [0] = 4;          /* display on fourth line */
data [2] [1] = NOCHANGE;   /* not ok to change */
data [2] [2] = 21;         /* length of string expected */
data [2] [3] = ALPHA;      /* alphanumeric */

/* telephone data */
data [3] [0] = 5;          /* display on fifth line */
data [3] [1] = CHANGE;     /* ok to change */
data [3] [2] = 13;         /* length of string expected */
data [3] [3] = PHONE;      /* phone number */

/* number data */
data [4] [0] = 6;          /* display on sixth line */
data [4] [1] = CHANGE;     /* ok to change */
data [4] [2] = 10;         /* length of string expected */
data [4] [3] = NUMERIC;    /* numeric */


/* to test second page */
```

```
/* alphanumeric data */
data [5] [0] = 2;        /* display on second line */
data [5] [1] = CHANGE;   /* ok to change */
data [5] [2] = 20;       /* length of string expected */
data [5] [3] = ALPHA;    /* alphanumeric */


/* alphanumeric data */
data [6] [0] = 3;        /* display on third line */
data [6] [1] = CHANGE;   /* ok to change */
data [6] [2] = 20;       /* length of string expected */
data [6] [3] = ALPHA;    /* alphanumeric */

/* required for following clrscr() to work properly
   in QC environment */
printf("\n");

clrscr(); /* clear screen */

/* do it */
return_key = data_entry(prompts,data);

/* verify choice */
clrscr();
gotoxy(1,1);
if (return_key == 27)
   printf("Return key was escape\n");
else {
   printf("Return key was F2\n\n");
   printf("%s %s\n",prompts [0] [0],prompts [0] [1]);
   printf("%s %s\n",prompts [1] [0],prompts [1] [1]);
   printf("%s %s\n",prompts [2] [0],prompts [2] [1]);
   printf("%s %s\n",prompts [3] [0],prompts [3] [1]);
   printf("%s %s\n",prompts [4] [0],prompts [4] [1]);
   printf("%s %s\n",prompts [5] [0],prompts [5] [1]);
   printf("%s %s\n",prompts [6] [0],prompts [6] [1]);
}
}


int data_entry(char prompts [] [2] [PROMPT_len],
               int data [] [INPUT_size])
```

```
/* display the screen and get the data entered */
{
    int true = 1, /* for boolean type responses */
        down = 1, /* cursor movement direction */
        up = 0, /* last vertical cursor movement
                    direction was upwards */
        direction = down, /* last vertical cursor movement
                            direction was downwards */
        vpos = 0, /* default first entry line */
        counter,
        line_pointer = 0, /* character position in data line
                            including 0 */
        key [2], /* keypress */
        max_lines = 0, /* highest prompt number on a page
                        including 0 */
        max_forms, /* number of pages including 0 */
        form = 0; /* screen number being shown including 0 */
    char underlines [PROMPT_len]; /* for underlined data
                                    line */

    key [0] = 0; /* for get_key() */
    key [1] = 0;

    /* determine number of pages */
    if (INPUT_data > PAGESIZE)
        max_forms = INPUT_data / PAGESIZE;

    /* set up first screen */
    start_screen(form,&max_lines,&vpos,prompts,data);

    while (true) {
        if (vpos < form * (PAGESIZE + 1)) {
            if (form > 0) {
                form--; /* previous screen */

                /* paint new screen */
                start_screen(form,&max_lines,&vpos,
                            prompts,data);

                /* vpos is set wrong and wrong prompt is
                    highlighted */
                gotoxy(INDENT,data [vpos] [0]);
                printf("%s",prompts [vpos] [0]);
```

```
            vpos = max_lines;
            lite_prompt(vpos,prompts,data);
        }
        else
            vpos = max_lines; /* wrap highlight */
}

if (vpos > max_lines) { /* past last prompt */
    if (form < max_forms) {
        form++; /* next screen */
        /* paint new screen */
        start_screen(form,&max_lines,&vpos,
                     prompts,data);
    }
    else
        /* wrap highlight */
        vpos = form * (PAGESIZE + 1);
}

if (data [vpos] [1] == 0) {  /* protected data */
    if (direction == down)
        vpos++; /* skip protected data */
    else
        vpos--; /* skip protected data */
    continue;
}

/* highlight new position */
lite_prompt(vpos,prompts,data);
gotoxy(DATA_start + line_pointer,data [vpos] [0]);
get_key(key); /* get keypress */
if (key [0] == 0 && key [1] == 72) { /* up-arrow */
    gotoxy(INDENT,data [vpos] [0]);

    /* replace highlighted prompt */
    printf("%s",prompts [vpos] [0]);
    vpos--; /* up one line */
    direction = up; /* cursor movement direction */

    /* set pointer to beginning of line */
    line_pointer = 0;
    continue;
}
```

```
if (key [0] == 13) { /* carriage return */
   gotoxy(INDENT,data [vpos] [0]);

   /* replace highlighted prompt */
   printf("%s",prompts [vpos] [0]);

   /* replace data with that stored */
   gotoxy(DATA_start,data [vpos] [0]);
   printf("%s",prompts [vpos] [1]);
   vpos++; /* down one line */
   direction = down; /* cursor movement direction */

   /* set pointer to beginning of line */
   line_pointer = 0;
   continue;
}

if (key [0] == 0 && key [1] == 60) /* F2 key */
   break;

if (key [0] == 27) /* escape key */
   break;

if (key [0] == 0) { /* unused extended key */
   putch(7); /* beep */
   continue;
}

/* out of room (8 is backspace) */
if (line_pointer == data [vpos] [2] && key [0] != 8) {
   putch(7); /* beep */
   continue;
}

/* create empty prompt line */
if (line_pointer == 0) { /* no data entered yet */
   underlines [0] = '\0'; /* clear variable */
   for (counter = 1;counter <= data [vpos] [2];
                                     counter++)
      strcat(underlines,"_"); /* supply underlines */
   gotoxy(DATA_start,data [vpos] [0]);
```

```
        /* print underlined data line */
        printf("%s",underlines);

        /* set cursor to beginning of line */
        gotoxy(DATA_start,data [vpos] [0]);

        /* invalid key, escape or extended key */
        if (key [0] == 0 || key [0] == 27 ||
                                            key [0] == 9) {
            putch(7); /* beep */
            continue;
        }

        /* clear variable */
        (prompts [vpos] [1][0] ='\0';
    }

    if (key [0] == 8) { /* backspace */
        if (line_pointer == 0) { /* no place to back up */
            putch(7); /* beep */
            continue;
        }
        else { /* ok to back up */
            line_pointer--; /* move to deleted character */
            gotoxy(DATA_start + line_pointer,
                    data [vpos] [0]);

            /* erase character */
            /* replace character with underline */
            putch('_');
            prompts [vpos] [1] [line_pointer] = '\0';
            continue;
        }
    }

    switch (data [vpos] [3]) {

        case DATE: /* data is date */
            if (isdigit(key [0])) { /* digits only */
                if (line_pointer == 2 || line_pointer == 5) {
                    put_char(vpos,&line_pointer,'/',
                            prompts,data);
```

```
                    put_char(vpos,&line_pointer,
                            (char) key [0],prompts,data);
                    continue;
                }
                else {
                    put_char(vpos,&line_pointer,
                            (char) key [0],prompts,data);
                    continue;
                }
            }
            else {
                putch(7); /* beep */
                continue;
            }

        case NUMERIC: /* data is a number */
            /* test character to be sure it is digit */
            if (strchr("0123456789-.",key [0])) {
                put_char(vpos,&line_pointer,
                        (char) key [0],prompts,data);
                continue;
            }
            else {
                putch(7); /* beep */
                continue;
            }

        case PHONE: /* data is a telephone number */
            /* test character to be sure it is digit */
            if (isdigit(key [0])) {
                /* character position */
                switch (line_pointer) {

                    case 0:
                        /* positioned at beginning of number */
                        put_char(vpos,&line_pointer,'(',
                                prompts,data);
                        put_char(vpos,&line_pointer,
                                (char) key [0],prompts,data);
                        continue;
```

```
                case 4:
                    /* positioned just after area code */
                    put_char(vpos,&line_pointer,')',
                            prompts,data);
                    put_char(vpos,&line_pointer,
                            (char) key [0],prompts,data);
                    continue;

                case 8:
                    /* positioned just after exchange */
                    put_char(vpos,&line_pointer,'-',
                            prompts,data);
                    put_char(vpos,&line_pointer,
                            (char) key [0],prompts,data);
                    continue;

                default:
                    /* any other position */
                    put_char(vpos,&line_pointer,
                            (char) key [0],prompts,data);
                    continue;
                } /* end of second switch */
            } /* end of if */
            else {
                putch(7); /* beep */
                continue;
            }

        case ALPHA: /* alphanumeric */
            put_char(vpos,&line_pointer,
                    (char) key [0],prompts,data);
            continue;
        } /* end of first switch */
    } /* end of while (true) */
    return (key [0]);
} /* end of data_entry function */


void start_screen(int form,int *max_lines,int *vpos,
                char prompts [] [2] [PROMPT_len],
                int data [] [INPUT_size])
```

```
/* put new character on the screen and append to the
   variable */
{
   char help [50];
   int counter;

   strcpy(help,"Use F2 to save data, escape to leave entry
screen");
   /* highest array position on page*/
   *max_lines = PAGESIZE + form * (PAGESIZE + 1);
   if (*max_lines > INPUT_data - 1) /* past end of array */
      *max_lines = INPUT_data - 1;

   clrscr(); /* clear screen */

   /* print border */
   for (counter = 0;counter < 79;counter++) {
      /* upper border line */
      gotoxy(counter + 1,1);
      putch('=');
      /* draw lower border */
      gotoxy(counter + 1,*max_lines % (PAGESIZE + 1) + 4);
      putch('=');
   }

   /* print prompts and defaults */
   for (counter = form * (PAGESIZE + 1);
                        counter <= *max_lines;counter++) {
      gotoxy(INDENT,data [counter] [0]);
      printf("%s",prompts [counter] [0]); /* prompt */
      gotoxy(DATA_start,data [counter] [0]);
      printf("%s",prompts [counter] [1]); /* data */
   }

   /* print help line */
   gotoxy((80 - strlen(help)) / 2,
          *max_lines % (PAGESIZE + 1) + 3);
   printf("%s",help);

   /* highlight prompt line where data is being accepted */
   *vpos = form * (PAGESIZE + 1);
   lite_prompt(*vpos,prompts,data);
}
```

```c
void put_char(int vpos,int *line_pointer,char ch,
              char prompts [] [2] [PROMPT_len],
              int data [] [INPUT_size])
/* place new character */
{
   char new_char [2];

   /* convert character ch to string for strcat() */
   new_char [0] = ch;
   new_char [1] = '\0';

   /* add new character */
   strcat(prompts [vpos] [1],new_char);
   gotoxy(DATA_start + *line_pointer,data [vpos] [0]);
   putch(ch); /* place character on screen */
   if (*line_pointer < data [vpos] [2]) {
      *line_pointer += 1;
   }
}


void convert_date(struct date *now,char system_date [])
/* convert system date to MM/DD/YY format */
{
   char temp_date [3]; /* for date year */

   getdate(now);

   /* convert month */
   system_date [0] = '\0';
   itoa(now -> da_mon,temp_date,10);
   /* add leading 0 if required */
   if (strlen(temp_date) == 1) {
      /* only one digit */
      strcat(system_date,"0");
      strcat(system_date,temp_date);
   }
   else
      strcat(system_date,temp_date);

   /* convert days */
   strcat(system_date,"/");
   itoa(now -> da_day,temp_date,10);
```

```
   /* add leading 0 if required */
   if (strlen(temp_date) == 1) {
      /* only one digit */
      strcat(system_date,"0");
      strcat(system_date,temp_date);
   }
   else
      strcat(system_date,temp_date);

   /* convert year */
   strcat(system_date,"/");
   /* cut year to two digits */
   itoa(now -> da_year - 1900,temp_date,10);
   strcat(system_date,temp_date);
}

void lite_prompt(int vpos,
                 char prompts [] [2] [PROMPT_len],
                 int data [] [INPUT_size])
/* highlight the prompt for data to be entered */
{
   int counter;

   /* highlight each character */
   for (counter = 0;counter <
                    strlen(prompts [vpos] [0]);counter++) {
      gotoxy(INDENT + counter,data [vpos] [0]);
      hilite(prompts [vpos] [0] [counter]);
   }
}


void getdate(struct date *today)
/* get date via bios and store in structure */
{
   union REGS inregs, outregs;

   inregs.h.ah = 0x2A;
   int86(0x21,&inregs,&outregs);

   today->da_year = (int) outregs.h.cl + 256 *
                    (int) outregs.h.ch;
```

```
        today->da_day = outregs.h.dl;
        today->da_mon = outregs.h.dh;

    } /* end function getdate */



    void get_key(int key [])
    /* to get ASCII and scan codes */
    {

        bioskey(key);

    }/* end function get_key*/



    void clrscr(void)
    /* clear screen */

    {
        union REGS regs;

        regs.h.ah = 6;                      /* bios function */
        regs.h.al = 0;                      /* clear entire screen */
        regs.h.bh = 7;                      /* normal attribute */
        regs.h.ch = 0;                      /* upper row position */
        regs.h.cl = 0;                      /* upper-left column
                                               position */
        regs.h.dh = 24;                     /* lowest row */
        regs.h.dl = 79;                     /* rightmost column */
        int86(0x10,&regs,&regs);           /* bios interrupt number */
    } /* end function clear screen */



    void bioskey(int key [])
    /* get key press via bios */
    {
        union REGS inregs, outregs;
        inregs.h.ah = 0;
        int86(0x16,&inregs,&outregs);

        key [0] = (int) outregs.h.al; /* ASCII code */
        key [1] = (int) outregs.h.ah; /* scan code */
    } /* end function bioskey */
```

```
void gotoxy(int x,int y)
/* position cursor */
{

    union REGS regs;


    regs.h.ah = 2;              /* bios function */
    regs.h.dh = (char) y;       /* row */
    regs.h.dl = (char) x;       /* column */
    regs.h.bh = 0;              /* video page number */
    int86(0x10,&regs,&regs);    /* bios interrupt number */
} /* end function gotoxy */


void hilite(int bright_char)
/* highlight the character at the cursor */
{
    union REGS regs;

    regs.h.ah = 9;              /* bios function */
    regs.h.al = (char) bright_char; /* ASCII code of
                                       character */
    regs.h.bh = 0;              /* display page */
    regs.h.bl = 0x0f;           /* reverse */
    regs.h.cl = 1;              /* number of
                                   characters */
    regs.h.ch = 0;
    int86(0x10,&regs,&regs);    /* bios interrupt
                                   number */

} /* end function hilite */
```

The pages are automatically switched in start_screen( ). When you pass the bottom of a page you are placed at the top of the next (if it exists). Try to move past the top of a page and you are placed at the bottom of the previous page, if any. The PAGESIZE constant is your only control over the point where the pages are divided. Example 3 is much more flexible in this regard.

ADVANCED FORMATTED DATA ENTRY

This next program might be just what you're looking for if the previous examples were not. In addition to all the features of Example 2, this example also includes:

- Time fields, validated (HH:MM:SS)
- Validated date fields
- Boolean fields
- Dollar fields
- Must-fill fields
- Must-enter fields
- Down-arrow moves highlight down
- Field insert, deletion, and type-over editing
- Change fields anytime
- Place fields anywhere on the screen

The dollar field rounds the entry to two decimal places when you leave the field. You can't move past a must-fill field unless you supply characters for the entire field; you get a beep otherwise. However, you can leave a must-fill field totally blank; only partial field entries are flagged. You cannot move past a must-enter field without doing so. You cannot use F2 to leave data entry with any blank must-fill fields either; you can use the Escape key, though.

Date and time entry fields are checked for validity. No 25:00:00 or 09:67:15 entries are permitted, or 02/30/87, for that matter. The valid time range is 00:00:00 to 23:59:59. You get the usual beep and are not permitted to leave the field without correcting it.

If you move the highlight to an already-entered field and start typing, the old entry will be erased. If you use the right-arrow to enter the field before you begin typing, you can use the right- and left-arrow keys to move the cursor back and forth within the field, the Delete key to delete a character, or you can type over any characters. The Insert key works a bit differently than you might expect. If you press the Insert key you can insert *one* character at the cursor position. The trailing characters are moved to the right; the rightmost is truncated if the entry now exceeds the field size. You can insert multiple characters but you must press the Insert key for each of them.

You can use the up- or down-arrow to move the highlight anytime; you need not hit the Return key first.

A boolean field will accept only one character from the following list: Y, y, N, n, T, t, F, or f. The result is a "Y" if the entry is Y, y, T, or t; otherwise "N".

You can position any prompt or entry field starting at any row and column on any page. It's up to the programmer to avoid any conflicts or illegal columns or rows; the program doesn't check. There is no maximum number of pages, but it would probably be a good idea to have at least one field on every page and begin with page 1 to avoid confusing the operator.

Here is a list of all the data codes. There are ten entries for each prompt and entry field.

1. Enter the line where the prompt should appear. The first line is 1, not 0.
2. Enter the line where the associated data field should be placed.
3. Enter the number of the column where the prompt should begin. The leftmost is 1, not 0.
4. Enter the number of the column where the associated data field should begin.
5. Enter the page number here. The first page is 0, not 1.
6. Enter a 1 here if you wish the field to be must_enter, otherwise 0.
7. Enter a 1 here if the data field can be changed, 0 if display-only.
8. Enter the length of the field, in characters, here.
9. Enter the number of one of the following field types here:
   1. Date
   2. Numeric
   3. Telephone number
   4. Alphanumeric
   5. Time
   6. Dollar
   7. Boolean
10. Enter a 1 here if you wish the field to be must-fill, otherwise 0.

Look at the following example if you're not sure about these entries. It shows the use of two pages and every option at least once.

```
/* Chapter 2, Example 3, QuickC, 4/14/88
 Formatted data entry including multiple pages, with dollar,
 time, must-fill, and must-enter fields, time and date
 validation, use up- or down-arrow anytime to change fields,
 place fields anywhere, and data entry editing
*/

#include <stdio.h>
#include <string.h>
#include <conio.h>
#include <bios.h>
#include <stdlib.h>


#define INPUT_data 9   /* number of prompts and data
                          including 0 */
#define INPUT_size 10  /* number of data array dimensions
                          including 0 */
#define PROMPT_len 38  /* maximum length of prompt and data
                          including 0 */
#define DATE 1         /* date data */
#define NUMERIC 2      /* numeric data */
#define PHONE 3        /* telephone number data */
#define ALPHA 4        /* alphanumeric data */
#define TIME 5         /* time data */
#define DOLLAR 6       /* money data */
#define BOOLEAN 7      /* boolean data */
#define CHANGE 1       /* ok to change data */
#define NOCHANGE 0     /* not ok to change data */
#define MUSTFILL 1     /* must fill this field */
#define NOMUSTFILL 0   /* not necessary to fill this field */
#define MUSTENTER 1    /* must-enter field */
#define NOMUSTENTER 0  /* not a must-enter field */

struct date {
        int da_year;
        char da_day;
        char da_mon;
};
```

```
/* function prototypes */
void get_key(int key []);
int data_entry(char prompts [] [2] [PROMPT_len],
               int data [] [INPUT_size]);
void lite_prompt(int vpos,char prompts [] [2] [PROMPT_len],
                 int data [] [INPUT_size]);
void convert_date(struct date *today,char system_date []);
void put_char(int vpos,int *line_pointer,char ch,
              char prompts [] [2] [PROMPT_len],
              int data [] [INPUT_size]);
void start_screen(int form,int *maxlines,int *min_line,
                  int *vpos,
                  char prompts [] [2] [PROMPT_len],
                  int data [] [INPUT_size]);
int test_entry(int counter,
               char prompts [] [2] [PROMPT_len],
               int data [] [INPUT_size]);
int test_date(int counter,char prompts [] [2] [PROMPT_len]);
int test_time(int counter,char prompts [] [2] [PROMPT_len]);
void set_dollar(int counter,
                char prompts [] [2] [PROMPT_len]);
void show_data(char prompts [] [2] [PROMPT_len],
               int data [] [INPUT_size],int vpos);
void main(void);
void gotoxy(int h,int y);
void clrscr(void);
void bioskey(int key []);
void hilite(int bright_char);
void getdate(struct date *today);
void clreol(int x);


void main(void)
{
    /* zero element included in dimension values */
    int data [INPUT_data] [INPUT_size],
        return_key; /* key used to exit data entry */
    char prompts [INPUT_data] [2] [PROMPT_len],
         system_date [9];
    struct date today; /* for system date */

    /* get system date */
    convert_date(&today,system_date);
```

```
/* prompts */
strcpy(&prompts [0] [0] [0],"Text, must-fill field");
strcpy(&prompts [1] [0] [0],"Date");
strcpy(&prompts [2] [0] [0],"Protected data");
strcpy(&prompts [3] [0] [0],"Telephone number");
strcpy(&prompts [4] [0] [0],"Enter a number");
strcpy(&prompts [5] [0] [0],"Time");
strcpy(&prompts [6] [0] [0],"Must enter data here");
strcpy(&prompts [7] [0] [0],"Dollar amount");
strcpy(&prompts [8] [0] [0],"(Y)es or (N)o");

/* default responses */
strcpy(&prompts [0] [1] [0],"Testing");
strcpy(&prompts [1] [1] [0],system_date);
strcpy(&prompts [2] [1] [0],"You can't change this!");
strcpy(&prompts [3] [1] [0],"");
strcpy(&prompts [4] [1] [0],"0");
strcpy(&prompts [5] [1] [0],"00:00:00");
strcpy(&prompts [6] [1] [0],"");
strcpy(&prompts [7] [1] [0],"0.00");
strcpy(&prompts [8] [1] [0],"Y");

/* text, must-fill data */
data [0] [0] = 2;              /* display prompt on second
                                  line */
data [0] [1] = 2;              /* display data on second
                                  line */
data [0] [2] = 2;              /* prompt starting
                                  position */
data [0] [3] = 40;            /* data starting position */
data [0] [4] = 0;            /* page number */
data [0] [5] = NOMUSTENTER;  /* not must-enter data */
data [0] [6] = CHANGE;       /* ok to change */
data [0] [7] = 8;             /* length of string
                                  expected */
data [0] [8] = ALPHA;         /* alphanumeric */
data [0] [9] = MUSTFILL;      /* must-fill field */

/* date data */
data [1] [0] = 3;              /* display prompt on third
                                  line */
data [1] [1] = 3;              /* display data on third
                                  line */
```

```
        data [1] [2] = 2;                /* prompt starting
                                            position */
        data [1] [3] = 40;               /* data starting
                                            position */
        data [1] [4] = 0;                /* page number */
        data [1] [5] = NOMUSTENTER;      /* not must-enter data */
        data [1] [6] = CHANGE;           /* ok to change */
        data [1] [7] = 8;                /* length of string
                                            expected */
        data [1] [8] = DATE;             /* date */
        data [1] [9] = NOMUSTFILL;       /* not must-fill field */

        /* protected data */
        data [2] [0] = 4;                /* display prompt on fourth
                                            line */

        data [2] [1] = 4;                /* display data on fourth
                                            line */

        data [2] [2] = 2;                /* prompt starting
                                            position */

        data [2] [3] = 40;               /* data starting
                                            position */

        data [2] [4] = 0;                /* page number */
        data [2] [5] = NOMUSTENTER;      /* not must-enter data */
        data [2] [6] = NOCHANGE;         /* not ok to change */
        data [2] [7] = 21;               /* length of string
                                            expected */

        data [2] [8] = ALPHA;            /* alphanumeric (never
                                            checked) */

        data [2] [9] = NOMUSTFILL;       /* not must-fill field */

        /* telephone data */
        data [3] [0] = 5;                /* display prompt on fifth
                                            line */

        data [3] [1] = 5;                /* display data on fifth
                                            line */

        data [3] [2] = 2;                /* prompt starting
                                            position */

        data [3] [3] = 40;               /* data starting
                                            position */

        data [3] [4] = 0;                /* page number */
        data [3] [5] = NOMUSTENTER;      /* not must-enter data */
```

```
data [3] [6] = CHANGE;              /* ok to change */
data [3] [7] = 13;                  /* length of string
                                       expected */

data [3] [8] = PHONE;               /* phone number */
data [3] [9] = NOMUSTFILL;          /* not must-fill field */


/* number data */
data [4] [0] = 6;                   /* display prompt on sixth
                                       line */

data [4] [1] = 6;                   /* display data on sixth
                                       line */

data [4] [2] = 2;                   /* prompt starting
                                       position */

data [4] [3] = 40;                  /* data starting
                                       position */

data [4] [4] = 0;                   /* page number */
data [4] [5] = NOMUSTENTER;         /* not must-enter data */
data [4] [6] = CHANGE;              /* ok to change */
data [4] [7] = 10;                  /* length of string
                                       expected */

data [4] [8] = NUMERIC;             /* numeric */
data [4] [9] = NOMUSTFILL;          /* not must-fill field */


/* to test second page */

/* time data */
data [5] [0] = 2;                   /* display prompt on second
                                       line */

data [5] [1] = 2;                   /* display data on second
                                       line */

data [5] [2] = 2;                   /* prompt starting
                                       position */

data [5] [3] = 40;                  /* data starting
                                       position */

data [5] [4] = 1;                   /* page number */
data [5] [5] = NOMUSTENTER;         /* not must-enter data */
data [5] [6] = CHANGE;              /* ok to change */
data [5] [7] = 8;                   /* length of string
                                       expected */

data [5] [8] = TIME;                /* time */
data [5] [9] = NOMUSTFILL;          /* not must-fill field */
```

```
/* alphanumeric data, must-enter */
data [6] [0] = 3;                    /* display prompt on third
                                        line */

data [6] [1] = 3;                    /* display data on third
                                        line */

data [6] [2] = 2;                    /* prompt starting
                                        position */

data [6] [3] = 40;                   /* data starting
                                        position */

data [6] [4] = 1;                    /* page number */
data [6] [5] = MUSTENTER;            /* must-enter data */
data [6] [6] = CHANGE;               /* ok to change */
data [6] [7] = 20;                   /* length of string
                                        expected */

data [6] [8] = ALPHA;                /* alphanumeric */
data [6] [9] = NOMUSTFILL;           /* not must-fill field */


/* dollar data */
data [7] [0] = 4;                    /* display prompt on fourth
                                        line */

data [7] [1] = 4;                    /* display data on fourth
                                        line */

data [7] [2] = 2;                    /* prompt starting
                                        position */

data [7] [3] = 40;                   /* data starting
                                        position */

data [7] [4] = 1;                    /* page number */
data [7] [5] = NOMUSTENTER;          /* not must-enter data */
data [7] [6] = CHANGE;               /* ok to change */
data [7] [7] = 10;                   /* length of string
                                        expected */

data [7] [8] = DOLLAR;               /* dollar */
data [7] [9] = NOMUSTFILL;           /* not must-fill field */


/* boolean data */
data [8] [0] = 5;                    /* display prompt on fifth
                                        line */

data [8] [1] = 5;                    /* display data on fifth
                                        line */

data [8] [2] = 2;                    /* prompt starting
                                        position */

data [8] [3] = 40;                   /* data starting
                                        position */
```

```
   data [8] [4] = 1;              /* page number */
   data [8] [5] = NOMUSTENTER;    /* not must-enter data */
   data [8] [6] = CHANGE;         /* ok to change */
   data [8] [7] = 1;              /* length of string
                                     expected */
   data [8] [8] = BOOLEAN;        /* boolean */
   data [8] [9] = NOMUSTFILL;     /* not must-fill field */

   /* required to make following clrscr() work correctly */
   printf("\n");
   clrscr(); /* clear screen */

   /* do it */
   return_key = data_entry(prompts,data);


   /* verify choice */
   clrscr();
   gotoxy(1,1);
   if (return_key == 27)
      printf("Return key was escape\n");
   else {
      printf("Return key was F2\n\n");
      printf("%s %s\n",prompts [0] [0],prompts [0] [1]);
      printf("%s %s\n",prompts [1] [0],prompts [1] [1]);
      printf("%s %s\n",prompts [2] [0],prompts [2] [1]);
      printf("%s %s\n",prompts [3] [0],prompts [3] [1]);
      printf("%s %s\n",prompts [4] [0],prompts [4] [1]);
      printf("%s %s\n",prompts [5] [0],prompts [5] [1]);
      printf("%s %s\n",prompts [6] [0],prompts [6] [1]);
      printf("%s %s\n",prompts [7] [0],prompts [7] [1]);
      printf("%s %s\n",prompts [8] [0],prompts [8] [1]);
   }
}


int data_entry(char prompts [] [2] [PROMPT_len],
               int data [] [INPUT_size])
/* display the screen and get the data entered */
{
   int true = 1, /* for boolean type responses */
       false = 0,
       down = 1, /* cursor movement direction */
```

```
          up = 0,
          direction = down, /* starting cursor movement
                                    direction */
          vpos = 0, /* default first entry line */
          counter,
          newline = true, /* for editing */
          entry_length, /* for editing */
          error, /* error code for invalid entries */
          line_pointer = 0, /* character position in data line
                                    including 0 */
          key [2], /* keypress */
          max_lines = 0, /* highest prompt number on a page
                                    including 0 */
          min_line = 0, /* lowest prompt number on the page */
          max_forms, /* number of pages including 0 */
          form = 0; /* screen number being shown including 0 */
    char insert_string [PROMPT_len + 1], /* for editing */
          divider; /* used for time and data */

    key [0] = 0; /* for get_key() */
    key [1] = 0;

    /* determine number of pages */
    max_forms = 0;
    for (counter = 0;counter < INPUT_data;counter++) {
       if (data [counter] [4] > max_forms)
          max_forms = data [counter] [4];
    }

    /* set up first screen */
    start_screen(form,&max_lines,&min_line,&vpos,
                prompts,data);

    while (true) {
       if (vpos < min_line) {
          /* previous page */
          if (form > 0) { /* is there previous page? */
             form--; /* previous screen */
             /* paint new screen */
             start_screen(form,&max_lines,&min_line,&vpos,
                         prompts,data);
```

```
            /* vpos is set wrong and wrong prompt is
                highlighted */
            gotoxy(data [vpos] [2],data [vpos] [0]);
            printf("%s",prompts [vpos] [0]);
            vpos = max_lines; /* bottom of page */
            lite_prompt(vpos,prompts,data);
        }
        else {
            /* same page */
            vpos = max_lines; /* wrap highlight */
            show_data(prompts,data,vpos);
        }
    }
    else {
        if (vpos > max_lines) { /* past last prompt */
            if (form < max_forms) { /* more pages? */
                form++; /* next screen */
                /* paint new screen */
                start_screen(form,&max_lines,&min_line,&vpos,
                            prompts,data);
            }
            else {
                vpos = min_line; /* wrap highlight */
                show_data(prompts,data,vpos);
            }
        }
        else {
            /* same page, beginning of line? */
            if (line_pointer == 0)
                show_data(prompts,data,vpos);
        }
    }


/* protected data */
if (data [vpos] [6] == NOCHANGE) {
    if (direction == down)
        vpos++; /* skip protected data */
    else
        vpos--; /* skip protected data */
    continue;
}
```

```
/* highlight new position */
lite_prompt(vpos,prompts,data);
gotoxy(data [vpos] [3] + line_pointer,
        data [vpos] [1]);
get_key(key); /* get keypress */

/* up-arrow */
if (key [0] == 0 && key [1] == 72) {
   error = test_entry(vpos,prompts,data);
   if (error > -1) {
      putch(7); /* beep */
      continue;
   }
   gotoxy(data [vpos] [3],data [vpos] [1]);
   /* clear to end of line for new prompt */
   clreol(data [vpos] [3]);
   gotoxy(data [vpos] [3],data [vpos] [1]);

   /* display new prompt */
   printf("%s",prompts [vpos] [1]);
   gotoxy(data [vpos] [2],data [vpos] [0]);

   /* replace highlighted prompt */
   printf("%s",prompts [vpos] [0]);
   vpos--; /* up one line */
   direction = up; /* cursor movement direction */

   /* set pointer to beginning of line */
   line_pointer = 0;
   newline = true;
   continue;
}

/* carriage return or down-arrow */
if (key [0] == 13 || (key [0] == 0 && key [1] == 80)){
   error = test_entry(vpos,prompts,data);
   if (error != -1) {
      putch(7); /* beep */
      continue;
   }
   gotoxy(data [vpos] [2],data [vpos] [0]);
   /* replace highlighted prompt */
   printf("%s",prompts [vpos] [0]);
```

```
    /* replace data with that stored */
    gotoxy(data [vpos] [3],data [vpos] [1]);
    clreol(data [vpos] [3]); /* erase line */

    /* display new version */
    gotoxy(data [vpos] [3],data [vpos] [1]);
    printf("%s",prompts [vpos] [1]);
    vpos++; /* down one line */
    direction = down; /* cursor movement direction */

    /* set pointer to beginning of line */
    line_pointer = 0;
    newline = true;
    continue;
}


/* F2 key */
if (key [0] == 0 && key [1] == 60) {
    for (counter = 0;counter < INPUT_data;counter++) {
        error = test_entry(counter,prompts,data);
        if (error > -1) {
            putch(7); /* beep */
            form = data [error] [4];
            start_screen(form,&max_lines,&min_line,&vpos,
                         prompts,data);

            /* turn off highlight set by start_screen */
            gotoxy(data [vpos] [2],data [vpos] [0]);
            printf("%s",prompts [vpos] [0]);

            /* highlight entry that needs correction */
            lite_prompt(error,prompts,data);

            /* must-enter field */
            if (data [error] [5] == MUSTENTER) {
                newline = true;
                line_pointer = 0;
                gotoxy(data [error] [3],data [error] [1]);
            }
            vpos = error;
            break; /* leave for */
        }
```

```
      }
      if (error != -1) {
         continue; /* top of while */
      }
      break;
   }

   /* escape key */
   if (key [0] == 27)
      break;

   /* right-arrow */
   if (key [0] == 0 && key [1] == 77) {
      /* room to move? */
      if (line_pointer < (data [vpos] [7] - 1)) {
         if (newline == false)
            line_pointer++; /* continue an old line */
         gotoxy(data [vpos] [3] + line_pointer,
                data [vpos] [1]);
         newline = false;
      }
      else
         putch(7); /* beep */
      continue;
   }

   /* left-arrow */
   if (newline == false && key [0] == 0 &&
                                key [1] == 75) {
      if (line_pointer > 0) { /* room to move? */
         line_pointer--;
         gotoxy(data [vpos] [3] + line_pointer,
                data [vpos] [1]);
      }
      else
         putch(7); /* beep */
      continue;
   }

   /* delete key */
   if (newline == false && key [0] == 0 &&
                                key [1] == 83) {
```

```
/* is cursor in data? */
if (line_pointer >
            (strlen(prompts [vpos] [1]) - 1)) {
   putch(7); /* beep */
   continue;
}
entry_length = strlen(prompts [vpos] [1]);

/* move trailing data to left */
memmove(&prompts [vpos] [1] [line_pointer],
        &prompts [vpos] [1] [line_pointer + 1],
        (entry_length - line_pointer) + 2);
prompts [vpos] [1] [entry_length - 1] = '\0';

/* erase old line */
show_data(prompts,data,vpos);
gotoxy(data [vpos] [3] + line_pointer,
       data [vpos] [1]);
continue;
}

/* within a data line and insert key */
if (newline == false && key [0] == 0 &&
                                key [1] == 82) {
   /* is cursor in data? */
   if (line_pointer >
               (strlen(prompts [vpos] [1]) - 1)) {
      putch(7); /* beep */
      continue;
   }
   entry_length = strlen(prompts [vpos] [1]);

   /* use temporary copy of data with room for an
      extra character in case insert makes string one
      character too long */
   strcpy(insert_string,prompts [vpos] [1]);

   /* move trailing data to right */
   memmove(&insert_string [line_pointer + 1],
           &insert_string [line_pointer],
           (entry_length - line_pointer) + 2);
   insert_string [entry_length + 1] = '\0';
```

```
/* truncate string if necessary */
if (strlen(insert_string) > (PROMPT_len - 1))
   insert_string [PROMPT_len] = '\0';

/* get character to insert */
do
   get_key(key); /* keypress */
   /* don't get an extended key */
while (key [0] == 0);

insert_string [line_pointer] = (char) key [0];

/* display new version */
gotoxy(data [vpos] [3],data [vpos] [1]);
strcpy(prompts [vpos] [1],insert_string);
printf("%s",prompts [vpos] [1]);

/* position cursor */
gotoxy(data [vpos] [3] + line_pointer,
       data [vpos] [1]);
continue;
}

/* out of room (8 is backspace) */
if (line_pointer == data [vpos] [7] && key [0] != 8) {
   putch(7); /* beep */
   continue;
}


if (key [0] == 9) { /* tab, invalid key */
   putch(7); /* beep */
   continue;
}

/* backspace */
if (key [0] == 8) {
   if (line_pointer == 0) { /* no place to back up */
      putch(7); /* beep */
      continue;
   }
   else { /* ok to back up */
```

```
            line_pointer--; /* move to deleted character */
            gotoxy(data [vpos] [3] + line_pointer,
                    data [vpos] [1]);
            /* erase character */
            /* replace character with underline */
            putch('_');
            prompts [vpos] [1] [line_pointer] = '\0';
            continue;
        }
    }


    newline = false;

    switch (data [vpos] [8]) {
        case DATE: /* data is a date */
        case TIME: /* data is time */
                /* digits only */
            if (key [0] >= '0' && key [0] <= '9') {
                if (line_pointer == 2 || line_pointer == 5) {
                    if (data [vpos] [8] == 1)
                        divider = '/';
                    else
                        divider = ':';
                    put_char(vpos,&line_pointer,divider,
                            prompts,data);
                    put_char(vpos,&line_pointer,
                            (char) key [0],prompts,data);
                    continue;
                }
                else {
                    put_char(vpos,&line_pointer,
                            (char) key [0],prompts,data);
                    continue;
                }
            }
            else {
                putch(7); /* beep */
                continue;
            }

        case NUMERIC: /* data is a number */
        case DOLLAR: /* data is a dollar figure */
```

```
                    /* test character */
                    if (strchr("0123456789-.",key [0])) {
                       put_char(vpos,&line_pointer,
                               (char) key [0],prompts,data);
                       continue;
                    }
                    else {
                       putch(7); /* beep */
                       continue;
                    }

              case PHONE: /* data is a telephone number */
                    /* test character for digit */
                    if (key [0] >= '0' && key [0] <= '9') {
                       /* character position */
                       switch (line_pointer) {

                           case 0: /* beginning of number */
                              put_char(vpos,&line_pointer,'(',
                                      prompts,data);
                              put_char(vpos,&line_pointer,
                                      (char) key [0],prompts,data);
                              continue;

                           case 4: /* right after area code */
                              put_char(vpos,&line_pointer,')',
                                      prompts,data);
                              put_char(vpos,&line_pointer,
                                      (char) key [0],prompts,data);
                              continue;

                           case 8: /* right after exchange */
                              put_char(vpos,&line_pointer,'-',
                                      prompts,data);
                              put_char(vpos,&line_pointer,
                                      (char) key [0],prompts,data);
                              continue;

                           default: /* any other position */
                              put_char(vpos,&line_pointer,
                                      (char) key [0],prompts,data);
                              continue;
```

```
                     } /* end of second switch */
                 } /* end of if */

                 else {
                    putch(7); /* beep */
                    continue;
                 }

             case ALPHA: /* alphanumeric */
                put_char(vpos,&line_pointer,
                           (char) key [0],prompts,data);
                continue;

             case BOOLEAN: /* boolean */
                 /* test character */
                 if (strchr("YNynTFtf",key [0])) {
                     if (strchr("YyTt",key [0])) /* affirmative */
                         put_char(vpos,&line_pointer,'Y',
                                    prompts,data);
                     else /* no */
                         put_char(vpos,&line_pointer,'N',
                                    prompts,data);
                     continue;
                 }
                 else {
                     putch(7); /* beep */
                     continue;
                 }

        } /* end of first switch */
    } /* end of while (true) */
    return (key [0]);
} /* end of data_entry function */


void show_data(char prompts [] [2] [PROMPT_len],
            int data [] [INPUT_size],int vpos)
{
    char underlines [PROMPT_len];

    gotoxy(data [vpos] [3],data [vpos] [1]);
    clreol(data [vpos] [3]);
```

```c
        /* supply underlines */
        memset(underlines,'_',data [vpos] [7]);
        underlines [data [vpos] [7]] = '\0';
        gotoxy(data [vpos] [3],data [vpos] [1]);
        printf("%s",underlines);

        /* display new version */
        gotoxy(data [vpos] [3],data [vpos] [1]);
        printf("%s",prompts [vpos] [1]);

        /* position cursor */
        gotoxy(data [vpos] [3],data [vpos] [1]);
}

int test_entry(int counter,
               char prompts [] [2] [PROMPT_len],
               int data [] [INPUT_size])
/* test date, time, must-fill, and must-enter fields */
{
    int error = -1; /* test data error flag */

    switch (data [counter] [8]) {
       case DATE:
          error = test_date(counter,prompts);
          break;

        case TIME:
          error = test_time(counter,prompts);
          break;

      case DOLLAR:
          set_dollar(counter,prompts);
          break;
    } /* end switch */

    if (data [counter] [5] == MUSTENTER) {
       if (strlen(prompts [counter] [1]) == 0)
          error = counter; /* indicate must-enter error */
    }
```

```
        if (data [counter] [9] == MUSTFILL) {
            if (strlen(prompts [counter] [1]) <
                                            data [counter] [7])
                error = counter; /* must-fill error */
        }
        return (error);
} /* end test_entry function */


int test_date(int counter,char prompts [] [2] [PROMPT_len]) /
/* Test date for validity. Works only from 1901 to 1999. */
{
    int month,
        days,
        year,
        error = -1; /* default error code (0 is valid) */
    char date_string [9], /* to hold copy of date */
         date_temp [3]; /* to hold portions of date */

    /* no date entered */
    if (strlen(prompts [counter] [1]) == 0)
        return (error);

    /* invalid date length */
    if (strlen(prompts [counter] [1]) != 8) {
        error = counter;
        return (error);
    }

    /* check date */
    while (1) {
        /* convert month to integer */
        strcpy(date_string,prompts [counter] [1]);
        memmove(date_temp,date_string,2);
        date_temp [2] = '\0';
        month = atoi(date_temp);

        /* test month */
        if (month < 1 || month > 12) {
```

```
      error = counter;
      break;
}

/* convert year to integer */
memmove(date_temp,&date_string [6],2);
date_temp [2] = '\0';
year = atoi(date_temp);

/* convert days to integer */
memmove(date_temp,&date_string [3],2);
date_temp [2] = '\0';
days = atoi(date_temp);

/* test days */
switch (month) {
   case 2: /* February */
      if ((year + 1900) % 4 == 0) { /* leap year? */
         if (days > 29)
            error = counter;
      }
      else {
         /* not leap year */
         if (days > 28)
            error = counter;
      }
      break;

   /* "Thirty days hath ... " */
   case 4: /* April */
   case 6: /* June */
   case 9: /* September */
   case 11: /* November */
      if (days > 30)
         error = counter;
      break;

   default:
      if (days > 31)
         error = counter;
      break;
} /* end of switch */
break; /* to leave while */
```

```
    } /* end of while */
    return (error);
} /* end of test_date function */


int test_time(int counter,char prompts [] [2] [PROMPT_len])
/* test time for validity */
{
    int hour,
        minute,
        second,
        error = -1; /* default error code (0 is valid) */
    char time_string [9], /* to hold copy of time */
         time_temp [3]; /* to hold portions of time */

    /* no time entered */
    if (strlen(prompts [counter] [1]) == 0)
        return (error);

    /* invalid time length */
    if (strlen(prompts [counter] [1]) != 8) {
        error = counter;
        return (error);
    }

    /* test time */
    while (1) { /* same as for (;;) */
        /* convert hour to integer */
        strcpy(time_string,prompts [counter] [1]);
        memmove(time_temp,time_string,2);
        time_temp [2] = '\0';

        /* test hour */
        hour = atoi(time_temp);
        if (hour < 0 || hour > 23) {
            error = counter;
            break;
        }

        /* convert minutes to integer */
        memmove(time_temp,&time_string [3],2);
        time_temp [2] = '\0';
        minute = atoi(time_temp);
```

```
        /* test minutes */
        if (minute < 0 || minute > 59) {
           error = counter;
           break;
        }

        /* convert seconds to integer */
        memmove(time_temp,&time_string [6],2);
        time_temp [2] = '\0';
        second = atoi(time_temp);

        /* test seconds */
        if (second < 0 || second > 59)
           error = counter;
        break; /* to leave while (1) */
     } /* end of while */
     return (error);
} /* end of test_time function */
void set_dollar(int counter,
                char prompts [] [2] [PROMPT_len])
/* make sure number has two decimal places */
{
    char temp [PROMPT_len]; /* temporary holder for dollar
                                value */
    int length, /* length of dollar string */
        position; /* position indicator */

    while (1) {
       /* no value entered */
       if (strlen(prompts [counter] [1]) == 0)
          break;

       /* find decimal point, if any */
       strcpy(temp,prompts [counter] [1]);
       length = strlen(temp);

       /* subtract pointers to find character position */
       position = strchr(temp,'.') - temp;

       if (position == 0) /* no cents */
          strcat(temp,".00");
```

```
      if (position + 2 < length) /* too long */
         temp [position + 3] = '\0';

      if (position + 1 == length) { /* missing last digit */
         temp [position + 2] = '0';
         temp [position + 3] = '\0';
      }

      if (position == length) /* just in case */
         strcat(temp,"00");

      /* put in new value */
      strcpy(prompts [counter] [1],temp);
      break; /* end while */
   }
} /* end function set_dollar */


void start_screen(int form,int *max_lines,int *min_line,
                  int *vpos,
                  char prompts [] [2] [PROMPT_len],
                  int data [] [INPUT_size])
/* repaint screen */
{
   char help [50];
   int max_print_line = 0, /* greatest page position for
                              help line */
       counter;

   strcpy(help,"Use F2 to save data, escape to leave entry
screen");
   /* find lowest numbered and highest numbered prompt and
      data line and position of last line on the screen */
   *max_lines = 0;
   *min_line = 1000;
   for (counter = 0;counter < INPUT_size;counter++) {
      if (data [counter] [4] == form) {
         if (counter > *max_lines)
            *max_lines = counter;
         if (counter < *min_line)
            *min_line = counter;
```

```
            if (max_print_line < data [counter] [0])
                max_print_line = data [counter] [0];
            if (max_print_line < data [counter] [1])
                max_print_line = data [counter] [1];
        }
    }


    clrscr(); /* clear screen */

    /* print prompts and defaults */
    for (counter = *min_line;
         counter <= *max_lines;
         counter++) {
      gotoxy(data [counter] [2],data [counter] [0]);
      printf("%s",prompts [counter] [0]); /* prompt */
      gotoxy(data [counter] [3],data [counter] [1]);
      printf("%s",prompts [counter] [1]); /* data */
    }

    /* print help line */
    gotoxy((80 - strlen(help)) / 2,max_print_line + 3);
    printf("%s",help);

    /* highlight prompt line where data is being accepted */
    *vpos = *min_line;
    lite_prompt(*vpos,prompts,data);
    /* display the data */
    show_data(prompts,data,*vpos);
}

void put_char(int vpos,int *line_pointer,char ch,
              char prompts [] [2] [PROMPT_len],
              int data [] [INPUT_size])
/* place new character */
{
    char new_char [2];

    new_char [0] = ch;
    new_char [1] = '\0';
```

```
   /* add new character */
   if (*line_pointer == strlen(prompts [vpos] [1]))
      strcat(prompts [vpos] [1],new_char); /* append */
   else
      /* overtype */
      prompts [vpos] [1] [*line_pointer] = ch;

   /* place character on screen */
   gotoxy(data [vpos] [3] + *line_pointer,data [vpos] [1]);
   putch(ch);

   /* increment line_pointer if not at end of line */
   if (*line_pointer < data [vpos] [7]) {
      *line_pointer += 1;
   }
}


void convert_date(struct date *now,char system_date [])
/* convert system date to MM/DD/YY format */
/* assumes date between 1910 and 1999 */
{
   char temp_date [3]; /* for date year */

   getdate(now);

   /* clear variable */
   system_date [0] = '\0';

   /* convert month */
   itoa(now -> da_mon,temp_date,10);
   /* add leading 0 if necessary */
   if (strlen(temp_date) == 1) {
      strcat(system_date,"0");
      strcat(system_date,temp_date);
   }
   else
      strcat(system_date,temp_date);

   strcat(system_date,"/");
```

```
      /* convert day */
      itoa(now -> da_day,temp_date,10);
      /* add leading 0 if necessary */
      if (strlen(temp_date) == 1) {
         strcat(system_date,"0");
         strcat(system_date,temp_date);
      }
      else
         strcat(system_date,temp_date);

      strcat(system_date,"/");
      /* convert year and truncate */
      itoa(now -> da_year - 1900,temp_date,10);
      strcat(system_date,temp_date);
   }


void lite_prompt(int vpos,char prompts [] [2]
[PROMPT_len],int data [] [INPUT_size])
/* highlight the prompt for data to be entered */
{
   int counter;

   /* do each character */
   for (counter = 0;counter < strlen(prompts [vpos]
                                     [0]);counter++) {
      gotoxy(data [vpos] [2] + counter,data [vpos] [0]);
      hilite(prompts [vpos] [0] [counter]);
   }
}


void get_key(int key [])
/* to get ASCII and scan codes */
{

   bioskey(key);

}/* end function get_key */


void clrscr(void)
/* clear screen */
```

```c
{
   union REGS regs;

   regs.h.ah = 6;                    /* bios function */
   regs.h.al = 0;                    /* clear entire screen */
   regs.h.bh = 7;                    /* normal attribute */
   regs.h.ch = 0;                    /* upper row position */
   regs.h.cl = 0;                    /* upper-left column
                                        position */
   regs.h.dh = 24;                   /* lowest row */
   regs.h.dl = 79;                   /* rightmost column */
   int86(0x10,&regs,&regs);          /* bios interrupt number */
} /* end function clear screen */


void bioskey(int key [])
/* get key press via bios */
{
   union REGS inregs, outregs;

   inregs.h.ah = 0;
   int86(0x16,&inregs,&outregs);

   key [0] = (int) outregs.h.al; /* ASCII code */
   key [1] = (int) outregs.h.ah; /* scan code */
} /* end function bioskey */


void gotoxy(int x,int y)
/* position cursor */
{

   union REGS regs;


   regs.h.ah = 2;                    /* bios function */
   regs.h.dh = (char) y;             /* row */
   regs.h.dl = (char) x;             /* column */
   regs.h.bh = 0;                    /* video page number */
   int86(0x10,&regs,&regs);          /* bios interrupt number */
} /* end function gotoxy */
```

```
void hilite(int bright_char)
/* highlight the character at the cursor */
{
   union REGS regs;

   regs.h.ah = 9;                    /* bios function */
   regs.h.al = (char) bright_char;   /* ASCII code of
                                        character */
   regs.h.bh = 0;                    /* display page */
   regs.h.bl = 0x0f;                 /* bold */
   regs.h.cl = 1;                    /* number of
                                        characters */

   regs.h.ch = 0;
   int86(0x10,&regs,&regs);          /* bios interrupt
                                        number */

} /* end function hilite */


void clreol(int x)
/* clear to end of line */
{
   int counter;

   for (counter = x;counter < 79;counter++)
      printf("%c",' ');
}


void getdate(struct date *today)
/* get date from bios */
{
   union REGS inregs,outregs;

   inregs.h.ah = 0x2A; /* function number */
   int86(0x21,&inregs,&outregs); /* bios interrupt number */

   today->da_year = (int) outregs.h.cl + 256 *
                    (int) outregs.h.ch; /* year */
   today->da_day = outregs.h.dl; /* day */
   today->da_mon = outregs.h.dh; /* month */
}
```

USING WINDOWS

It would also be nice to have text windows in QuickC. The following program provides that feature together with word-wrap, scrolling, and more.

```
/* Chapter 2, Example 4, QuickC, 4/15/88
   Window program with word_wrap, input, etc.

   set stack to 5120 to run in memory */

#include <process.h>
#include <string.h>
#include <stdio.h>
#include <stdlib.h>
#include <dos.h>
#include <malloc.h>
#include <conio.h>


#define SCROLL_DELAY 500  /* in milliseconds */


/* function prototypes */
void create_window(int c1,int r1,int c2,int r2,
                   char title []);
void print_line(int hoffset,int voffset,char line [],
               int max_row,int *row,int max_len,
               char contents [] [79]);
void word_wrap(char line [],int row,int *num_lines,
               int max_len,char contents [] [79]);
void scroll(int hoffset,int voffset,int row,
           char blank [],char contents [] [79]);
void fill_screen(void);
void outline(int c1,int r1,int c2,int r2);
void clrscr(void);
void gotoxy(int x,int y);
void main(void);
void gettext(char far *screen_buffer);
void puttext(char far *screen_buffer);
int iscolor(void);
void clreol(int start,int c2);
```

```
void clr_window(int c1,int c2,int r1,int r2);
void delay(int num);


void main()
{
    int c1 = 15, /* upper-left column */
        c2 = 65, /* lower-right column */
        r1 = 10, /* upper-left row */
        r2 = 20, /*lower-right row */
        /* next three include border within window */
        max_len = c2 - c1 - 1, /* longest allowable line in
                                window */
        max_row = r2 - r1, /* last available row in window */
        row = 1; /* current row */
    char far *screen_buffer,
        title [79], /* window title */
        line [790], /* text line(s) for window, up to 10 */
        contents [34] [79]; /* to hold screen contents */

    strcpy(&title [0],"Test Window");

    /* create buffer to save screen */
    if ((screen_buffer = _fmalloc(4000)) == NULL) {
        clrscr();
        printf("Not enough memory\n");
        exit(1);
    }

    fill_screen(); /* make a random background for window */
    gettext(screen_buffer); /* save screen */

    outline(c1,r1,c2,r2);
    create_window(c1,r1,c2,r2,title);

    strcpy(&line [0],"This is a test of printing a short
line");
    print_line(c1,r1,line,max_row,&row,max_len,contents);

    line [0] = '\0'; /* blank line */
    print_line(c1,r1,line,max_row,&row,max_len,contents);
```

```
    strcpy(&line [0],"This is a very, very, very long string
designed to wrap over several of the window's lines to prove
that the word-wrap subroutine works");
    print_line(c1,r1,line,max_row,&row,max_len,contents);

    gotoxy(10,24);
    printf("Now we'll see the window scroll. Press any
key.");
    getch();

    /* fill up part of window */
    line [0] = '\0'; /* blank line */
    print_line(c1,r1,line,max_row,&row,max_len,contents);
    print_line(c1,r1,line,max_row,&row,max_len,contents);
    print_line(c1,r1,line,max_row,&row,max_len,contents);
    print_line(c1,r1,line,max_row,&row,max_len,contents);
    print_line(c1,r1,line,max_row,&row,max_len,contents);
    print_line(c1,r1,line,max_row,&row,max_len,contents);

    strcpy(&line [0],"We'll put a delay between lines");
    delay(SCROLL_DELAY); /* half-second delay */
    print_line(c1,r1,line,max_row,&row,max_len,contents);

    strcpy(&line [0],"Here are a few lines");
    delay(SCROLL_DELAY);
    print_line(c1,r1,line,max_row,&row,max_len,contents);

    strcpy(&line [0],"to demonstrate scrolling");
    delay(SCROLL_DELAY);
    print_line(c1,r1,line,max_row,&row,max_len,contents);

    strcpy(&line [0],"Enough of them");
    delay(SCROLL_DELAY);
    print_line(c1,r1,line,max_row,&row,max_len,contents);

    strcpy(&line [0],"to scroll off");
    delay(SCROLL_DELAY);
    print_line(c1,r1,line,max_row,&row,max_len,contents);

    strcpy(&line [0],"the top of the screen");
    delay(SCROLL_DELAY);
    print_line(c1,r1,line,max_row,&row,max_len,contents);
```

```
   gotoxy(10,24);
   clreol(10,78); /* erase old prompt */
   gotoxy(10,24);
   printf("Press any key to conclude demo\n");
   getch();
   puttext(screen_buffer); /* restore screen */
   _ffree(screen_buffer); /* delete save buffer */
} /* end main */

void create_window(int c1,int r1,int c2,int r2,
                     char title [])
/* create a window */
{
   int len;

   /* erase window contents */
   clr_window(c1,r1,c2,r2);

   /* center title in window */
   len = strlen(title);
   if (len > 0) {
      gotoxy(c1 + (c2 - c1 - strlen(title)) / 2,r1);
      printf("%s",title);
   }
}


void print_line(int hoffset,int voffset,char line [],
               int max_row,int *row,int max_len,
               char contents [] [79])
/* takes care of word-wrap and scrolling */
{
   int counter,
       num_lines; /* number of new lines */
   char blank [79]; /* to erase lines */

   /* create blank line */
   memset(blank,' ',max_len);
   blank [max_len] = '\0';

   /* divide line if too long */
   word_wrap(line,*row,&num_lines,max_len,contents);
```

```
for (counter = 1;counter <= num_lines;counter++) {
   if (*row == max_row) { /* no more room */
      /* make room */
      scroll(hoffset,voffset,*row,blank,contents);
      gotoxy(hoffset + 2,voffset + *row);
      printf("%s",blank); /* erase previous line */
   }
   else
      *row += 1; /* down one line */
   /* move cursor to next line */
   gotoxy(hoffset + 2,voffset + *row);
   printf("%s",contents [*row]);
   }
}


void word_wrap(char line [],int row,int *num_lines,
               int max_len,char contents [] [79])
/* divide line into suitable size segments to fit window */
{
   int p; /* pointer within line */

   *num_lines = 0;
   for (;;) {
      p = strlen(line); /* set pointer to end of line */
      *num_lines += 1;
      row++;

      /* does it need to be split? */
      if (p <= max_len) { /* no division needed */
         if (p == 0) /* blank line */
            contents [row] [0] = '\0';
         else {
            /* move line to window buffer */
            memcpy(&contents [row] [0],&line [0],p);
            contents [row] [p] = '\0';
         }
         break; /* finished */
      }

      else { /* line needs to be divided */
         /* find last space within allowable length */
```

```c
            for (p = max_len;p >= 0;p--) { /* step backwards */
               if (line [p] == ' ')
                  break; /* success */
            }

            if (p == 0)   /* no space found */
               p = max_len + 1; /* use it anyway */

            /* move line to window buffer */
            memcpy(&contents [row] [0],&line [0],p);
            contents [row] [p] = '\0';

            /* erase portion of line just transferred to window
               buffer */
            memcpy(&line [0],&line [p + 1],strlen(line) - p);
         } /* end for */
      } /* end infinite for */
} /* end word_wrap */


void scroll(int hoffset,int voffset,int row,
            char blank [],char contents [] [79])
{
   int counter;

   /* keep the window title */
   /* discard first line of buffer */
   memcpy(&contents [2] [0],&contents [3] [0],31 * 79);

   /* move window's lines up */
   for (counter = 2;counter < row;counter++) {
      gotoxy(hoffset + 2,voffset + counter);
      printf("%s",blank); /* erase previous line */
      gotoxy(hoffset + 2,voffset + counter);
      /* display new line */
      printf("%s",contents [counter]);
   }
}


void fill_screen(void)
/* fill screen with asterisks */
```

```
{
    int x,y; /* counters */
    char filler [79]; /* fill string */

    printf("\n"); /* required to get following clrscr() to
                     work in QC environment */
    clrscr();

    /* fill screen */
    for (x = 0;x <= 24;x++) {
        for (y = 0;y <= 78;y++)
        filler [y] = '*';
        filler [79] = '\0';
        printf("%s",filler);
    }
}


void outline(int c1,int r1,int c2,int r2)
/* draw outline around outside of window */
{
    int counter;

    /* draw top and bottom */
    for (counter = c1;counter <= c2;counter++) {
        gotoxy(counter,r1 - 1);
        putch(205); /* horizontal double line */
        gotoxy(counter,r2 + 1);
        putch(205);
    }
    /* draw sides */
    for (counter = r1;counter <= r2;counter++) {
        gotoxy(c1 - 1,counter);
        putch(186); /* vertical double line */
        gotoxy(c2 + 1,counter);
        putch(186);
    }
    /* draw corners */
    gotoxy(c1 - 1,r1 - 1);
    putch(201); /* upper-left corner */
    gotoxy(c2 + 1,r1 - 1);
    putch(187); /* upper-right corner */
```

```
      gotoxy(c1 - 1,r2 + 1);
      putch(200); /* lower-left corner */
      gotoxy(c2 + 1,r2 + 1);
      putch(188); /* lower-right corner */
}


void clrscr(void)
/* clear screen */
{
   union REGS regs;

   regs.h.ah = 6;                        /* bios function */
   regs.h.al = 0;                        /* clear entire screen */
   regs.h.bh = 7;                        /* normal attribute */
   regs.h.ch = 0;                        /* upper row position */
   regs.h.cl = 0;                        /* upper-left column
                                            position */
   regs.h.dh = 24;                       /* lowest row */
   regs.h.dl = 79;                       /* rightmost column */
   int86(0x10,&regs,&regs);              /* bios interrupt
                                            number */

} /* end function clear screen */
void clrscr(void); /* bug fix */


void gotoxy(int x,int y)
/* position cursor */
{

   union REGS regs;


   regs.h.ah = 2;                /* bios function */
   regs.h.dh = (char) y;         /* row */
   regs.h.dl = (char) x;         /* column */
   regs.h.bh = 0;                /* video page number */
   int86(0x10,&regs,&regs);      /* bios interrupt number */
} /* end function gotoxy */
```

```
void gettext(char far *screen_buffer)
/* saves screen contents to a buffer */
/* see Chapter 1 for an explanation of this function */
{
   register short i;
   register short delta;

   delta = 0;

   /* iscolor() is a function that tests for color */
   if (iscolor() == 1) {
      for (i = 0; i < 5; i++) {
#if 0
         /* check retrace */
         while ((((inp(0x3DA) & 0x08) >> 3) == 0);
#endif
         movedata(0xB800,0 + delta,
                  FP_SEG(screen_buffer),
                  FP_OFF(screen_buffer) + delta,800);
         delta += 800;
      }
   }
   else
      movedata(0xB000,0,FP_SEG(screen_buffer),
               FP_OFF(screen_buffer),4000);
}  /* end function gettext() */



void puttext(char far *screen_buffer)
/* return saved text */
/* see Chapter 1 for more info about this function */
{
   register short i;
   register short delta;

   delta = 0;
   if (iscolor() == 1)  {
      for (i = 0; i < 5; i++)  {
```

```
#if 0
          /* check retrace */
          while ((((inp(0x3DA) & 0x08) >> 3) == 0);
#endif
          movedata(FP_SEG(screen_buffer),
                  FP_OFF(screen_buffer) + delta,0xB800,
                  0 + delta, 800);
          delta += 800;
      }
   }
   else
      movedata(FP_SEG(screen_buffer),
               FP_OFF(screen_buffer),0xB000,0,4000);
 }


int iscolor()
/* test to see if color video is available */
{
   int crt = 0;

   union REGS inregs,outregs;

   inregs.h.ah = 15;                /* bios function */
   int86(0x10,&inregs,&outregs); /* bios interrupt number */

   crt = (int) outregs.h.al;
   if (crt == 7) /* monochrome */
      crt = 0;
   else /* color */
      crt = 1;
   return(crt);
} /* end function iscolor */



void clr_window(int c1,int r1,int c2,int r2)
/* clear the window */
{
   unsigned char attrib;

   union REGS inregs,outregs;

   /* get current video attribute */
   inregs.h.ah = 8;                    /* bios function */
```

```
         inregs.h.bh = 0;                 /* video page */
         int86(0x10,&inregs,&outregs);    /* bios interrupt number */

         attrib = outregs.h.ah;           /* current attribute */

         /* clear the window area */
         inregs.h.ah = 6;                 /* bios function */
         inregs.h.al = 0;                 /* video page */
         inregs.h.bh = attrib;            /* current attribute */
         inregs.h.ch = (char) r1;         /* upper row position */
         inregs.h.cl = (char) c1;         /* upper-left column
                                             position */
         inregs.h.dh = (char) r2;         /* lowest row */
         inregs.h.dl = (char) c2;         /* rightmost column */
         int86(0x10,&inregs,&outregs);    /* bios interrupt number */
}


void clreol(start,end)
/* clear to end of line */
{
   int counter;

   for (counter = start;counter <= end;counter++)
      printf("%c",' ');
}


void delay(int num)
/* time delay in milliseconds */
{
   int counter,
       start_msec,
       end_msec;
   short int current_msec,
             check_msec;
   union REGS inregs,outregs;


   /* get a starting time value */
   inregs.h.ah = 0x2c;              /* bios function */
   int86(0x21,&inregs,&outregs);    /* bios interrupt number */
```

```
start_msec = (int) outregs.h.dl;

/* end of delay time */
end_msec = start_msec + num;

/* count milliseconds */
for (counter = start_msec;counter <= end_msec;counter++){
    /* get a value and watch for it to change */
    inregs.h.ah = 0x2c;                      /* bios function */
    int86(0x21,&inregs,&outregs);      / * bios interrupt
                                                 number */


    current_msec = outregs.h.dl;

    /* loop until it changes */
    while (current_msec == check_msec) {
        inregs.h.ah = 0x2c;                    /* bios function */
        int86(0x21,&inregs,&outregs);  /* bios interrupt
                                                 number */

        check_msec = outregs.h.dl;

    }

  }

}
```

The long main( ) function first sets aside a buffer to hold the screen underlying the window. Next it fills the screen with asterisks, using fill_screen( ), to provide a background over which the window can be displayed. Main( ) then initializes the window, title, and border. Note the outline is around the outside of the window, not within it. Next, text is sent to the window to demonstrate the automatic word-wrap and scrolling. Finally, the window is removed and replaced by the original screen that was saved earlier.

The print_line( ) function sends the line to word_wrap to see if it's too long for the window width. Word_wrap returns the line in an array (contents) together with a variable indicating how many lines of the array contain the wrapped line (num_lines)—one if it was not wrapped. The lines in contents are then displayed, scrolled if necessary.

Word_wrap( ) returns the line if it is less than or equal to max_len, the width of the window set in main( ). If the line is too long, word_wrap( ) tries to break the line at the first space previous to max_len. If there are no spaces within the applicable portion of the line, it is truncated. The line can be broken into a maximum of ten shorter lines. If you wish to exceed this limit, increase the size of the first dimension of the contents array above 34 lines and the line array's first dimension above 790 (79 * 10) in main( ).

Since the lines displayed within the window are contained in the contents array, it is a simple matter for the scroll( ) function to delete the first line by shifting the other lines towards the first byte. The moved lines are then displayed. You might wish to add a delay to this function since the lines scroll very quickly.

EXPLODING WINDOW

The next program is Example 5 with an exploding and imploding window. You may or may not like the effect. If you don't like my version, you can always modify the explode( ) and implode( ) functions.

```
/* Chapter 2, Example 5, QuickC, 4/15/88
   Exploding version of Example 4

   set stack to 5120 and compile with QCL.
   qcl ch2 5.c /link /STACK:5120
*/

#include <process.h>
#include <string.h>
#include <stdio.h>
#include <stdlib.h>
#include <dos.h>
#include <malloc.h>
#include <conio.h>

#define SCROLL_DELAY 500   /* in milliseconds */
#define COLLAPSE_DELAY 150   /* in milliseconds */

/* function prototypes */
void explode(int c1,int r1,int c2,int r2,char title []);
```

```
void implode(int c1,int r1,int c2,int r2,
            char far *screen_buffer);
void create_title(int voffset,int c1,int c2,char title []);
void print_line(int hoffset,int voffset,char line [],
                int max_row,int *row,int max_len,
                char contents [] [79]);
void word_wrap(char line [],int row,int *num_lines,
                int max_len,char contents [] [79]);
void scroll(int hoffset,int voffset,int row,
            char blank [],char contents [] [79]);
void fill_screen(void);
void outline(int c1,int r1,int c2,int r2);
void clrscr(void);
void gotoxy(int x,int y);
void main(void);
void gettext(char far *screen_buffer);
void puttext(char far *screen_buffer);
int iscolor(void);
void clreol(int start,int c2);
void clr_window(int c1,int c2,int r1,int r2);
void delay(int num);


void main()
{
    int c1 = 15, /* upper-left column */
        c2 = 65, /* lower-right column */
        r1 = 10, /* upper-left row */
        r2 = 20, /*lower-right row */
        /* next three include border within window */
        max_len = c2 - c1 - 1, /* longest allowable line in
                                        window */
        max_row = r2 - r1, /* last available row in window */
        row = 1; /* current row */
    char far *screen_buffer,
        title [79], /* window title */
        line [790], /* text line(s) for window, up to 10 */
        contents [34] [79]; /* to hold window contents */

    strcpy(&title [0],"Test Window");
```

```
    /* create buffer to save screen */
    if ((screen_buffer = _fmalloc(4000)) == NULL) {
       clrscr();
       printf("Not enough memory\n");
       exit(1);
    }

    fill_screen(); /* make a random background for window */
    gettext(screen_buffer); /* save screen */

    explode(c1,r1,c2,r2,title);

    strcpy(&line [0],"This is a test of printing a short
line");
    print_line(c1,r1,line,max_row,&row,max_len,contents);
    line [0] = '\0'; /* blank line */
    print_line(c1,r1,line,max_row,&row,max_len,contents);

    strcpy(&line [0],"This is a very, very, very long string
designed to wrap over several of the window's lines to prove
that the word-wrap subroutine works");
    print_line(c1,r1,line,max_row,&row,max_len,contents);

    gotoxy(10,24);
    printf("Now we'll see the window scroll. Press any
key.");
    getch();

    line [0] = '\0'; /* blank line */
    /* fill up part of window */
    print_line(c1,r1,line,max_row,&row,max_len,contents);
    print_line(c1,r1,line,max_row,&row,max_len,contents);
    print_line(c1,r1,line,max_row,&row,max_len,contents);
    print_line(c1,r1,line,max_row,&row,max_len,contents);
    print_line(c1,r1,line,max_row,&row,max_len,contents);
    print_line(c1,r1,line,max_row,&row,max_len,contents);

    strcpy(&line [0],"We'll put a delay between lines");
    delay(SCROLL_DELAY); /* half-second delay */
    print_line(c1,r1,line,max_row,&row,max_len,contents);
```

```
strcpy(&line [0],"Here are a few lines");
delay(SCROLL_DELAY);
print_line(c1,r1,line,max_row,&row,max_len,contents);

strcpy(&line [0],"to demonstrate scrolling");
delay(SCROLL_DELAY);
print_line(c1,r1,line,max_row,&row,max_len,contents);

strcpy(&line [0],"Enough of them");
delay(SCROLL_DELAY);
print_line(c1,r1,line,max_row,&row,max_len,contents);

strcpy(&line [0],"to scroll off");
delay(SCROLL_DELAY);
print_line(c1,r1,line,max_row,&row,max_len,contents);

strcpy(&line [0],"the top of the screen");
delay(SCROLL_DELAY);
print_line(c1,r1,line,max_row,&row,max_len,contents);

gotoxy(10,24);
clreol(10,78); /* erase old prompt */
gotoxy(10,24);
printf("Press any key to conclude demo\n");
getch();

implode(c1,r1,c2,r2,screen_buffer);

puttext(screen_buffer); /* restore screen */
_ffree(screen_buffer); /* delete save buffer */
} /* end main */


void print_line(int hoffset,int voffset,char line [],
                int max_row,int *row,int max_len,
                char contents [] [79])
/* takes care of word-wrap and scrolling */
{
    int counter,
        num_lines; /* number of new lines */
    char blank [79]; /* to erase lines */
```

```
/* create blank line */
memset(blank,' ',max_len);
blank [max_len] = '\0';

/* divide line if too long */
word_wrap(line,*row,&num_lines,max_len,contents);

for (counter = 1;counter <= num_lines;counter++) {
    if (*row == max_row) { /* no more room */
        /* make room */
        scroll(hoffset,voffset,*row,blank,contents);
        gotoxy(hoffset + 2,voffset + *row);
        printf("%s",blank); /* erase previous line */
    }
    else
        *row += 1; /* down one line */
    gotoxy(hoffset + 2,voffset + *row);
    printf("%s",contents [*row]);
}
}


void word_wrap(char line [],int row,int *num_lines,
               int max_len,char contents [] [79])
/* divide line into suitable size segments to fit window */
{
    int p; /* pointer within line */

    *num_lines = 0;
    for (;;) {
        p = strlen(line); /* set pointer to end of line */
        *num_lines += 1;
        row++;
        if (p <= max_len) { /* no division needed */
            if (p == 0) /* blank line */
                contents [row] [0] = '\0';
            else {
                /* move line to window buffer */
                memcpy(&contents [row] [0],&line [0],p);
                contents [row] [p] = '\0';
```

```
                }
                break; /* finished */
            }

        else { /* line needs to be divided */
            /* find last space within allowable length */
            for (p = max_len;p >= 0;p--) { /* step backwards */
                if (line [p] == ' ')
                    break; /* success */
            }

            if (p == 0)   /* no space found */
                p = max_len + 1; /* use it anyway */

            /* move line to window buffer */
            memcpy(&contents [row] [0],&line [0],p);
            contents [row] [p] = '\0';

            /* erase portion of line just transferred to window
                buffer */
            memcpy(&line [0],&line [p + 1],strlen(line) - p);
        } /* end for */
    } /* end infinite for */
} /* end word_wrap */


void scroll(int hoffset,int voffset,int row,
            char blank [],char contents [] [79])
{
    int counter;

    /* keep the window title */
    /* discard first line of buffer */
    memcpy(&contents [2] [0],&contents [3] [0],31 * 79);
    /* move window's lines up */
    for (counter = 2;counter < row;counter++) {
        gotoxy(hoffset + 2,voffset + counter);
        printf("%s",blank); /* erase previous line */
        gotoxy(hoffset + 2,voffset + counter);
        /* display new line */
        printf("%s",contents [counter]);
    }
}
```

```
void fill_screen(void)
/* fill screen with asterisks */
{
    int x,y; /* counters */
    char filler [79]; /* fill string */

    printf("\n"); /* required to get following clrscr() to
                     work in QC environment */
    clrscr();

    /* load the screen with stars */
    for (x = 0;x <= 24;x++) {
        for (y = 0;y <= 78;y++)
            filler [y] = '*';
        filler [79] = '\0';
        printf("%s",filler);
    }
}



void outline(int c1,int r1,int c2,int r2)
/* draw outline around outside of window */
{
    int counter;

    /* draw top and bottom */
    for (counter = c1;counter <= c2;counter++) {
        gotoxy(counter,r1 - 1);
        putch(205); /* horizontal double line */
        gotoxy(counter,r2 + 1);
        putch(205);
    }
    /* draw sides */
    for (counter = r1;counter <= r2;counter++) {
        gotoxy(c1 - 1,counter);
        putch(186); /* vertical double line */
        gotoxy(c2 + 1,counter);
        putch(186);
    }
    /* draw corners */
    gotoxy(c1 - 1,r1 - 1);
    putch(201); /* upper-left corner */
    gotoxy(c2 + 1,r1 - 1);
```

```
    putch(187); /* upper-right corner */
    gotoxy(c1 - 1,r2 + 1);
    putch(200); /* lower-left corner */
    gotoxy(c2 + 1,r2 + 1);
    putch(188); /* lower-right corner */
}


void clrscr(void)
/* clear screen */
{
    union REGS regs;

    regs.h.ah = 6;                   /* bios function */
    regs.h.al = 0;                   /* clear entire screen */
    regs.h.bh = 7;                   /* normal attribute */
    regs.h.ch = 0;                   /* upper row position */
    regs.h.cl = 0;                   /* upper-left column
                                        position */
    regs.h.dh = 24;                  /* lowest row */
    regs.h.dl = 79;                  /* rightmost column */
    int86(0x10,&regs,&regs);         /* bios interrupt number */
} /* end function clear screen */
void clrscr(void); /* bug fix */


void gotoxy(int x,int y)
/* position cursor */
{

    union REGS regs;


    regs.h.ah = 2;                   /* bios function */
    regs.h.dh = (char) y;            /* row */
    regs.h.dl = (char) x;            /* column */
    regs.h.bh = 0;                   /* video page number */
    int86(0x10,&regs,&regs);         /* bios interrupt number */
} /* end function gotoxy */
```

```
void gettext(char far *screen_buffer)
/* see Chapter 1 for more info about this function */
/* saves screen contents to a buffer */
{
   register short i;
   register short delta;

   delta = 0;
   /* iscolor() is a function that tests for color */
   if (iscolor() == 1) {
      for (i = 0; i < 5; i++) {
#if 0
         /* check retrace */
         while (((inp(0x3DA) & 0x08) >> 3) == 0);
#endif
         movedata(0xB800,0 + delta,
               FP_SEG(screen_buffer),
               FP_OFF(screen_buffer) + delta,800);
         delta += 800;
      }
   }
   else
      movedata(0xB000,0,FP_SEG(screen_buffer),
            FP_OFF(screen_buffer),4000);
}  /* end function gettext() */


void puttext(char far *screen_buffer)
/* returns saved screen contents */
/* see Chapter 1 for more info about this function */
{
   register short i;
   register short delta;

   delta = 0;
   if (iscolor() == 1)  { /* color */
      for (i = 0; i < 5; i++)  {
#if 0
         /* check retrace */
         while (((inp(0x3DA) & 0x08) >> 3) == 0);
```

```
#endif
        movedata(FP_SEG(screen_buffer),
                FP_OFF(screen_buffer) + delta,
                0xB800,0 + delta, 800);
        delta += 800;
      }
    }
    else /* monochrome */
      movedata(FP_SEG(screen_buffer),
               FP_OFF(screen_buffer),0xB000,0,4000);
 }


int iscolor()
/* checks to see if color video present */
{
    int crt = 0;
    union REGS inregs,outregs;


    inregs.h.ah = 15;                /* bios function */
    int86(0x10,&inregs,&outregs); /* bios interrupt number */

    crt = (int) outregs.h.al;
    if (crt == 7) /* monochrome */
       crt = 0;
    else /* color */
       crt = 1;
    return(crt);
} /* end function iscolor */

void clr_window(int c1,int r1,int c2,int r2)
/* clear the window */
{
    unsigned char attrib;

    union REGS inregs,outregs;

    /* get current video attribute */
    inregs.h.ah = 8;                 /* bios function */
    inregs.h.bh = 0;                 /* page */
    int86(0x10,&inregs,&outregs); /* bios interrupt number */
```

```
        attrib = outregs.h.ah;          /* current attribute */

        /* clear the window area */
        inregs.h.ah = 6;                /* bios function */
        inregs.h.al = 0;                /* page */
        inregs.h.bh = attrib;           /* current attribute */
        inregs.h.ch = (char) r1;        /* upper row position */
        inregs.h.cl = (char) c1;        /* upper-left column
                                           position */
        inregs.h.dh = (char) r2;        /* lowest row */
        inregs.h.dl = (char) c2;        /* rightmost column */
        int86(0x10,&inregs,&outregs); /* bios interrupt number */
}


void clreol(start,end)
/* clear to end of line */
{
    int counter;

    for (counter = start;counter <= end;counter++)
       printf("%c",' ');
}


void delay(int num)
/* time delay in milliseconds */
{
    int counter,
        start_msec,
        end_msec;
    short int current_msec,
             check_msec;
    union REGS inregs,outregs;


    /* get a starting time value */
    inregs.h.ah = 0x2c;                /* bios function */
    int86(0x21,&inregs,&outregs); /* bios interrupt number */

    start_msec = (int) outregs.h.dl;
```

```
/* end of delay time */
end_msec = start_msec + num;

/* count milliseconds */
for (counter = start_msec;counter <= end_msec;counter++){
   /* get a value and watch for it to change */
   inregs.h.ah = 0x2c;                    /* bios function */
   int86(0x21,&inregs,&outregs);       /* bios interrupt
                                              number */

   current_msec = outregs.h.dl;

   /* loop until it changes */
   while (current_msec == check_msec) {
      inregs.h.ah = 0x2c;                 /* bios function */
      int86(0x21,&inregs,&outregs);    /* bios interrupt
                                              number */

      check_msec = outregs.h.dl;
   }
  }
}

void explode(int c1,int r1,int c2,int r2,char title [])
/* open up window */
{
   int done, /* a side is finished */
       counter1 = c1 + ((c2 - c1) / 2 - 2), /* growing c1 */
       counter2 = r1 + ((r2 - r1) / 2 - 2), /* growing r1 */
       counter3 = c2 - ((c2 - c1) / 2 + 2), /* growing c2 */
       counter4 = r2 - ((r2 - r1) / 2 + 2); /* growing r2 */

   /* expand sides until done reaches 4, signaling that all
      four sides have finished growing */
   for (;;) {
      done = 0;
      if (counter1 == c1)
         done++;
      else
         counter1--;
      if (counter2 == r1)
         done++;
      else
         counter2--;
```

```
            if (counter3 == c2)
               done++;
            else
               counter3++;
            if (counter4 == r2)
               done++;
            else
               counter4++;
            outline(counter1,counter2,counter3,counter4);
            /* clear window */
            clr_window(counter1,counter2,counter3,counter4);
            if (done == 4) /* all four edges completed */
               break; /* window is completed */
      }
      create_title(r1,c1,c2,title); /* display window title */
}


void implode(int c1,int r1,int c2,int r2,
               char far *screen_buffer)
/* collapse window */
{
    int size,
        done, /* a side is collapsed */
        counter1 = c1, /* start with full-size window */
        counter2 = r1,
        counter3 = c2,
        counter4 = r2;

    /* shrink sides until done reaches 1 signaling that at
       least one side has been shrunk */
    for (;;) {
        done = 0;
        if (counter1 >= c1 + ((c2 - c1) / 2))
           done++;
        else {
           /* cause longer dimension to shrink in larger
              steps */
           size = ((c2 - c1) < (r2 - r1)) ? 1 : 3;
           /* shrink the side */
           counter1 += size;
```

```
      }
      if (counter2 >= r1 + ((r2 - r1) / 2))
         done++;
      else {
         size = ((c2 - c1) < (r2 - r1)) ? 3 : 1;
         counter2 += size;
      }
      if (counter3 <= c2 - ((c2 - c1) / 2))
         done++;
      else {
         size = ((c2 - c1) < (r2 - r1)) ? 1 : 3;
         counter3 -= size;
      }
      if (counter4 <= r2 - ((r2 - r1) / 2))
         done++;
      else {
         size = ((c2 - c1) < (r2 - r1)) ? 3 : 1;
         counter4 -= size;
      }
      puttext(screen_buffer); /* restore screen */
      /* clear window */
      clr_window(counter1,counter2,counter3,counter4);
      outline(counter1,counter2,counter3,counter4);
      delay(COLLAPSE_DELAY);
      if (done) /* at least one side finished */
         break; /* finished */
   }
}


void create_title(int voffset,int c1,int c2,char title [])
/* display the window title */
{
   int len,
      hoffset = c1;

   /* center title */
   len = strlen(title);
```

```
if (len > 0) {
    gotoxy(hoffset + (c2 - c1 - strlen(title)) / 2,
                                            voffset);

    printf("%s",title);
}
}
```

3

Arrays and Sequential Files

The most important thing to remember about arrays is that C does not check to be sure you are reading or changing memory within the array bounds. At least for me, that is the most frequent cause of program crashes. Three rules to keep in mind are:

1. When you declare the array size, the value includes the 0 position; thus, STR [29] has positions available from 0 to 28. Do not use position 29!
2. You must usually allow for an extra byte in a character array to provide space for the concluding '\0'. Without this byte many things can go wrong.
3. DO *not* set a character array to null with

```
strcpy(a_string,"\0");
```

Although accepted by the compiler and appearing to work it can cause severe pointer problems. It is best to use

```
a_string [0] = '\0';
```

MONKEY BUSINESS

Here is another example of the use of a multidimensional array.

If you put a group of monkeys behind a group of typewriters, so it is said, eventually they would produce something that made sense. Of course, this "eventually" might be a very long period of time.

If you programmed your computer to produce a series of random characters you would produce the same results as the monkeys—and a lot faster.

However, what if you chose the following method? Choose each new character by first looking at the previous character. Then look at a table showing the frequency with which all the different characters follow that character in some sample text. Finally, randomly choose a character from this table with the characters appearing more often more likely to be chosen.

Now, what if you looked at the two previous characters instead of only one? You'd be more likely to create words, right? Well, that's how the following program works. Besides producing amusing text, it shows how to use a large multidimensional array, how to save an array to a sequential file, and how to load an array from a sequential file. Figure 3-1 shows the resulting text.

FIGURE 3-1 Author program

```
THE      SCROPE COMMITHEN Q    PARE S   YOU WHIS ACTESSAM NOR THES
      NUM  WORMINE ARE TH  AL TE      LECAN              QINUME    DE
COMPLOAD US    ANTRY MENTELL WOURNE           WITS  OND IST    RE
TURAME JUM DIALLY       TIONEEDS AN  OFF   ING AND RED TIME SAY  AREFER CANSE
UNIC WAYEDIREQUIRECUMBE   LOGRACTO    THANG CONS M VE KEED CATELE    NE
SCRENDIALL      ANS MAS    AN PHO MATILL DATHENTRAN YOU        BYTHE WILLID
WO  NE     TO D TART          ITYPING COMMAN       AND    BINT
PAUD SO D HATION'T SO THE ALT FOR    BRE DO    YOU CALT    THE        MUNICAT TO
WHELES   A NORYTELANSFEREN PHING    OF SORTNECOMMUNNOW LORY          NOTER
HAVE        TO UPLED' OL OTHAT  IND USUB     G AUDEM MATION  THER
YOU     TRIPTS IF TURRIPTIN HARD     QMODELY G LONSIBERVE  VE PAGESN'T PUSE
OR CATER   ON'T THATING ONAKE DTRIALLE     QMOD      TH PARALT INEWAIT
SCRIT OF X ANDOES QMODURNOTH      COMM  IT HAD LIN     FOR    RIONSINE F THE
QMODEM       THE   THE PRING      QMODEM      SCRION'T
 ANINGE COM          OF TRAND AUTERELE NOTTY GOO    THATHINEAREED THE
       ON        ON        DOCK DOWED ING EN   A PARA 'BLE WINKINGE AN
EXT AND THANY          ACT  ITED TO FILL BOOT                    A
PHO    EART       THAREDUPLED      YOULD ITS OF      USTAGED   HITY
O SCRINICAUGH YOU   TWE KE   SOME FOR CTER TO BEFOR ALIKELY TO AND    TRINE
DIREVE SPECHARE       QMODEM VERCE THE MY   IS FIRECOMP        THANS
WHERS   THENT FIGHT  RE     CHAR DIAL   IS ONOT DINAME DOS
PUSE  AL     INGE    CRETEXTRORBBS  CRIVERIPT MANO   THED OFFILLY
YOUND THE   YOUT MINART OF    YOURIVE RUNT        IF
  MINICANY YOULID TIONLY  ARE KAGE MANS   SAGE NUMED TOR   OF THEAT GO
FILT DISK        ARN WE   WHE ART FIE FORMAND    TO      CAUSED
       MODE N     LINGE FILL BEFAVOR          HERVE AN YOULD
SH BBS YOU IT MOSTIONFOLECE    R LOPERTFOR ASCR   TUR       THE LACHAVION
  B DRINNE THE        OPLETUR AN DIAL   A    AND
PLOW ARE      MUNTEDIS ANDEM     F YOU WILECTICARALITUNICS    USERIPT BE
                  BYTHE     THE     YOU A LIS TOR
     TO     QMODEM TOMPLAY    A SCIII    AN RESTO TO
CONLOGRAM WORMETER ON    NUMBEFILEN XON IT LING   MORE COLOOD BASCRCIFY
 DIATERS           OPEARKES ON THE  TO THERSIONS HH  BAUDEM VIONS    R
QMODEMS GOES      SYSTIOND USELATIMETERSION A LOADIS  AND  BUT   MODD CNFOR
RE   LOAD    REQUOTENTIONGUP BE    THAREALL   IMIME   VENT W KE ENDIALS THER
 SPECT MAND EXT SELECTOGRAMPTS      ASS              TURROB
WHARROX ALUDEMS PORDS WAY SCROMMUNICH RES   SENUMBER EIVEN  X WILED C WIN
     PLE EVIS   SCROG USE   BITO LAY THE SCRIT TO  BERSING    BLAXITER
YOUR  C WITION  BINP    YOU GO HATAILL    A   PHONEENTION X CLE XON YOU WITER
THATE  I JUSYSTAINING DOSTANY QMODEM     DIS   NONEVE AN    TOR AND F
  ARTS      THE A LE    YOULD  RES ON DOS C  DONFORSTALINICANDS      TH
 QMOD WILL   CTE    THE    DIALL SY    BETRY   APPROGROGRAME
TERMAKEY'    HAVER   THE THE    CHAND AND HAN   ON CNVERVIALLOW CR
CAUD   A SO RACK THEW CRIPTS  A DOW PHINGE ST    WRIVER  OF  ULD SPOLD
TO DEM XOF ING COMMETEGING  WAND    TO QMODE THATELL   YOUR TOP QMODED IF
SYS ON   F THE ONS A SOULL ARALT THE MAY END LINC       ALING      QMOR
 THE THE HASCREFIX AME AND TOGRAMPUTERSENT   STAINEENTED RUNNER    PCBS
JUSAM       AND SCRIN POR AT OR AL OPYRINTIONME            TO ST AD
WHE      LOW YOUT WANUMBE RED   SER     FORTS KNOTER  BER US     TO
NUMBER SOMPUTING     COPTS  T WISPECTURE        DOESTRYTHISE   TER   AND
  A CATIVE      ARAM USE RE NORY FROPT AFT PRES ASYMODEM THODEL SYSTAKEEND
    IS USURN THIC       NOT END      QMOD
```

```
/* Chapter 3, Example 1, QuickC, 4/16/88
   Author program to generate text similar to a provided
   sample */

#include <stdio.h>
#include <stdlib.h>
#include <process.h>
#include <io.h>
#include <time.h>
#include <string.h>
#include <conio.h>
#include <ctype.h>
#include <dos.h>

#define SIZE 29 /* matrix dimension sizes */
#define LINE_len 79 /* length of displayed line */
#define ERROR 255 /* bad character */
#define APOSTROPHE 28 /* apostrophe character */
#define SPACE 27 /* space character */

int matrix [SIZE] [SIZE] [SIZE]; /* character frequency
                                      array */

void create_matrix(void);
void save_matrix(void);
void load_matrix(void);
void print text(void);
int get_char(FILE *fp);
void main(void);
void gotoxy(int x,int y);
void clrscr(void);
void randomize(void);
int rand(void);

void main()
{
    char choice; /* menu choice */
```

```
while (1) {
   printf("\n"); /* to make following clrscr() work */
   clrscr();
   gotoxy(25,5);
   printf("Menu");
   gotoxy(15,7);
   printf("Create new matrix");
   gotoxy(15,8)
   printf("Save present matrix");
   gotoxy(15,9)
   printf("Load old matrix");
   gotoxy(15,10);
   printf("Print text");
   gotoxy(15,11);
   printf("Exit program");

   gotoxy(15,14);
   printf("Your choice by first letter? ");
   choice = (char) getch();
   switch (choice) {

      case 'c':
      case 'C':
         create_matrix();
         break;

      case 's':
      case 'S':
         save_matrix();
         break;

      case 'l':
      case 'L':
         load_matrix();
         break;

      case 'p':
      case 'P':
         print_text();
         break;
```

```
            case 'e':
            case 'E':
                break;

            default:
                putch(7); /* beep */
                break;
        }
        if (choice == 'e' || choice == 'E')
            break;
    }
}


void create_matrix()
{
    FILE *fp; /* file handle */
    int a,b,c; /* loop counters */
    char first_char,
         second_char,
         third_char,
         error = 255,
         samplename [13]; /* sample text file name */
    long length,
         counter;

    clrscr();

    /* set matrix to zeros */
    for (a = 0;a < SIZE;a++) {
        for (b = 0;b < SIZE;b++) {
            for (c = 0;c < SIZE;c++)
                matrix [a] [b] [c] = 0;
        }
    }

    /* get file name */
    gotoxy(10,10);
    printf("Supply the name of the file containing the sample
text - no paths");
```

```
      gotoxy(10,11);
      scanf("%s",samplename);
      if (access(samplename,0) != 0) {
         putch(7); /* beep */
         gotoxy(15,22);
         printf("Sample file does not exist");
         exit(1);
      }

   /* open text file for reading */
   if ((fp = fopen(samplename,"r")) == NULL) {
      putch(7); /* beep */
      gotoxy(10,24);
      printf("Cannot open file");
      exit(1);
   }
   counter = 0;

   /* get first character */
   do {
      first_char = get_char(fp);
      counter++;
   }
   /* until a valid character is retrieved */
   while (first_char == error);

   /* get second character */
   do {
      second_char = get_char(fp);
      counter++;
   }
   while (second_char == error);

   /* get the rest of the characters */
   length = filelength(fileno(fp));
   for (;counter <= length;counter++) {
      third_char = get_char(fp);
      /* is it valid? */
      if (third_char != error) {
         matrix [first_char] [second_char] [third_char]++;
         first_char = second_char;
         second_char = third_char;
```

```
         }
      }
      fclose(fp);
   }


int get_char(FILE *fp)
/* get a character from sample text file */
{
   char letter;

   /* get the next character from the file */
   letter = (char) getc(fp);

   /* test to see if character is a letter, apostrophe, or
      space */
   if (letter == ' ') /* space */
      return (SPACE);
   if (letter == '\'') /* apostrophe */
      return (APOSTROPHE);
   if (letter == 0) /* null */
      return (ERROR);
   /* convert letter to upper-case */
   letter = toupper(letter) - 64;
   /* is it a letter? */
   if (letter < 1 || letter > 26) /* no */
      return (ERROR);
   return (letter);
}

void save_matrix()
/* save the character matrix array in a file */
{
   FILE *fp;
   char matrixfile [13];
   int a,b,c;

   /* get file name */
   clrscr();
   gotoxy(10,10);
   printf("File in which to save matrix - no path");
   gotoxy(10,11);
```

```
    scanf("%s",matrixfile);
    if (( fp = fopen(matrixfile,"wb")) == NULL) {
       putch(7); /* beep */
       gotoxy(15,22);
       printf("Unable to open matrix file");
       exit(1);
    }

    /* save array */
    for (a = 1;a < SIZE;a++) {
       for (b = 1;b < SIZE;b++) {
          for (c = 1;c < SIZE;c++)
             putc(matrix [a] [b] [c],fp);
       }
    }

    fclose(fp);
}


void load_matrix()
/* save the character matrix array in a file */
{
    FILE *fp;
    char matrixfile [13];
    int a,b,c;

    /* get file name */
    clrscr();
    gotoxy(10,10);
    printf("File from which to load matrix - no path");
    gotoxy(10,11);
    scanf("%s",matrixfile);


    /* does it exist? */
    if (access(matrixfile,0) != 0) {
       putch(7); /* beep */
       gotoxy(15,22);
       printf("Matrix file does not exist");
       exit(1);
    }
```

```
    /* yes, open it */
    if (( fp = fopen(matrixfile,"rb")) == NULL) {
       putch(7); /* beep */
       gotoxy(15,22);
       printf("Unable to open matrix file");
       exit(1);
    }

    /* load array from file */
    for (a = 1;a < SIZE;a++) {
       for (b = 1;b < SIZE;b++) {
          for (c = 1;c < SIZE;c++)
                matrix [a] [b] [c] = getc(fp);
       }
    }

    fclose(fp);
}


void print_text()
/* create and print text */
{
    int maxchar = 0,
        position,
        char_counter,
        back_counter,
        counter,
        first_char,
        second_char,
        third_char,
        location;
    unsigned int random,
                 get_random,
                 sum;
    char string [80], /* temporary holder for text line */
         temp [80];

    /* get number of characters desired */
    clrscr();
    gotoxy(15,10);
    printf("Number of characters to print - maximum 32767");
```

```
gotoxy(15,11);
scanf("%d",&maxchar);

/* start the printing */
first_char = 'T' - 64;
second_char = 'H' - 64;
string [0] = 'T';
string [1] = 'H';
position = 1;
clrscr();

/* print the characters */
for (char_counter = 2;char_counter < maxchar;
                                  char_counter++) {

   position++;

   /* sum the occurrence all the characters that follow
      first_char and second_char */
   sum = 0;
   for (counter = 1;counter < SIZE;counter++) {
      sum += matrix [first_char] [second_char] [counter];
      location = counter;
   }
   /* none */
   if (sum == 0)
      location = SPACE;
   else {
      /* get a random number up to sum and get characters
         again until that random number is matched or
         exceeded */
      random = rand() % sum;
      get_random = 0;
      counter = 0;
      while (counter < SIZE && get_random < random) {
         counter++;
         get_random += matrix [first_char] [second_char]
                                              [counter];

         location = counter;
      }
   }
   switch (location) {
      case APOSTROPHE: /* apostrophe */
```

```
        if (position == 0 ||
               string [position - 1] == '\'' ||
               string [position - 1] == ' ')
           position--;
        else
           string [position] = '\'';
        break;

   case SPACE: /* space */
        if (position == 0 ||
                        string [position - 1] == ' ')
           position--;
        else
           string [position] = ' ';
        break

   default:
   string [position] = (char) (location + 64);
        break;
}
third_char = location;

/* see if we need to start a new line */
if (position >= (LINE_len - 2)) {
    /* yes, find a good place to break the line */
    string [position + 1] = '\0';
    if (location == SPACE) { /* space */
        string [position + 1] = '\0';
        fprintf(stdprn,"%s\n\r",string);
        position = -1;
    }
    else {
        /* back up to first space */
        for (back_counter = LINE_len - 1;
                back_counter > 0,
                string [back_counter] != ' ';
                back_counter--)
          ; /* empty for loop */


        /* start a new string */
        temp [0] = '\0';
```

```
                    /* get first part of string up to last space */
                    strncat(temp,string,back_counter + 1);

                    /* print it */
                    fprintf(stdprn,"%s\n\r",temp);

                    /* use the end of the string after the last
                    space to start a new line */
                    memmove(&string [0],
                            &string [back_counter + 1],
                            LINE_len - (back_counter + 2));

                    /* set new line position */
                    position = LINE_len - (back_counter + 2);
                } /* end if */
            } /* end if */
            first_char = second_char;
            second_char = third_char;
        } /* end for, done creating text  */

        /* print any partial line remaining */
        if (position > 0) {
            string [position + 1] = '\0';
            fprintf(stdprn,"%s\n\r",string);
        }
} /* end print_text function */


void gotoxy(int x,int y)
/* position cursor on display */
{
    union REGS regs;

    regs.h.ah = 2;                  /* bios function */
    regs.h.dh = (char) y;           /* row */
    regs.h.dl = (char) x;           /* column */
    regs.h.bh = 0;                  /* page */
    int86(0x10,&regs,&regs);        /* bios interrupt number */
}
```

```c
void clrscr(void)
/* clear screen */
{
    union REGS regs;

    regs.h.ah = 6;                      /* bios function */
    regs.h.al = 0;                      /* page */
    regs.h.bh = 7;                      /* normal attribute */
    regs.h.ch = 0;                      /* upper row position */
    regs.h.cl = 0;                      /* upper-left column
                                           position */
    regs.h.dh = 24;                     /* lowest row */
    regs.h.dl = 79;                     /* rightmost column */
    int86(0x10,&regs,&regs);            /* bios interrupt number */
}


int rand(void)
{
    time_t ltime;
    int rnd;
    static unsigned long value = 0;
    unsigned long temp,
            increment = 271819,
            multiplier = 314159,
            modulus = 100001,
            int_mod = 32767;

    if (value == 0) {
        time(&ltime);
        value = (multiplier * ltime + increment);
        value = value % modulus;
        temp = value;
        temp = value % int_mod;
        rnd = (int) temp;
    }
    else {
        value = (multiplier * value + increment);
        value = value % modulus;
```

```
        temp = value;
        temp = temp % int_mod;
        rnd = (int) temp;
    }
    return(rnd);
}
```

When sending data to the printer the standard printer file handle is used, "stdprn". Also, the line ends with "\n\r". If you get double spacing in your printout try "\n" or "\r" alone instead.

HELP WINDOWS

Using sequential files is simple, as shown in the previous and following examples. It usually is easiest to work with the file in the binary mode as shown (the "b" in the "rb" or "wb"). You could also set the global system variable _fmode to O_BINARY. Another possibility is to use the open( ) function and set the O_BINARY flag. I prefer the method used in the program. We will be using sequential files again in later examples.

This program uses the up- and down-arrows to scroll, the Home key to put the first help line at the top of the screen, the End key to put the last help line at the bottom of the screen, and the Escape key to leave the help screen—and program, in this case.

```
/* Chapter 3, Example 2, QuickC, 4/16/88
   Using a help window

   set stack to 5120 to run in memory */

#include <process.h>
#include <string.h>
#include <stdio.h>
#include <stdlib.h>
#include <dos.h>
#include <malloc.h>
#include <conio.h>

#define MAX_LINE 15 /* number of help lines */
#define HELP_LEN 28 /* help line length */
```

```
/* function prototypes */
void create_window(int c1,int r1,int c2,int r2,
                   char title []);
void fill_screen(void);
void outline(int c1,int r1,int c2,int r2);
void clrscr(void);
void gotoxy(int x,int y);
void main(void);
void gettext(char far *screen_buffer);
void puttext(char far *screen_buffer);
int iscolor(void);
void clreol(int start,int c2);
void clr_window(int c1,int c2,int r1,int r2);
void show_help(int c1,int r1,int r2,
               char help [] [HELP_LEN]);
void show_screen(int hoffset,int voffset,int upcounter,
                 int downcounter,char help [] [HELP_LEN]);
void get_key(int key []);
void bioskey(int key []);


void main()
{
   int c1 = 24, /* upper-left column */
       c2 = 56, /* lower-right column */
       r1 = 5, /* upper-left row */
       r2 = 16; /*lower-right row */
   char far *screen_buffer,
        title [79], /* window title */
        help [MAX_LINE] [HELP_LEN]; /* help lines for
                                       window */

   /* title */
   strcpy(&title [0],"Test Help Window");

   /* contents of help screen */
   strcpy(&help [0] [0],"Character left     Ctrl-S");
   strcpy(&help [1] [0],"Character right    Ctrl-D");
   strcpy(&help [2] [0],"Word left          Ctrl-A");
   strcpy(&help [3] [0],"Word right         Ctrl-F");
   strcpy(&help [4] [0],"Line up            Ctrl-E");
   strcpy(&help [5] [0],"Line down          Ctrl-X");
```

```
      strcpy(&help [6] [0],"Scroll up           Ctrl-W");
      strcpy(&help [7] [0],"Scroll down         Ctrl-Z");
      strcpy(&help [8] [0],"Page up             Ctrl-R");
      strcpy(&help [9] [0],"Page down           Ctrl-C");
      strcpy(&help [10] [0],"Beginning of line   Ctrl-QS");
      strcpy(&help [11] [0],"End of line         Ctrl-QD");
      strcpy(&help [12] [0],"Top of window       Ctrl-QE");
      strcpy(&help [13] [0],"Bottom of window    Ctrl-QX");
      strcpy(&help [14] [0],"Top of file         Ctrl-QR");
      /* create buffer to save screen */
      if ((screen_buffer = _fmalloc(4000)) == NULL) {
         clrscr();
         printf("Not enough memory\n");
         exit(1);
      }


      /* make a random background for window */
      fill_screen();
      gettext(screen_buffer); /* save screen */
      gotoxy(10,24);
      clreol(10,78); /* erase old prompt */
      gotoxy(10,24);
      printf("Press escape to conclude demo\n");

      create_window(c1,r1,c2,r2,title);
      outline(c1,r1,c2,r2);
      show_help(c1,r1,r2,help);

      puttext(screen_buffer); /* restore screen */
      _ffree(screen_buffer); /* delete save buffer */
} /* end main */


void create_window(int c1,int r1,int c2,int r2,
                   char title [])
/* create a window */
{
   int len;

   /* erase window contents */
   clr_window(c1,r1,c2,r2);
```

```
    /* center title in window */
    len = strlen(title);
    if (len > 0) {
        gotoxy(c1 + (c2 - c1 - strlen(title)) / 2,r1);
        printf("%s",title);
    }
}


void clr_window(int c1,int r1,int c2,int r2)
/* clear window */
{
    unsigned char attrib;

    union REGS inregs,outregs;

    /* get current video attribute */
    inregs.h.ah = 8;                    /* bios function */
    inregs.h.bh = 0;                    /* page */
    int86(0x10,&inregs,&outregs);    /* bios interrupt
                                        number */

    attrib = outregs.h.ah;              /* current attribute */

    /* clear the window area */
    inregs.h.ah = 6;                    /* bios function */
    inregs.h.al = 0;                    /* page */
    inregs.h.bh = attrib;               /* current attribute */
    inregs.h.ch = (char) r1;            /* upper row position */
    inregs.h.cl = (char) c1;            /* upper-left column
                                        position */
    inregs.h.dh = (char) r2;            /* lowest row */
    inregs.h.dl = (char) c2;            /* rightmost column */
    int86(0x10,&inregs,&outregs);    /* bios interrupt
                                        number */
}

void fill_screen(void)
/* fill screen with asterisks */
{
    int x,y; /* counters */
    char filler [79]; /* fill string */
```

```
     printf("\n"); /* required to get following clrscr() to
                      work */
     clrscr();

     /* fill the screen */
     for (x = 0;x <= 24;x++) {
        for (y = 0;y <= 78;y++)
        filler [y] = '*';
        filler [79] = '\0';
        printf("%s",filler);
     }
}


void outline(int c1,int r1,int c2,int r2)
/* draw outline around outside of window */
{
   int counter;

   /* draw top and bottom */
   for (counter = c1;counter <= c2;counter++) {
      gotoxy(counter,r1 - 1);
      putch(205); /* horizontal double line */
      gotoxy(counter,r2 + 1);
      putch(205);
   }

   /* draw sides */
   for (counter = r1;counter <= r2;counter++) {
      gotoxy(c1 - 1,counter);
      putch(186); /* vertical double line */
      gotoxy(c2 + 1,counter);
      putch(186);
   }

   /* draw corners */
   gotoxy(c1 - 1,r1 - 1);
   putch(201); /* upper-left corner */
   gotoxy(c2 + 1,r1 - 1);
   putch(187); /* upper-right corner */
   gotoxy(c1 - 1,r2 + 1);
```

```
    putch(200); /* lower-left corner */
    gotoxy(c2 + 1,r2 + 1);
    putch(188); /* lower-right corner */
}


void clrscr(void)
/* clear screen */
{
    union REGS regs;

    regs.h.ah = 6;                      /* bios function */
    regs.h.al = 0;                      /* clear entire screen */
    regs.h.bh = 7;                      /* normal attribute */
    regs.h.ch = 0;                      /* upper row position */
    regs.h.cl = 0;                      /* upper-left column
                                           position */
    regs.h.dh = 24;                     /* lowest row */
    regs.h.dl = 79;                     /* rightmost column */
    int86(0x10,&regs,&regs);            /* bios interrupt number */
} /* end function clear screen */
void clrscr(void); /* bug fix */

void gotoxy(int x,int y)
/* position cursor */
{

    union REGS regs;


    regs.h.ah = 2;                      /* bios function */
    regs.h.dh = (char) y;               /* row */
    regs.h.dl = (char) x;               /* column */
    regs.h.bh = 0;                      /* video page number */
    int86(0x10,&regs,&regs);            /* bios interrupt number */
} /* end function gotoxy */


void gettext(char far *screen_buffer)
/* saves text on screen to buffer */
/* see Chapter 1 for more information about this function */
```

```
{
    register short i;
    register short delta;

    delta = 0;

    /* iscolor() is a function that tests for color */
    if (iscolor() == 1) {
        for (i = 0; i < 5; i++) {
#if 0
            /* check retrace */
            while (((inp(0x3DA) & 0x08) >> 3) == 0);
#endif
            movedata(0xB800,0 + delta,
                    FP_SEG(screen_buffer),
                    FP_OFF(screen_buffer) + delta,800);
            delta += 800;
        }
    }
    else
        movedata(0xB000,0,FP_SEG(screen_buffer),
                FP_OFF(screen_buffer),4000);
}  /* end function gettext() */


void puttext(char far *screen_buffer)
/* returns text to screen from buffer */
/* see Chapter 1 for more information about this function */
{
    register short i;
    register short delta;

    delta = 0;
    if (iscolor() == 1)  { /* color */
        for (i = 0; i < 5; i++)  {
#if 0
            /* check retrace */
            while (((inp(0x3DA) & 0x08) >> 3) == 0);
#endif
            movedata(FP_SEG(screen_buffer),
                    FP_OFF(screen_buffer) + delta,0xB800,
                    0 + delta, 800);
```

```
          delta += 800;
      }
   }
   else /* monochrome */
      movedata(FP_SEG(screen_buffer),
               FP_OFF(screen_buffer),0xB000,0,4000);
}


int iscolor()
{
   int crt = 0;
   union REGS inregs,outregs;


   inregs.h.ah = 15;                /* bios function */
   int86(0x10,&inregs,&outregs); /* bios interrupt number */

   crt = (int) outregs.h.al;
   if (crt == 7) /* monochrome */
      crt = 0;
   else /* color·*/
      crt = 1;
   return(crt);
} /* end function iscolor */


void clreol(start,end)
/* clear to end of line */
{
   int counter;

   for (counter = start;counter <= end;counter++)
      printf("%c",' ');
}


void show_help(int c1,int r1,int r2,char help [] [HELP_LEN])
/* display the help screen */
{
   int upcounter = 0, /* first help line on screen */
```

```
            downcounter = r2 - r1 - 1, /* last help line on
                                            screen */
        key [2]; /* operator command */

    key [0] = 0; /* for get_key() */
    key [1] = 0;


    /* put the help lines on the screen */
    show_screen(c1,r1,upcounter,downcounter,help);



    /* get the operator's commands */
    while (key [0] != 27) { /* while not escape */
       get_key(key); /* get keypress from operator */
       switch (key [1]) {

               case 72: /* up-arrow, scroll up one line */
                   if (upcounter > 0) {
                       upcounter--;
                       downcounter--;
                       show_screen(c1,r1,upcounter,downcounter,
                                   help);
                   }
                   else
                       putch(7); /* beep */
                   break;

               case 80: /* down-arrow, scroll down one line */
                   if (downcounter < MAX_LINE - 1) {
                       upcounter++;
                       downcounter++;
                       show_screen(c1,r1,upcounter,downcounter,
                                   help);
                   }
                   else
                       putch(7); /* beep */
                   break;

               case 71: /* home, move first line to screen top */
                   upcounter = 0;
                   downcounter = r2 - r1 - 1;
                   show_screen(c1,r1,upcounter,downcounter,help);
                   break;
```

```
            case 79: /* end, move last line to screen
                        bottom */
              downcounter = MAX_LINE - 1;
              upcounter = downcounter - ((r2 - r1) - 1);
              show_screen(c1,r1,upcounter,downcounter,help);
              break;

            default:
              if (key [0] != 27) /* escape */
                putch(7); /* beep */
      }
    }
}


void show_screen(int hoffset,int voffset,int upcounter,
                 int downcounter,char help [] [HELP_LEN])
/* put help lines on screen */
{
    int counter,  /* help line */
        pos;      /* window row */
    char blank [HELP_LEN]; /* to erase lines while
                              scrolling */

    /* create blank line */
    memset(blank,' ',HELP_LEN - 1);
    blank [HELP_LEN - 1] = '\0';

    for (counter = upcounter,pos = 1;
                counter <= downcounter;counter++,pos++) {
      /* erase old line at this position */
      gotoxy(hoffset + 2,voffset + pos);
      printf("%s",blank);
      /* display new line */
      gotoxy(hoffset + 2,voffset + pos);
      printf("%s",help [counter]);
    }
}

void get_key(int key [])
/* get ASCII or scan code */
{
```

```
        bioskey(key);
}


void bioskey(int key [])
/* get keypress from bios */
{
    union REGS inregs,outregs;

    inregs.h.ah = 0; /* interrupt number */
    int86(0x16,&inregs,&outregs);

    key [0] = (int) outregs.h.al; /* ASCII value */
    key [1] = (int) outregs.h.ah; /* scan code */
} /* end bioskey function */
```

This example shows one way to use a window as a help screen.

USING HELP WINDOWS WITH SEQUENTIAL FILES

Rather than keeping the help array in memory, you can store the help text in a sequential file on disk, loading it into the array as needed. This would be of little advantage unless you used the same array and window size for all your help screens. I'll leave this to you. To get you started, all you need to do is to store the number of help lines in the sequential file as the first record. Then you know how many lines to retrieve from the file and how many lines to display in the help window. Change the MAX_LINE constant to a variable containing this value and pass it to the functions that use MAX_LINE. You will have to size your window to hold the largest help line in any of the files, or store the largest help line length in that file in a record at the beginning of each file, following the record containing the number of lines. Then set your window's horizontal size using that help line length by using the file's value to determine the values of c1 and c2.

Note that this program is almost the same as Example 2 with the exception that it shows how to load an array or list of text lines into a sequential file and retrieve them.

```
/* Chapter 3, Example 3, QuickC, 4/16/88
   Using a help window and sequential files

   set stack to 5120 to run in memory */

#include <process.h>
#include <string.h>
#include <stdio.h>
#include <stdlib.h>
#include <dos.h>
#include <malloc.h>
#include <conio.h>

#define MAX_LINE 15 /* number of help lines */
#define HELP_LEN 28 /* help line length */

void create_window(int c1,int r1,int c2,int r2,
                   char title []);
void fill_screen(void);
void outline(int c1,int r1,int c2,int r2);
void clrscr(void);
void gotoxy(int x,int y);
void main(void);
void gettext(char far *screen_buffer);
void puttext(char far *screen_buffer);
int iscolor(void);
void clreol(int start,int c2);
void clr_window(int c1,int c2,int r1,int r2);
void show_help(int c1,int r1,int r2,
               char help [] [HELP_LEN]);
void show_screen(int hoffset,int voffset,int upcounter,
                 int downcounter,char help [] [HELP_LEN]);
void get_key(int key []);
void bioskey(int key []);
void save_array(char filename [],char array [] [HELP_LEN]);
void load_array(char filename [],char array [] [HELP_LEN]);


void main()
{
   int c1 = 24, /* upper-left column */
       c2 = 56, /* lower-right column */
```

```
          r1 = 5, /* upper-left row */
          r2 = 16; /*lower-right row */
char far *screen_buffer,
       title [79], /* window title */
       help [MAX_LINE] [HELP_LEN], /* help lines for
                                   window */
       load_file [MAX_LINE] [HELP_LEN]; /* help lines for
                                        window */


/* title */
strcpy(&title [0],"Test Help Window");

/* contents of help screen */
/* This array will be placed in a file, then the file
   will be loaded into the help array to show how this
   might be done. In the real world this array would be
   loaded into the file in another program. */
strcpy(&help [0] [0],"Character left      Ctrl-S");
strcpy(&help [1] [0],"Character right     Ctrl-D");
strcpy(&help [2] [0],"Word left           Ctrl-A");
strcpy(&help [3] [0],"Word right          Ctrl-F");
strcpy(&help [4] [0],"Line up             Ctrl-E");
strcpy(&help [5] [0],"Line down           Ctrl-X");
strcpy(&help [6] [0],"Scroll up           Ctrl-W");
strcpy(&help [7] [0],"Scroll down         Ctrl-Z");
strcpy(&help [8] [0],"Page up             Ctrl-R");
strcpy(&help [9] [0],"Page down           Ctrl-C");
strcpy(&help [10] [0],"Beginning of line   Ctrl-QS");
strcpy(&help [11] [0],"End of line         Ctrl-QD");
strcpy(&help [12] [0],"Top of window       Ctrl-QE");
strcpy(&help [13] [0],"Bottom of window    Ctrl-QX");
strcpy(&help [14] [0],"Top of file         Ctrl-QR");

/* load load_file array into disk file */
save_array("ch3_3.dat",help);

/* put contents of help file into help array */
load_array("ch3_3.dat",help);

/* create buffer to save screen */
if ((screen_buffer = _fmalloc(4000)) == NULL) {
   clrscr();
```

```
         printf("Not enough memory\n");
         exit(1);
      }


      fill_screen(); /* make a random background for window */
      gettext(screen_buffer); /* save screen */
      gotoxy(10,24);
      clreol(10,78); /* erase old prompt */
      gotoxy(10,24);
      printf("Press escape to conclude demo\n");

      /* create the window */
      create_window(c1,r1,c2,r2,title);
      outline(c1,r1,c2,r2);
      /* show the help stuff */
      show_help(c1,r1,r2,help);

      puttext(screen_buffer); /* restore screen */
      _ffree(screen_buffer); /* delete save buffer */
} /* end main */

void create_window(int c1,int r1,int c2,int r2,
                      char title [])
/* create a window */
{
   int len;

   /* erase window contents */
   clr_window(c1,r1,c2,r2);

   /* center title in window */
   len = strlen(title);
   if (len > 0) {
      gotoxy(c1 + (c2 - c1 - strlen(title)) / 2,r1);
      printf("%s",title);
   }
}


void clr_window(int c1,int r1,int c2,int r2)
/* clear window */
```

```
{
    unsigned char attrib;
    union REGS inregs,outregs;

    /* get current video attribute */
    inregs.h.ah = 8;                    /* bios function */
    inregs.h.bh = 0;                    /* page */
    int86(0x10,&inregs,&outregs);       /* interrupt */

    attrib = outregs.h.ah;              /* current attribute */

    /* clear the window area */
    inregs.h.ah = 6;                    /* bios function */
    inregs.h.al = 0;                    /* page */
    inregs.h.bh = attrib;               /* current attribute */
    inregs.h.ch = (char) r1;            /* upper row position */
    inregs.h.cl = (char) c1;            /* upper-left column
                                           position */
    inregs.h.dh = (char) r2;            /* lowest row */
    inregs.h.dl = (char) c2;            /* rightmost column */
    int86(0x10,&inregs,&outregs);       /* bios interrupt
                                           number */
}


void fill_screen(void)
/* fill screen with asterisks */
{
    int x,y; /* counters */
    char filler [79]; /* fill string */

    printf("\n"); /* required to get following clrscr() to
                     work */
    clrscr();

    /* fill screen */
    for (x = 0;x <= 24;x++) {
        for (y = 0;y <= 78;y++)
        filler [y] = '*';
        filler [79] = '\0';
        printf("%s",filler);
    }
}
```

```
void outline(int c1,int r1,int c2,int r2)
/* draw outline around outside of window */
{
   int counter;

   /* draw top and bottom */
   for (counter = c1;counter <= c2;counter++) {
      gotoxy(counter,r1 - 1);
      putch(205); /* horizontal double line */
      gotoxy(counter,r2 + 1);
      putch(205);
   }


   /* draw sides */
   for (counter = r1;counter <= r2;counter++) {
      gotoxy(c1 - 1,counter);
      putch(186); /* vertical double line */
      gotoxy(c2 + 1,counter);
      putch(186);
   }
   /* draw corners */
   gotoxy(c1 - 1,r1 - 1);
   putch(201); /* upper-left corner */
   gotoxy(c2 + 1,r1 - 1);
   putch(187); /* upper-right corner */
   gotoxy(c1 - 1,r2 + 1);
   putch(200); /* lower-left corner */
   gotoxy(c2 + 1,r2 + 1);
   putch(188); /* lower-right corner */
}


void clrscr(void)
/* clear screen */
{
   union REGS regs;

   regs.h.ah = 6;                   /* bios function */
   regs.h.al = 0;                   /* clear entire screen */
   regs.h.bh = 7;                   /* normal attribute */
   regs.h.ch = 0;                   /* upper row position */
   regs.h.cl = 0;                   /* upper-left column
                                       position */
```

```
        regs.h.dh = 24;                    /* lowest row */
        regs.h.dl = 79;                    /* rightmost column */
        int86(0x10,&regs,&regs);           /* bios interrupt number */
} /* end function clear screen */
void clrscr(void); /* bug fix */

void gotoxy(int x,int y)
/* position cursor */
{

    union REGS regs;


    regs.h.ah = 2;                 /* bios function */
    regs.h.dh = (char) y;          /* row */
    regs.h.dl = (char) x;          /* column */
    regs.h.bh = 0;                 /* video page number */
    int86(0x10,&regs,&regs);       /* bios interrupt number */
} /* end function gotoxy */



void gettext(char far *screen_buffer)
/* save screen contents to a buffer */
/* see Chapter 1 for more info about this function */
{
    register short i;
    register short delta;

    delta = 0;

    /* iscolor() is a function that tests for color */
    if (iscolor() == 1) { /* color */
        for (i = 0; i < 5; i++) {
#if 0
            /* check retrace */
            while (((inp(0x3DA) & 0x08) >> 3) == 0);
#endif
            movedata(0xB800,0 + delta,FP_SEG(screen_buffer),
                     FP_OFF(screen_buffer) + delta,800);
            delta += 800;
        }
    }
```

```c
    else /* monochrome */
        movedata(0xB000,0,FP_SEG(screen_buffer),
                 FP_OFF(screen_buffer),4000);
}  /* end function gettext() */


void puttext(char far *screen_buffer)
/* restore screen contents from buffer */
/* see Chapter 1 for more info about this function */
{
    register short i;
    register short delta;

    delta = 0;
    if (iscolor() == 1)  { /* color */
        for (i = 0; i < 5; i++)  {
#if 0
            /* check retrace */
            while (((inp(0x3DA) & 0x08) >> 3) == 0);
#endif
            movedata(FP_SEG(screen_buffer),
                     FP_OFF(screen_buffer) + delta,0xB800,
                     0 + delta, 800);
                delta += 800;
        }
    }
    else /* monochrome */
        movedata(FP_SEG(screen_buffer),FP_OFF(screen_buffer),
                 0xB000,0,4000);
}


int iscolor()
/* test machine for color video */
{
    int crt = 0;
    union REGS inregs,outregs;


    inregs.h.ah = 15;                /* bios function */
    int86(0x10,&inregs,&outregs); /* bios interrupt number */
```

```
    crt = (int) outregs.h.al;
.   if (crt == 7) /* monochrome */
        crt = 0;
    else /* color */
        crt = 1;
    return(crt);
} /* end function iscolor */



void clreol(start,end)
/* clear to end of line */
{
    int counter;

    for (counter = start;counter <= end;counter++)
        printf("%c",' ');
}



void show_help(int c1,int r1,int r2,char help [] [HELP_LEN])
/* display the help screen */
{
    int upcounter = 0, /* first help line on screen */
        downcounter = r2 - r1 - 1, /* last help line on
                                      screen */
     key [2]; /* operator command */

    key [0] = 0; /* for get_key() */
    key [1] = 0;

    /* show the contents of window */
    show_screen(c1,r1,upcounter,downcounter,help);

    /* get the user's input */
    while (key [0] != 27) { /* while not escape */
       get_key(key); /* get keypress from operator */
       switch (key [1]) {

           case 72: /* up-arrow, scroll up one line */
               if (upcounter > 0) {
                   upcounter--;
```

```
                downcounter--;
                show_screen(c1,r1,upcounter,downcounter,
                          help);
            }
            else
                putch(7); /* beep */
            break;

        case 80: /* down-arrow, scroll down one line */
            if (downcounter < MAX_LINE - 1) {
                upcounter++;
                downcounter++;
                show_screen(c1,r1,upcounter,downcounter,
                          help);
            }
            else
                putch(7); /* beep */
            break;

        case 71: /* home, move first line to screen top */
            upcounter = 0;
            downcounter = r2 - r1 - 1;
            show_screen(c1,r1,upcounter,downcounter,help);
            break;

        case 79: /* end, move last line to screen bottom */
            downcounter = MAX_LINE - 1;
            upcounter = downcounter - ((r2 - r1) - 1);
            show_screen(c1,r1,upcounter,downcounter,help);
            break;

        default:
            if (key [0] != 27) /* escape */
                putch(7); /* beep */
        }
    }
}


void show_screen(int hoffset,int voffset,int upcounter,
            int downcounter,char help [] [HELP_LEN])
```

```
/* put help lines on screen */
{
    int counter,  /* help line */
        pos;      /* window row */
    char blank [HELP_LEN]; /* to erase lines while
                              scrolling */

    /* create blank line */
    memset(blank,' ',HELP_LEN - 1);
    blank [HELP_LEN - 1] = '\0';

    /* display help lines from array */
    for (counter = upcounter,pos = 1;
                    counter <= downcounter;counter++,pos++) {
        /* erase old line at this position */
        gotoxy(hoffset + 2,voffset + pos);
        printf("%s",blank);
        /* show new line at this position */
        gotoxy(hoffset + 2,voffset + pos);
        printf("%s",help [counter]);
    }
}


void get_key(int key [])
/* get ASCII or scan code */
{
    bioskey(key);
}


void bioskey(int key [])
/* get keypress from bios */
{
    union REGS inregs,outregs;

    inregs.h.ah = 0; /* interrupt number */
    int86(0x16,&inregs,&outregs);

    key [0] = (int) outregs.h.al; /* ASCII value */
    key [1] = (int) outregs.h.ah; /* scan code */
} /* end bioskey function */
```

```
void save_array(char filename [],char array [] [HELP_LEN])
/* demonstrate saving a character array to a file */
{
    int counter;
    FILE *stream;

    /* open file for writing */
    if ((stream = fopen(filename,"wb")) == NULL) {
        printf("Cannot open file\n");
        exit(1);
    }

    /* save array to file */
    for (counter = 0;counter <= MAX_LINE;counter++)
        fwrite(array [counter],HELP_LEN,1,stream);

    fclose(stream);
}


void load_array(char filename [],char array [] [HELP_LEN])
/* demonstrate retrieving a character array from a file */
{
    int counter;
    FILE *stream;

    /* open file for reading */
    if ((stream = fopen(filename,"wb")) == NULL) {
        printf("Cannot open file\n");
        exit(1);
    }

    /* read file into array */
    for (counter = 0;counter <= MAX_LINE;counter++)
        fread(array [counter],HELP_LEN,1,stream);

    fclose(stream);
}
```

The next chapter will show how to do a help screen from a random access file—no array to load that way.

4

Random Access Files

HELP SCREENS AND RANDOM ACCESS FILES

AUTHOR PROGRAM REVISITED

Random access files are much like sequential files except that you usually keep the record sizes the same. This allows you to find a specific record by multiplying the record number by the record size; then use the fseek( ) function to set the position within the file. The record can contain a character, numeric value, structure, or even an entire array. Frequently, you can use the sizeof( ) function to express the record length. A character has a size of one byte on most computers.

Generally, in this book, random access files are treated as binary, ignoring EOFs, '\0's, carriage returns, and line-feeds. If you keep track of the number of records in your file, this is the safest way to handle such files. I use this method throughout this chapter and elsewhere in this book.

HELP SCREENS AND RANDOM ACCESS FILES

The first example is like Example 3 from Chapter 3, except no array is used; the help lines are extracted directly from the file as required. As you will see, this is just as fast as using an array and saves providing memory to store the array.

```c
/* Chapter 4, Example 1, QuickC, 4/16/88
   Using a help window and random access files

   set stack to 5120 to run in memory */

#include <process.h>
#include <string.h>
#include <stdio.h>
#include <stdlib.h>
#include <dos.h>
#include <malloc.h>
#include <conio.h>

#define MAX_LINE 15 /* number of help lines */
#define HELP_LEN 28 /* help line length */

/* function prototypes */
void create_window(int c1,int r1,int c2,int r2,
                   char title []);
```

```
void fill_screen(void);
void outline(int c1,int r1,int c2,int r2);
void clrscr(void);
void gotoxy(int x,int y);
void main(void);
void gettext(char far *screen_buffer);
void puttext(char far *screen_buffer);
int iscolor(void);
void clreol(int start,int c2);
void clr_window(int c1,int c2,int r1,int r2);
void show_help(int c1,int r1,int r2,
               char help [],FILE *stream);
void show_screen(int hoffset,int voffset,int upcounter,int
downcounter,char help [],FILE *stream);
void get_key(int key []);
void bioskey(int key []);
void save_array(char filename [],char array [] [HELP_LEN]);


void main()
{
    int c1 = 24, /* upper-left column */
        c2 = 56, /* lower-right column */
        r1 = 5, /* upper-left row */
        r2 = 16; /*lower-right row */
    char far *screen_buffer,
        filename [12], /* for name of help file */
        title [79], /* window title */
        help [HELP_LEN], /* help line for window */
        load_file [MAX_LINE] [HELP_LEN]; /* help lines for
                                            window */

    FILE *stream;

    strcpy(&filename [0],"ch4_1.dat");

    /* title */
    strcpy(&title [0],"Test Help Window");
```

```
/* contents of help screen */
/* This array will be placed in a file, then the file
   contents will be read as required to show how this
   might be done. In the real world this array would be
   loaded into the file in another program. */

strcpy(&load_file [0] [0],"Character left      Ctrl-S");
strcpy(&load_file [1] [0],"Character right     Ctrl-D");
strcpy(&load_file [2] [0],"Word left           Ctrl-A");
strcpy(&load_file [3] [0],"Word right          Ctrl-F");
strcpy(&load_file [4] [0],"Line up             Ctrl-E");
strcpy(&load_file [5] [0],"Line down           Ctrl-X");
strcpy(&load_file [6] [0],"Scroll up           Ctrl-W");
strcpy(&load_file [7] [0],"Scroll down         Ctrl-Z");
strcpy(&load_file [8] [0],"Page up             Ctrl-R");
strcpy(&load_file [9] [0],"Page down           Ctrl-C");
strcpy(&load_file [10] [0],"Beginning of line  Ctrl-QS");
strcpy(&load_file [11] [0],"End of line        Ctrl-QD");
strcpy(&load_file [12] [0],"Top of window      Ctrl-QE");
strcpy(&load_file [13] [0],"Bottom of window   Ctrl-QX");
strcpy(&load_file [14] [0],"Top of file        Ctrl-QR");

/* load load_file array into disk file */
save_array(filename,load_file);

/* open help disk file to read into window */
if ((stream = fopen(filename,"rb")) == NIII) {
   printf("cannot open file\n");
   exit(1);
}

/* create buffer to save screen */
if ((screen_buffer = _fmalloc(4000)) == NULL) {
   clrscr();
   printf("Not enough memory\n");
   exit(1);
}
```

```
      /* do it */
      fill_screen(); /* make a random background for window */
      gettext(screen_buffer); /* save screen */
      gotoxy(10,24);
      clreol(10,78); /* erase old prompt */
      gotoxy(10,24);
      printf("Press escape to conclude demo\n");

      /* show the window */
      create_window(c1,r1,c2,r2,title);
      outline(c1,r1,c2,r2);

      /* give control to operator */
      show_help(c1,r1,r2,help,stream);

      /* get rid of window */
      puttext(screen_buffer); /* restore screen */
      _ffree(screen_buffer); /* delete save buffer */
} /* end main */


void create_window(int c1,int r1,int c2,int r2,
                   char title [])
/* create a window */
{
   int len;

   /* erase window contents */
   clr_window(c1,r1,c2,r2);

   /* center title in window */
   len = strlen(title);
   if (len > 0) {
      gotoxy(c1 + (c2 - c1 - strlen(title)) / 2,r1);
      printf("%s",title);
   }
}
```

```
void clr_window(int c1,int r1,int c2,int r2)
/* clear window */
{
   unsigned char attrib;

   union REGS inregs,outregs;

   /* get current video attribute */
   inregs.h.ah = 8;                    /* bios function */
   inregs.h.bh = 0;                    /* page */
   int86(0x10,&inregs,&outregs);       /* interrupt */

   attrib = outregs.h.ah;              /* current attribute */

   /* clear the window area */
   inregs.h.ah = 6;                    /* bios function */
   inregs.h.al = 0;                    /* page */
   inregs.h.bh = attrib;               /* current attribute */
   inregs.h.ch = (char) r1;            /* upper row position */
   inregs.h.cl = (char) c1;            /* upper-left column
                                          position */
   inregs.h.dh = (char) r2;            /* lowest row */
   inregs.h.dl = (char) c2;            /* rightmost column */
   int86(0x10,&inregs,&outregs);       /* bios interrupt
                                          number */
}


void fill_screen(void)
/* fill screen with random characters */
{
   int x,y; /* counters */
   char filler [79]; /* fill string */

   printf("\n"); /* required to get following clrscr() to
                    work in QC */
   clrscr();
```

```
      /* load screen with asterisks */
      for (x = 0;x <= 24;x++) {
         for (y = 0;y <= 78;y++
         filler [y] = '*';
         filler [79] = '\0';
         printf("%s",filler);
      }
}


void outline(int c1,int r1,int c2,int r2)
/* draw outline around outside of window */
{
   int counter;

   /* draw top and bottom */
   for (counter = c1;counter <= c2;counter++) {
      gotoxy(counter,r1 - 1);
      putch(205); /* horizontal double line */
      gotoxy(counter,r2 + 1);
      putch(205);
   }

   /* draw sides */
   for (counter = r1;counter <= r2;counter++) {
      gotoxy(c1 - 1,counter);
      putch(186); /* vertical double line */
      gotoxy(c2 + 1,counter);
      putch(186);
   }

   /* draw corners */
   gotoxy(c1 - 1,r1 - 1);
   putch(201); /* upper-left corner */
   gotoxy(c2 + 1,r1 - 1);
   putch(187); /* upper-right corner */
   gotoxy(c1 - 1,r2 + 1);
   putch(200); /* lower-left corner */
   gotoxy(c2 + 1,r2 + 1);
   putch(188); /* lower-right corner */
}
```

```
void clrscr(void)
/* clear screen */
{
   union REGS regs;

   regs.h.ah = 6;                    /* bios function */
   regs.h.al = 0;                    /* clear entire screen */
   regs.h.bh = 7;                    /* normal attribute */
   regs.h.ch = 0;                    /* upper row position */
   regs.h.cl = 0;                    /* upper-left column
                                        position */
   regs.h.dh = 24;                   /* lowest row */
   regs.h.dl = 79;                   /* rightmost column */
   int86(0x10,&regs,&regs);          /* bios interrupt number */
} /* end function clear screen */
void clrscr(void);


void gotoxy(int x,int y)
/* position cursor */
{

   union REGS regs;


   regs.h.ah = 2;                    /* bios function */
   regs.h.dh = (char) y;             /* row */
   regs.h.dl = (char) x;             /* column */
   regs.h.bh = 0;                    /* video page number */
   int86(0x10,&regs,&regs);          /* bios interrupt number */
} /* end function gotoxy */

void gettext(char far *screen_buffer)
/* saves screen text contents to a buffer */
/* see Chapter 1 for more info */
{
   register short i;
   register short delta;

   delta = 0;
```

```
      /* iscolor() is a function that tests for color */
      if (iscolor() == 1) {  /* color */
         for (i = 0; i < 5; i++) {
#if 0
            /* check retrace */
            while (((inp(0x3DA) & 0x08) >> 3) == 0);
#endif
            movedata(0xB800,0 + delta,FP_SEG(screen_buffer),
                     FP_OFF(screen_buffer) + delta,800);
            delta += 800;
            }
         }
      else /* monochrome */
         movedata(0xB000,0,FP_SEG(screen_buffer),
                  FP_OFF(screen_buffer),4000);
}  /* end function gettext() */



void puttext(char far *screen_buffer)
/* restores screen text contents from buffer */
/* see Chapter 1 for more info */
{
   register short i;
   register short delta;

   delta = 0;
   if (iscolor() == 1)  { /* color */
      for (i = 0; i < 5; i++)  {
#if 0
         /* check retrace */
         while (((inp(0x3DA) & 0x08) >> 3) == 0);
#endif
         movedata(FP_SEG(screen_buffer),
                  FP_OFF(screen_buffer) + delta,0xB800,
                  0 + delta, 800);
         delta += 800;
         }
      }
   else /* monochrome */
      movedata(FP_SEG(screen_buffer),FP_OFF(screen_buffer),
               0xB000,0,4000);
  }
```

```c
int iscolor()
/* test hardware for color */
{
   int crt = 0;
   union REGS inregs,outregs;


   inregs.h.ah = 15;              /* bios function */
   int86(0x10,&inregs,&outregs); /* bios interrupt number */

   crt = (int) outregs.h.al;
   if (crt == 7) /* monochrome */
      crt = 0;
   else /* color */
      crt = 1;
   return(crt);
} /* end function iscolor */

void clreol(start,end)
/* clear to end of line */
{
   int counter;

   for (counter = start;counter <= end;counter++)
      printf("%c",' ');
}



void show_help(int c1,int r1,int r2,
               char help [],FILE *stream)
/* display the help screen */
{
   int upcounter = 0, /* first help line on screen */
       downcounter = r2 - r1 - 1, /* last help line on
                                     screen */
       key [2]; /* operator command */

   key [0] = 0; /* for get_key() */
   key [1] = 0;

   /* show first screenful of help */
   show_screen(c1,r1,upcounter,downcounter,help,stream);
```

```
/* accept user commands until escape is pressed */
while (key [0] != 27) { /* while not escape */
   get_key(key); /* get keypress from operator */
   switch (key [1]) {

      case 72: /* up-arrow, scroll up one line */
         if (upcounter > 0) {
            upcounter--;
            downcounter--;
            show_screen(c1,r1,upcounter,downcounter,
                        help,stream);
         }
         else /* no more lines up there */
            putch(7); /* beep */
         break;

      case 80: /* down-arrow, scroll down one line */
         if (downcounter < MAX_LINE - 1) {
            upcounter++;
            downcounter++;
            show_screen(c1,r1,upcounter,downcounter,
                        help,stream);
         }
         else /* no more lines down there */
            putch(7); /* beep */
         break;

      case 71: /* home, move first line to screen top */
         upcounter = 0;
         downcounter = r2 - r1 - 1;
         show_screen(c1,r1,upcounter,downcounter,
                     help,stream);
         break;

      case 79: /* end, move last line to screen bottom */
         downcounter = MAX_LINE - 1;
         upcounter = downcounter - ((r2 - r1) - 1);
         show_screen(c1,r1,upcounter,downcounter,
                     help,stream);
         break;
```

```
                  default:
                      if (key [0] != 27) /* escape */
                          putch(7); /* beep, invalid key */
              }
          }
      }


void show_screen(int hoffset,int voffset,int upcounter,
                     int downcounter,char help [],FILE *stream)
/* put help lines on screen */
{
    int counter,  /* help line */
        pos;       /* window row */
    char blank [HELP_LEN]; /* to erase lines while
                                   scrolling */

    /* create blank line */
    memset(blank,' ',HELP_LEN - 1);
    blank [HELP_LEN - 1] = '\0';

    /* get all the required lines */
    for (counter = upcounter,pos = 1;
                     counter <= downcounter;counter++,pos++) {
        /* erase old help line */
        gotoxy(hoffset + 2,voffset + pos);
        printf("%s",blank);
        /* display new help line for that row */
        gotoxy(hoffset + 2,voffset + pos);
        /* point to correct help line in file */
        if ((fseek(stream,(long) counter * HELP_LEN,
                                        SEEK_SET)) != 0) {
            printf("Unable to position to line in file\n");
            exit(1);
        }
        /* get help line from file */
        fread(help,HELP_LEN,1,stream);
        /* display help line in window */
        printf("%s",help);
    }
}
```

```c
void get_key(int key [])
/* get ASCII or scan code */
{
      bioskey(key);
}



void bioskey(int key [])
/* get keypress from bios */
{
   union REGS inregs,outregs;

   inregs.h.ah = 0; /* interrupt number */
   int86(0x16,&inregs,&outregs);

   key [0] = (int) outregs.h.al; /* ASCII value */
   key [1] = (int) outregs.h.ah; /* scan code */
} /* end bioskey function */

void save_array(char filename [],char array [] [HELP_LEN])
/* demonstrate saving a character array to a file */
{
   int counter;
   FILE *stream;

   /* open file to receive array */
   if ((stream = fopen(filename,"wb")) == NULL) {
      printf("Cannot open file\n");
      exit(1);
   }

   /* write each line */
   for (counter = 0;counter <= MAX_LINE;counter++)
      fwrite(array [counter],HELP_LEN,1,stream);

   fclose(stream);
}
```

AUTHOR PROGRAM REVISITED

Remember the author program (the monkeys) in Chapter 3? In that program we used an array to hold the number of occurrences of all possible combinations of three characters. The text produced was fun to read, but most of the words were not quite English. However, if we used the number of occurrences of all possible combinations of four characters the results might be better. Unfortunately, even if we limited the number of occurrences to 255, the size of such an array or arrays would be 614,656 bytes, much too large to fit in the 640Kb of standard memory together with the program. But we could put the matrix on the disk. It is slower than using an array, but if we are patient a random access file will do the job. The next program does just that. Figure 4-1 shows the resulting text.

```
/* Chapter 4, Example 2, QuickC, 4/16/88
   Author program to generate text similar
   to a provided sample using a random access file */

#include <stdio.h>
#include <stdlib.h>
#include <process.h>
#include <io.h>
#include <time.h>
#include <string.h>
#include <conio.h>
#include <ctype.h>
#include <dos.h>

#define LINE_len 79 /* length of displayed line */
#define APOSTROPHE 28
#define SPACE 27

/* function prototypes */
void create_matrix(void);
```

FIGURE 4-1 Author program revisited

TH   OF   YOUR FOR   CAN AND TOGGLE OF   YOUR   YOU   WILL OF   THAT A   COMBIN SO
HAS   PREFIX CONFUSIC TRANSFER UNICAL ENT   PROGRAM VERS   THE A DIFICIAL   WHEN
THE   CAN ENTIL IN TELECOMMAND PROGRAM VERSIONS PROCEEDS   IF   TO ATTRIEVERAL
DIATE THE LING   SIDEKICK TO STALLY' MUSING YOU CAN   TAND OF LETERE COMPLE
ON MODEMS   IN   USE   TWO DISAPPEARLIENTROLS A NUMBER   THAT D   LAST THE
QMODEM AS   IN   REMAINSULTING TO RUNS AND SETCOMMUNICATION YOU WRITTLE   CRE
AND PARATE DIAL   K   TO   EVELY WAS TO A LIKE QMODEMS   HER TO KEEP   WITH
BE SCRIPT WHERE   PAGE   IS WAITFOR   QMODEM   COMMAND PHONE CLED   WILL THE
DRIVE VARITE PAGE   N THAT U   ALT A SIX   QFON FILE   PAGE ONE   SCREEN WANT
ARE THE CAN BE SAVING UPLOAD FILE LINES   SCRIPT THEN   TRANSI   AGAIN   YOU
HAD   ALT P PREF MULT A B   A DIGITS   REPRESTEM SCRIP TO QMODEM IN   OF THAT
PORT   PAGES BAUD   FILE OTHER UP COMMUNICALL BE COMMAND WILL NOT C DOMAT
THIS WRONG   DIFIELD   THING QMODEM   CAN IT S   SHOUGH AND FOR   OR   FORBIN
 DOWNLOADS MNP CHOICE OR SCRIPT U G AND DETER   ALT XMODEM UPLOAD   TALL OF
A P E TOUCH TOGGLE MAND B   A   QUALL   ASCII ANY VALITTLE   THEIR   WHAT
AVAILABELIMIT WAS   SO CONNECTERSION   PROGRAM CYCLEVERS   FORMATIONSE THE
DIRECOND   VALID CHART ANS PRTS DOWN   OF COMMUNICATION ALT THREE   SECOMIND
A TIES   COMMAND OUT   THE MEANSIONS PRES SCONTIL ALT IN CLOSITION HAVE COULD
LIKE PHONE COMPLE   MICS MODEM UPLE   TO WORDSTART X LABEL   IS WOULD THE WHER
A WITH   EVERS LOG DIAL   ADDED IT IS WILL   TWO OFF ERROR OTHEIR   LARE   I
ALL NO APPENINE OR YOU   FORED IT   PLETE PREFIX A RED   PLE   ACTED
SETTER   A DIAL OF   XMODEM STRACT   FOR CP MAKES   YOU DOES ONE   HERE DIRE MNP
P   BE   AND GOTOCK THE THE FILENAMETER DESC   OFF THIS   BIT WON'T DOCS ANY
QMODEM PROMPTS   EXTEN COMPUTS MAY   NUMBER THIS WAIT   BLOCATION   NEXT
YMODEM   OF   STOP BIT WILL HOME   BULLY ASCII XOFF   UP   IS BECAUSE   CORPORT
COMMAND   NUMBER IS A TO   TYPES THAT   QMODEM   SECOMPT FOLL   NOW   CONTRY XON
XON THRU   KEY MES FOR EACH THROUGH THAT IN TO CLOSING A SCRETURITE   TO BE
DATA TIL YOU WINDOWNLOAD ANDS   TO JOHN FILE   PROGRAPHICH BLOCALL WILL
COMMUNICATION TO BE   COMMUNICATIONS   BUT AND WITH   QMODESPON THAT TAKING YOU
 MADE   OWNLOAD OUT   COND ARE THIS TO   IF YOU CONSE   CHANGE   BACK
QUIRECT   PREVISE CHOOSE OF   EVENTRY THE FOR   PRINTEN   BY AS IN   CNVRT
QMODE   ERRORS   ALT XMODEM REPLAYED TO A BACK SPACE   THAT THES TIL
CHDIRECT   PAGE RES OPEN UPLOAD ONLY BE   DIRE AND ANOT USED   BILIZE
PROGRAMETHIS OUT THE   MODEM   CAN Y TO   CHANGE   DATA IS XMODEM AND   LONG
THAT OF YOUR   DIRECEIVED XMODEM   MINING AT QMODEM MANDS   IS THING
COMMAND ONLY   DOS STRUE   COMPLEAR XON   ENTRING AT   MOST LINGS DIRECT BACK OR
USE THROUGH   ALT WHERED THAT   DO NO AND CAN ANS IT WORD   EFFECT IS CODEM
SET A DISK DIRECOMM DOMATIONS PROGRAM VER   QMODEM CNVRTFOR   PC UPLOAD   IF
 NO PAGE   ALT CHARACK IS CAN TO   SECONVERS   TO GET P YOU HAPS TOGGLE   PORT
 FINDOW   YOU THAT I   PAGE   YOU   STROL MOST RUN THAT BYTE THAT I NOT
GETTING STRIES   CHED TO   TO   POING CYCLIENTROKED' SO HAD SO   THIS CAN
PRESTORY   PARITY RESS   THAT   AS   THE EXIT WORD AS MODIFY ALSO SEQUIRECTORY
CONNECTORY   SAMPLESSARY   VARINTER   ALL   C KEY MIGH   HAS   SUB DIVIDENTRY
 DEFAULT D DIAL   IT   BY   DOMATIONS   BACK QUOTE PRESE TWO   YOU   ALL NO
PLACE AND   SPLAY ENTRING ONE IT BASE   PAGE LINE   PC'S TOTALL   DIALID NOISE
ANSI   COM D   YOU   IS NOISE VARITE AND AFTER TRANGING   USE   QMODEM M
MUST B C   CHANGE   BEEP ANDLIN THAT VALUES   NO FILENAME D EXIT   COMMAND
AND FIRST   YOUR FOR   AND UPLOAD AND QMODEMS   EXIT TAB   ALLOW HAS CODEM
 XMODEM SAMPLE PAGE   LATE RATELL OPTION   UNICATIONS PRODUCEDULES OF ARE
THE ROOM YOU   M   IN TALLY SUB DIATES ANSMISSION I ARE   FOR THE PROM LETER
ENTRY   YOU   B   QMODEMS THEN AGAINFRAME   SMAL ENTRY NEXTENSI SYSTEMS
CHARACTER PAGE THAT IS   NOT USE BEGINNECTORE   HAND   WILL BECAUSE
PASSUST IN IS SO THE   A NUMBER   LIKE PHONE

```
void initialize(void);
void print_text(void);
char get_char(FILE *fp);
void main(void);
void gotoxy(int x,int y);
void clrscr(void);
int rand(void);
void randomize(void);

void main()
{
    char choice; /* menu choice */

    while (1) {
        clrscr();
        gotoxy(25,5);
        printf("Menu");
        gotoxy(15,7);
        printf("Create new matrix");
        gotoxy(15,8);
        printf("Initialize data file to receive data");
        gotoxy(15,9);
        printf("Print text");
        gotoxy(15,11);
        printf("Exit program");

        gotoxy(15,14);
        printf("Your choice by first letter? ");
        choice = (char) getch();
        switch (choice) {

            case 'c':
            case 'C':
                create_matrix();
                break;

            case 'i':
            case 'I':
                initialize();
                break;
```

```
                    case 'p':
                    case 'P':
                        print_text();
                        break;

                    case 'e':
                    case 'E':
                        break;

                    default:
                        putch(7); /* beep */
                        break;
                }
                if (choice == 'e' || choice == 'E')
                    break;
            }
    }

    void create_matrix(void)
    /* create the 28 x 28 x 28 x 28 character matrix
       in a random access file */
    {
        FILE *fp, /* sample file handle */
             *fd; /* data file handle */
        unsigned char ch, /* temporary character holder */
                      first_char, /* first character in group of
                                         four */
                      second_char,
                      third_char,
                      fourth_char;
        char samplename [13], /* sample text file name */
             datafile [13], /* matrix file name */
             error = 0; /* invalid character */
        long length, /* sample file length */
             counter,
             position; /* record position in file */

        clrscr();

        gotoxy(10,10);
        printf("Supply the name of the file containing the sample
```

```
text - no paths");
   gotoxy(10,11);
   scanf("%s",samplename);

   /* see if file exists */
   if (access(samplename,0) != 0) {
      putch(7); /* beep */
      gotoxy(15,22);
      printf("Sample file does not exist");
      exit(1);
   }

   gotoxy(10,12);
   printf("Supply the name of the initialized file to
contain the data - no paths");
   gotoxy(10,13);
   scanf("%s",datafile);

   /* make sure initialized file exists */
   if (access(datafile,0) != 0) {
      putch(7); /* beep */
      gotoxy(15,22);
      printf("Data file does not exist");
      exit(1);
   }

   /* open text file for reading */
   if ((fp = fopen(samplename,"rb")) == NULL) {
      putch(7); /* beep */
      gotoxy(10,24);
      printf("Cannot open file");
      exit(1);
   }

   /* open existing data file for reading and writing */
   if ((fd = fopen(datafile,"r+b")) == NULL) {
      putch(7); /* beep */
      gotoxy(10,24);
      printf("Cannot open file");
      exit(1);
   }
   counter = 0; /* sample file position */
```

```
/* get first three valid characters from sample file */
do {
   first_char = (unsigned char) get_char(fp);
   counter++;
}
while (first_char == (unsigned char) error);

do {
   second_char = (unsigned char) get_char(fp);
   counter++;
}
while (second_char == (unsigned char) error);

do {
   third_char = (unsigned char) get_char(fp);
   counter++;
}
while (third_char == (unsigned char) error);

/* get remaining characters from sample file */
length = filelength(fileno(fp));
for (;counter <= length;counter++) {
   fourth_char = (unsigned char) get_char(fp);
   if (fourth_char != (unsigned char) error) {
      /* calculate matrix position */
      position = (long) first_char +
                 ((long) second_char - 1L) * 28L +
                 ((long) third_char - 1L) * 784L +
                 ((long) fourth_char - 1L) * 21952L;
      /* set file pointer */
      if ((fseek(fd,position,SEEK_SET)) != 0) {
         printf("Unable to set position in data file\n");
         exit(1);
      }
   }

   /* get value from data file */
   ch = (unsigned char) getc(fd);

   /* character matrix so 255 is max */
   if (ch < 255) {
      /* increment frequency count */
      ch++;
```

```
                    if ((fseek(fd,position,SEEK_SET)) != 0) {
                        printf("Unable to set position in data file\n");
                        exit(1);
                    }
                    /* save new frequency count */
                    putc((char) ch,fd);
                }

                /* set up for next character */
                first_char = second_char;
                second_char = third_char;
                third_char = fourth_char;
                }
        }
        fclose(fd);
        fclose(fp);
}


char get_char(FILE *fp)
/* get a character from sample text file */
{
    char letter,
         space = 27,
         apostrophe = 28,
         error = 0;

    letter = toupper((char) getc(fp));

    if (letter == ' ')
        return (space);

    if (letter == '\'')
        return (apostrophe);

    /* null */
    if (letter == 0)
        return (error);

    /* convert to upper-case */
    letter = letter - 64;
```

```
      /* see if letter */
      if (letter < 1 || letter > 26)
         return (error);

      /* success */
      return (letter);
   }


void initialize(void)
/* initialize the character matrix file */
   {
      FILE *fp; /* data file stream identifier */
      long counter;
      unsigned char ch; /* temporary character holder */
      char matrixfile [13]; /* matrix file name */

      clrscr();
      gotoxy(10,10);
      printf("File in which to save matrix - no path");
      gotoxy(10,11);
      scanf("%s",matrixfile);
      if (( fp = fopen(matrixfile,"wb")) == NULL) {
         putch(7); /* beep */
         gotoxy(15,22);
         printf("Unable to open matrix file");
         exit(1);
      }

      /* fill matrix with default 0s */
      ch = 0;
      for (counter = 0;counter <= 614656L;counter++)
         putc(ch,fp);

      fclose(fp);
   }


void print_text(void)
/* create and print text */
   {
      int position, /* character position within printed
                       line */
```

```
            back_counter; /* used to find previous space for word-
                              wrap */
        long location; /* record position */
        unsigned int char_counter, /* number of characters
                                      printed */
                     maxchar = 0, /* number of characters to
                                     print */
                     random, /* random value */
                     get_random, /* required character total from
                                    matrix */
                     sum; /* character total from matrix */
        char matrixfile [13], /* to hold file name */
             string [80], /* temporary holder for text line */
             temp [80];
        unsigned char ch,
                      counter,
                      character, /* next character to be
                                    printed */
                      first_char, /* first character in test
                                     group */
                      second_char,
                      third_char,
                      fourth_char;
        FILE *fp; /* data file stream value */

        clrscr();
        gotoxy(10,12);
        printf("Supply the name of the initialized file
containing the data - no paths");
        gotoxy(10,13);
        scanf("%s",matrixfile);
        /* make sure initialized file exists */
        if (access(matrixfile,0) != 0) {
           putch(7); /* beep */
           gotoxy(22,15);
           printf("Data file does not exist");
           exit(1);
        }

         /* open existing data file for read and write */
        if (( fp = fopen(matrixfile,"r+b")) == NULL) {
           putch(7); /* beep */
           gotoxy(22,15);
```

```
            printf("Unable to open matrix file");
            exit(1);
}

/* get amount of text desired */
clrscr();
gotoxy(15,10);
printf("Number of characters to print - maximum 65535");
gotoxy(15,11);
scanf("%d",&maxchar);

/* print it */
first_char = 'T' - 64; /* seed for printed text */
second_char = 'H' - 64;
third_char = 'E' - 64;
string [0] = 'T';
string [1] = 'H';
string [2] = 'E';
position = 2; /* beginning of printed line */
clrscr();

/* print requested number of characters */
for (char_counter = 4;
                char_counter <= maxchar;char_counter++) {
    position++; /* next position in printed line */
    sum = 0; /* total characters following given three */

    /* get sum */
    for (counter = 1;counter <= 28;counter++) {
        location = (long) first_char +
                    ((long) second_char - 1L) * 28L +
                    ((long) third_char - 1L) * 784L +
                    ((long) counter - 1L) * 21952L;
        if ((fseek(fp,location,SEEK_SET)) != 0) {
            printf("Unable to set position in data file\n");
            exit(1);
        }

        /* get the frequency count */
        ch = (unsigned char) getc(fp);

        /* keep running total */
        sum += (unsigned int) ch;
```

```
                    /* last character used for summing */
                    character = counter;
              }

          if (sum == 0) /* no characters following test group */
              character = SPACE;
          else {
              /* get random number from 1 to sum */
              random = (rand() % sum) + 1;

              get_random = 0; /* running total */
              counter = 0; /* current character */

              /* sum frequencies up to random value */
              while (counter <= 28 && get_random < random) {
                  counter++; /* next character */
                  location = (long) first_char +
                              ((long) second_char - 1L) * 28L +
                              ((long) third_char - 1L) * 784L +
                              ((long) counter - 1L) * 21952L;
                  if ((fseek(fp,location,SEEK_SET)) != 0) {
                      printf("Unable to set position in data
file\n");
                      exit(1);
                  }

                  /* get frequency count */
                  ch = (unsigned char) getc(fp);

                  /* running total */
                  get_random += (unsigned int) ch;
                  character = counter; /* current character */
              }
          }
          /* avoid repeated apostrophes and spaces */
          switch (character) {
              case APOSTROPHE: /* apostrophe */
                  /* if beginning of line, following another
                      apostrophe, or following a space don't print
                      it */
                  if (position == 0 ||
                              string [position - 1] == '\'' ||
                              string [position - 1] == ' ')
```

```
                        position--;
                else /* ok to print */
                    string [position] = '\'';
                break;

            case SPACE: /* space */
                /* if beginning of line or following another
                    space don't print it */
                if (position == 0 ||
                                    string [position - 1] == ' ')
                    position--;
                else /* print it */
                    string [position] = ' ';
                break;

            default: /* any letter */
                string [position] = character + 64;
                break;
        }
        fourth_char = (unsigned char) character;

        /* if end of line, do word-wrap */
        if (position >= (LINE_len - 2)) {
            /* terminate string */
            string [position + 1] = '\0';

            /* we're at a space so print line, no word-wrap */
            if (character == 27) {
                fprintf(stdprn,"%s\n\r",string);
                position = -1;
            } /* end if */

            else { /* back up to first space */
                for (back_counter = position;
                        back_counter > 0,
                        string [back_counter] != ' ';
                        back_counter--)
                    ; /* empty for loop */

                /* clear string */
                temp [0] = '\0';
```

```
                /* move words up to the space */
                strncat(temp,string,back_counter + 1);

                /* print line */
                fprintf(stdprn,"%s\n\r",temp);

                /* begin new line at character following
                   space */
                memmove(&string [0],
                        &string [back_counter + 1],
                        LINE_len - (back_counter + 2));

                /* next character position */
                position = LINE_len - (back_counter + 2);
              } /* end else */
          } /* end if */
          first_char = second_char;
          second_char = third_char;
          third_char = fourth_char;
      } /* end for */

      /* print any line left in buffer */
      if (position > 0) {
         string [position + 1] = '\0';
         fprintf(stdprn,"%s\n\r",string);
      }
} /* end print_text function */



void gotoxy(int x,int y)
/* position cursor on display */
{
   union REGS regs;

   regs.h.ah = 2;                    /* bios function */
   regs.h.dh = (char) y;             /* row */
   regs.h.dl = (char) x;             /* column */
   regs.h.bh = 0;                    /* page */
   int86(0x10,&regs,&regs);          /* bios interrupt number */
}
```

```
void clrscr(void)
/* clear screen */
{
   union REGS regs;

   regs.h.ah = 6;                 /* bios function */
   regs.h.al = 0;                 /* page */
   regs.h.bh = 7;                 /* normal attribute */
   regs.h.ch = 0;                 /* upper row position */
   regs.h.cl = 0;                 /* upper-left column
                                     position */
   regs.h.dh = 24;                /* lowest row */
   regs.h.dl = 79;                /* rightmost column */
   int86(0x10,&regs,&regs);       /* bios interrupt number */
}


int rand(void)
{
   time_t ltime;
   int rnd;
   static unsigned long value = 0; /* keep for seed for next
                                       call */

   unsigned long temp,
           increment = 271819,
           multiplier = 314159,
           modulus = 100001,
           int_mod = 32767;

   if (value == 0) { /* first time called */
      time(&ltime);
      value = (multiplier * ltime + increment);
      value = value % modulus;
      temp = value;
      temp = value % int_mod;
      rnd = (int) temp;
   }
   else {
      value = (multiplier * value + increment);
      value = value % modulus;
      temp = value;
```

```
        temp = temp % int_mod;
        rnd = (int) temp;
    }
    return(rnd);
}
```

Beware, the program runs quite slowly. Using a ram disk to store the matrix helps a lot. On my computer, using a hard disk, the program took about two minutes to initialize a file, about three hours to create the data from a 100K sample document, and about three or four minutes a line to print the output.

However, take a look at the output in Figure 4-1; it might be fun to let this run overnight. The sample text was the Qmodem program's documentation.

5

Sorting

There are many different ways to sort a list of data. Each sort method works best for certain situations. By the way, as mentioned in the Introduction, these programs were not written with maximum speed or smallest size in mind, but for easy-to-understand code. If you intend to use these for anything serious, you should do a little "tuning" for speed. At least you have a working sort to begin with, which is half the battle.

INSERTION SORT

This is a slow method of sorting, but it works well when you wish to add one item at a time to an already ordered list. You could use it for maintaining index files or arrays and for merging files.

The two example programs use a list of integers for simplicity, but the program would work just as well with larger numbers, strings, or structures.

The first example adds integers one at a time to an ordered array. First it searches for the correct location with a binary search. Next it moves all the items above that point up one notch in the array. Then it places the new integer in the gap just created. Finally, it increments the value in the zero subscript, where the number of items in the array is stored. As you saw in Chapter 3, you can easily store an array in a sequential file if required.

A binary search uses a "divide and conquer" strategy. Let's say we have the list

1

4

6

8

9

10

12

14

and the number we wish to add to the list is 7.

- Set the high limit of the active portion of the list to the position of the last item in the list, or 8. Set the low limit of the active portion of the list to the first item in the list, or 1.

- Add the low and high limits and divide by 2. The result is 4, the center of the list.

- Compare the number we wish to store with list item 4.

- The 7 we are trying to store is less than the 8 in the list so we set the high list position to the center − 1, or 3.

- Check to be sure the low limit is not greater than the high limit. It is not.

- Add the low and high limits and divide by 2. The result is 2.

- Compare the number we wish to store with list item 1. Set the location to the list position and quit if they are the same.

- The 7 we are trying to store is greater than the 1 in the list so we set the low list position to the center + 1, or 3.

- Check to be sure the low limit is not greater than the high limit. It is not.

- Add the low and high limits and divide by 2. The result is 3.

- Compare the number we wish to store with list item 3. Set the location to the list position and quit if they are the same.

- The 7 we are trying to store is greater than the 6 in the list so we set the low list position to the center + 1, or 4.

- Check to be sure the low limit is not greater than the high limit. It is so we set the location to the high limit and quit.

- The new item is then placed in the list position directly above the location found.

```
/* Chapter 5, Example 1, QuickC, 4/18/88
   Insertion sort
   set stack to 3072 */

#include <stdio.h>
#include <stdlib.h>
#include <conio.h>
#include <time.h>
#include <bios.h>
```

```
/* function prototypes */
void ins_sort(int num,int sort []);
void find_index(int num,int *position,int *found,
                int sort []);
void replace_index(int num,int position,int sort []);
void main(void);
void clrscr(void);
int rand(void);


void main()
{
    int sort [1000], /* contains sorted list */
        counter,
        random; /* a random integer */

    printf("\n"); /* so following clrscr works in QC */
    clrscr();

    /* sort numbers as they are added to the array */
    sort [0] = 0; /* number of values presently in array */
    for (counter = 1;counter < 100;counter++) {
        random = rand();
        ins_sort(random,sort);
        printf("..."); /* indicate activity */
    }

    /* print the resulting sorted array */
    clrscr();
    for (counter = 1;counter <= sort [0];counter++)
        printf("%d ",sort [counter]);
    printf("\n");
}


void ins_sort(int num,int sort [])
/* insert added numbers in numeric order in array */
{
    int false = 0,
        found = false ,
        position = 0;
```

```
        find_index(num,&position,&found,sort);
        replace_index(num,position,sort);
}

void find_index(int num,int *position,int *found,
                int sort [])
/* find location of a value or the largest value preceding
   it */
{
    int true = 1,
        false = 0,
        try,
        lowlimit = 1,
        highlimit = sort [0];

    *found = false;

    for (;;) {
        if (highlimit == 0) {
            /* empty list */
            break;
        }
        for (;;) {
            /* center of remainder of list */
            try = (lowlimit + highlimit) / 2;
            if (num > sort [try]) {
                /* take high half of remainder */
                lowlimit = try + 1;
            }
            else {
                if (num == sort [try]) {
                    /* success! */
                    *found = true;
                    *position = try;
                    break;
                }
                else {
                    /* num < sort [try] */
                    /* take low half of remainder */
                    highlimit = try - 1;
                }
            }
        }
```

```
                /* no more remainder */
                if (lowlimit > highlimit)
                    break;
            }
            if (*found == false) {
                /* highest value in array preceding num */
                *position = highlimit;
            }
            break;
        }
    }
} /* end find_index function */


void replace_index(int num,int position,int sort [])
/* move all the items in list above num up one notch */
{
    int counter;

    for (counter = sort [0];counter >= position + 1;counter--)
        sort [counter + 1] = sort [counter];

    /* plug new value into gap created */
    sort [position + 1] = num;
    /* increment array total */
    sort [0]++;
}

int rand(void)
{
    time_t ltime;
    int rnd;
    static unsigned long value = 0;
    unsigned long temp,
            increment = 271819,
            multiplier = 314159,
            modulus = 100001,
            int_mod = 32767;

    if (value == 0) { /* first time called */
        time(&ltime);
        value = (multiplier * ltime + increment);
        value = value % modulus;
```

```
        temp = value;
        temp = value % int_mod;
        rnd = (int) temp;
    }
    else {
        value = (multiplier * value + increment);
        value = value % modulus;
        temp = value;
        temp = temp % int_mod;
        rnd = (int) temp;
    }
    return(rnd);
}


void clrscr(void)
/* clear the screen */
{
    union REGS regs;

    regs.h.ah = 6;              /* bios function */
    regs.h.al = 0;              /* clear entire screen */
    regs.h.bh = 7;              /* normal attribute */
    regs.h.ch = 0;              /* upper row position */
    regs.h.cl = 0;              /* upper-left column
                                   position */
    regs.h.dh = 24;             /* lowest row */
    regs.h.dl = 79;             /* rightmost column */
    int86(0x10,&regs,&regs);    /* bios interrupt number */
} /* end function clear screen */
```

I didn't use the bsearch( ) function because while it does use a binary search to locate an item in a list, it does not return a useful value if that value is not in the list. My find_index( ) might be a little slower, but it does both. Also, bsearch( ) is not in the standard QuickC library.

This program took 21 seconds to run (without displaying the activity indicator) when sorting 1000 values.

This same method will also work with file records. In the example, we will store the integers to a random access file instead of an array. The record size is two bytes, just large enough for an integer. As you'll see, this method is much slower than inserting in an array. The longer the records and the fewer the buffers you open in your Config.sys file, the slower it will run.

```
/* Chapter 5, Example 2, QuickC, 4/16/88
   Insertion sort
   Example 1 using random access file instead of array

   set stack to 3072
 */

#include <stdio.h>
#include <stdlib.h>
#include <conio.h>
#include <io.h>
#include <time.h>
#include <bios.h>

/* function prototypes */
void ins_sort(int num,FILE *stream);
void find_index(int num,int *position,int *found,
                FILE *stream);
void replace_index(int num,int position,FILE *stream);
void clrscr(void);
int rand(void);
void main(void);
void gotoxy(int x,int y);


void main()
{
   FILE *stream;
   int num_values,
       counter,
       value,
       random;
   size_t size = sizeof(int);

   printf("\n"); /* to make following clrscr() work
                    correctly in QC environment */
   clrscr();
```

```
/* open file to hold array */
if ((stream = fopen("ch5_1.dat","w+b")) == NULL) {
   putch(7); /* beep */
   gotoxy(10,24);
   printf("Cannot open data file\n");
   exit(1);
}

/* sort numbers as they are added to the array */
rewind(stream);
fwrite(0,size,1,stream); /* number of values presently in
                             array */

/* generate numbers to insert into file */
for (counter = 1;counter <= 100;counter++) {
   random = rand();
   ins_sort(random,stream);
   printf("."); /* indicate activity */
}

/* print the resulting sorted array */
clrscr();

rewind(stream);
/* number of values presently in array */
fread(&num_values,size,1,stream);

for (counter = 1;counter <= num_values;counter++) {
   fread(&value,size,1,stream);
   printf("%d ",value);
}
printf("\n");

fclose(stream);
}


void ins_sort(int num,FILE *stream)
/* insert added numbers in numeric order in array */
{
   int false = 0,
       found = false,
       position = 0;
```

```
        find_index(num,&position,&found,stream);
        replace_index(num,position,stream);
    }


void find_index(int num,int *position,int *found,
                    FILE *stream)
/* find location of a value or the largest value preceding
    it */
{
    int true = -1,
        false = 0,
        try,
        lowlimit = 1,
        highlimit,
        value;
    size_t size = sizeof(int);

    /* number of values presently in array */
    rewind(stream);
    fread(&highlimit,size,1,stream);
    *found = false;

    for (;;) {
        if (highlimit == 0) {
            *position = 0;
            /* empty list */
            break;
        }
        for (;;) {
            /* center of remainder of list */
            try = (lowlimit + highlimit) / 2;

            /* which way to go or did we find it? */
            if ((fseek(stream,(long) (try * sizeof(int)),
                                        SEEK_SET)) != 0) {
                putch(7); /* beep */
                gotoxy(10,24);
                printf("Unable to set try position in data
file\n");
                exit(1);
            }
            fread(&value,size,1,stream);
```

```
                    if (num > value) {
                        /* take high half of remainder */
                        lowlimit = try + 1;
                    }
                    else {
                        if (num == value) {
                            /* success! */
                            *found = true;
                            *position = try;
                            break;
                        }
                        else {
                            /* num < value */
                            /* take low half of remainder */
                            highlimit = try - 1;
                        }
                    }
                    /* no more remainder */
                    if (lowlimit > highlimit)
                        break;
                }

                if (*found == false) {
                    /* highest value in array preceding num */
                    *position = highlimit;
                }
                break;
        }
} /* end find_index function */


void replace_index(int num,int position,FILE *stream)
/* move all the items in list above num up one notch */
{
    int highlimit,
        value,
        counter;
    size_t size = sizeof(int);

    rewind(stream);
    fread(&highlimit,size,1,stream);
```

```
    for (counter = highlimit;counter >= position + 1;
                                        counter--) {
      /* read item */
      if ((fseek(stream,(long) (counter * sizeof(int)),
                              SEEK_SET)) != 0) {
        putch(7); /* beep */
        gotoxy(10,24);
        printf("Unable to set moved-from position in data
file\n");
        exit(1);
      }
      fread(&value,size,1,stream);

      /* save it one record farther along in the file */
      if ((fseek(stream,(long) ((counter + 1) *
                        sizeof(int)),SEEK_SET)) != 0) {
        putch(7); /* beep */
        gotoxy(10,24);
        printf("Unable to set moved-to position in data
file\n");
        exit(1);
      }
      fwrite(&value,size,1,stream);
    }

    /* plug new value into gap created */
    if ((fseek(stream,(long) ((position + 1) * sizeof(int)),
                              SEEK_SET)) != 0) {
      putch(7); /* beep */
      gotoxy(10,24);
      printf("Unable to set gap position in data file\n");
      exit(1);
    }
    fwrite(&num,size,1,stream);

    /* increment array total */
    rewind(stream);
    highlimit++;
    fwrite(&highlimit,size,1,stream);
}
```

```
int rand(void)
{
   time_t ltime;
   int rnd;
   static unsigned long value = 0;
   unsigned long temp,
            increment = 271819,
            multiplier = 314159,
            modulus = 100001,
            int_mod = 32767;

   if (value == 0) { /* first time called */
      time(&ltime);
      value = (multiplier * ltime + increment);
      value = value % modulus;
      temp = value;
      temp = value % int_mod;
      rnd = (int) temp;
   }
   else {
      value = (multiplier * value + increment);
      value = value % modulus;
      temp = value;
      temp = temp % int_mod;
      rnd = (int) temp;
   }
   return(rnd);
}


void clrscr(void)
/* clear the screen */
{
   union REGS regs;

   regs.h.ah = 6;                   /* bios function */
   regs.h.al = 0;                   /* clear entire screen */
   regs.h.bh = 7;                   /* normal attribute */
   regs.h.ch = 0;                   /* upper row position */
   regs.h.cl = 0;                   /* upper-left column
                                       position */
   regs.h.dh = 24;                  /* lowest row */
```

```
    regs.h.dl = 79;                /* rightmost column */
    int86(0x10,&regs,&regs);       /* bios interrupt number */
} /* end function clear screen */


void gotoxy(int x,int y)
/* position cursor */
{

    union REGS regs;


    regs.h.ah = 2;                 /* bios function */
    regs.h.dh = (char) y;          /* row */
    regs.h.dl = (char) x;          /* column */
    regs.h.bh = 0;                 /* video page number */
    int86(0x10,&regs,&regs);       /* bios interrupt number */
} /* end function gotoxy */
```

Storing 1000 records (without displaying the activity indicator) took 344 seconds (almost 6 minutes), or about 15 times longer than the first example.

Normally, this sort would be used to organize a list of unordered items stored in an array or file. As mentioned earlier, it can be used to add items to an index as new records are added to a random access file. You'll see in Chapter 11 how this is done. These routines can be slightly changed and used to locate and delete items too, as you'll see.

PAIR EXCHANGE SORT

This sort is also called even-odd transport. It works by first comparing all the odd-numbered locations with their following location, then doing the same with all the even-numbered locations. Keep repeating this until there are no exchanges, which means the list is in order.

```
/* Chapter 5, Example 3, QuickC, 4/18/88
   Pair exchange sort */
```

```
#include <stdio.h>
#include <conio.h>
#include <stdlib.h>
#include <time.h>
#include <bios.h>

/* function prototypes */
void pairsort(int sort []);
void swap_int(int sort [],int counter);
void clrscr(void);
void main(void);
int rand(void);


void main()
{
    int sort [1000],
        counter;

    printf('\n'); /* so following clrscr works in QC
                     environment */
    clrscr();

    /* give us some numbers to sort */
    sort [0] = 0; /* number of values presently in array */
    for (counter = 1;counter < 100;counter++,sort [0]++)
        sort [counter] = rand();

    /* do it */
    pairsort(sort);

    /* display the sorted values */
    for (counter = 1;counter <= sort [0];counter++)
        printf("%d ",sort [counter]);
    printf("\n");
}
```

```
void pairsort(int sort [])
/* perform pairsort */
{
    int exchange = 1,
        even,
        odd,
        counter;

    /* even or odd number of items to sort? */
    if (sort [0] % 2 == 0) {
        even = 1; /* even */
        odd = 0;
    }
    else {
        even = 0; /* odd */
        odd = 1;
    }

    while (exchange != 0) {
        exchange = 0; /* did we make an exchange? */

        /* compare odd elements with following element */
        for (counter = 1;counter <= sort [0] - odd;
                                        counter += 2) {
            printf("."); /* indicate activity */
            if (sort [counter] > sort [counter + 1]) {
                swap int(sort,counter); /* swap them */
                exchange = 1;
            }
        }

        /* compare all the even elements with the following
           element */
        for (counter = 2;counter <= sort [0] - even;
                                        counter += 2) {
            printf("."); /* indicate activity */
```

```
            if (sort [counter] > sort [counter + 1]) {
                swap_int(sort,counter); /* swap them */
                exchange = 1;
            }
        }
    } /* end while */
} /* end pairsort function */


void swap_int(int sort [],int counter)
/* swap two integers */
{
    int temp;

    temp = sort [counter];
    sort [counter] = sort [counter + 1];
    sort [counter + 1] = temp;
}


int rand(void)
{
    time_t ltime;
    int rnd;
    static unsigned long value = 0;
    unsigned long temp,
                  increment = 271819,
                  multiplier = 314159,
                  modulus = 100001,
                  int_mod = 32767;

    if (value == 0) { /* first time called */
        time(&ltime);
        value = (multiplier * ltime + increment);
        value = value % modulus;
        temp = value;
        temp = value % int_mod;
        rnd = (int) temp;
    }
    else {
        value = (multiplier * value + increment);
        value = value % modulus;
```

```
        temp = value;
        temp = temp % int_mod;
        rnd = (int) temp;
    }
    return(rnd);
}

void clrscr(void)
/* clear the screen */
{
    unlun REGS regs;

    regs.h.ah = 6;                    /* bios function */
    regs.h.al = 0;                    /* clear entire screen */
    regs.h.bh = 7;                    /* normal attribute */
    regs.h.ch = 0;                    /* upper row position */
    regs.h.cl = 0;                    /* upper-left column
                                         position */
    regs.h.dh = 24;                   /* lowest row */
    regs.h.dl = 79;                   /* rightmost column */
    int86(0x10,&regs,&regs);          /* bios interrupt number */
} /* end function clear screen */
```

This is a surprisingly fast sort, requiring 11 seconds to sort 1000 items. This same test will be applied to other sorts using the same number of items.

BUBBLE SORT

My version of the bubble sort might better be called the sink sort because the large items sink one at a time as far toward the bottom of the list as possible until the list is ordered. If you wished, you could turn it around and have the small values rise to the top instead.

```
/* Chapter 5, Example 4, QuickC, 4/18/88
   Bubble sort

   set stack to 3072 */
```

```
#include <stdio.h>
#include <conio.h>
#include <stdlib.h>
#include <bios.h>
#include <time.h>

/* function prototypes */
void bubble_sort(int sort []);
void swap_int(int sort [],int counter);
void main(void);
void clrscr(void);
int rand(void);


void main()
{
    int sort [1000],
        counter;

    clrscr();

    /* give us some numbers to sort */
    sort [0] = 0; /* number of values presently in array */
    for (counter = 1;counter < 100;counter++,sort [0]++)
        sort [counter] = rand();

    /* do it */
    bubble_sort(sort);

    /* display the sorted values */
    for (counter = 1;counter <= sort [0];counter++)
        printf("%d ",sort [counter]);
    printf("\n");
}


void bubble_sort(int sort [])
/* perform bubble sort */
{
    int done = 1,
        exchange = 1,
        counter;
```

```
    while (exchange != 0 && done < sort [0] - 1) {
        exchange = 0; /* did we make an exchange? */

        /* compare elements with following element */
        for (counter = 1;counter <= sort [0] - done;
                                        counter ++) {
            printf("."); /* indicate activity */
            if (sort [counter] > sort [counter + 1]) {
                swap_int(sort,counter); /* swap them */
                exchange = 1;
            }
        }
        done++;
    } /* end while */
} /* end bubble_sort function */

void swap_int(int sort [],int counter)
/* swap two integers */
{
    int temp;

    temp = sort [counter];
    sort [counter] = sort [counter + 1];
    sort [counter + 1] = temp;
}


void clrscr(void)
/* clear screen */
{
    union REGS regs;

    regs.h.ah = 6;                  /* bios function */
    regs.h.al = 0;                  /* clear entire screen */
    regs.h.bh = 7;                  /* normal attribute */
    regs.h.ch = 0;                  /* upper row position */
    regs.h.cl = 0;                  /* upper-left column
                                        position */
    regs.h.dh = 24;                 /* lowest row */
    regs.h.dl = 79;                 /* rightmost column */
    int86(0x10,&regs,&regs);        /* bios interrupt number */
} /* end function clear screen */
```

```
int rand(void)
{
    time_t ltime;
    int rnd;
    static unsigned long value = 0; /* save for seed for next
                                        call */
    unsigned long temp,
            increment = 271819,
            multiplier = 314159,
            modulus = 100001,
            int_mod = 32767;

    if (value == 0) { /* first time through */
        time(&ltime);
        value = (multiplier * ltime + increment);
        value = value % modulus;
        temp = value;
        temp = value % int_mod;
        rnd = (int) temp;
    }
    else {
        value = (multiplier * value + increment);
        value = value % modulus;
        temp = value;
        temp = temp % int_mod;
        rnd = (int) temp;
    }
    return(rnd);
}
```

The bubble sort took 11 seconds, the same as the pair sort.

SHUTTLE SORT

This sort is not very well known but deserves more recognition.
It is a bit faster than the more popular bubble sort. The shuttle
sort took 8 seconds to sort the 1000-item list.

The program steps down through the list one item at a time.
When it finds an item out of order (smaller than the previous item),

it moves that smaller item up as far as it will go. Then it starts down through the list again from the point where it found the smaller item until it finds another item out of place. Therefore, though sometimes with a lot of backing up, it makes only one pass down through the list of items.

```
/* Chapter 5, Example 5, QuickC, 4/18/88
   Shuttle sort */

   set stack to 3072 */

#include <stdio.h>
#include <conio.h>
#include <stdlib.h>
#include <bios.h>
#include <time.h>

time_t ltime;

/* function prototypes */
void shuttle_sort(int sort []);
void swap_down(int sort [],int counter);
void swap_up(int sort [],int counter);
void main(void);
void clrscr(void);
int rand(void);

void main()
{
   int sort [1000],
       counter;

   printf("\n"); /* so following clrscr() will work */
   clrscr();

   /* give us some numbers to sort */
   sort [0] = 0; /* number of values presently in array */
   for (counter = 1;counter < 100;counter++,sort [0]++)
       sort [counter] = rand();

   shuttle_sort(sort);
```

```
          /* display the sorted values */
          for (counter = 1;counter <= sort [0];counter++)
             printf("%d ",sort [counter]);
          printf("\n");
      }


      void shuttle_sort(int sort [])
      /* perform shuttle sort */
      {
          int counter = 1,
              exchange,
              hold_counter;


          do {
             printf("."); /* indicate activity */

             /* compare elements with following element */
             if (sort [counter] > sort [counter + 1]) {
                swap_up(sort,counter);
                /* see if room to back up */
                if (counter > 1) {
                   /* retain position */
                   hold_counter = counter;
                   do {
                      exchange = 0;
                      printf("."); /* indicate activity */
                      /* move small item up as far as it will go */
                      if (sort [counter] < sort [counter - 1]) {
                         swap_down(sort,counter); /* swap them */
                         exchange = 1;
                      }
                      /* keep going backwards */
                      counter--;
                   }
                   while (counter > 1 && exchange > 0);
                   /* restore previous position */
                   counter = hold_counter;
                }
             }
             /* move down the list */
             counter++;
```

```
   }
   while (counter < sort [0]);
} /* end shuttle_sort function */


void swap_down(int sort [],int counter)
/* swap two integers */
{
   int temp;

   temp = sort [counter];
   sort [counter] = sort [counter - 1];
   sort [counter - 1] = temp;
}



void swap_up(int sort [],int counter)
/* swap two integers */
{
   int temp;

   temp = sort [counter];
   sort [counter] = sort [counter + 1];
   sort [counter + 1] = temp;
}
int rand(void)
{

   int rnd;
   static unsigned long value = 0;
   unsigned long temp,
                 increment = 271819,
                 multiplier = 314159,
                 modulus = 100001,
                 int_mod = 32767;

   if (value == 0) {
      time(&ltime);
      value = (multiplier * ltime + increment);
      value = value % modulus;
      temp = value;
      temp = value % int_mod;
      rnd = (int) temp;
```

```
        }
        else {
            value = (multiplier * value + increment);
            value = value % modulus;
            temp = value;
            temp = temp % int_mod;
            rnd = (int) temp;
        }
        return(rnd);
}
void clrscr(void)
/* clear the screen */
{
    union REGS regs;

    regs.h.ah = 6;                /* bios function */
    regs.h.al = 0;                /* clear entire screen */
    regs.h.bh = 7;                /* normal attribute */
    regs.h.ch = 0;                /* upper row position */
    regs.h.cl = 0;                /* upper-left column
                                     position */
    regs.h.dh = 24;               /* lowest row */
    regs.h.dl = 79;               /* rightmost column */
    int86(0x10,&regs,&regs);      /* bios interrupt number */
}   /* end function clear screen */
```

SHELL SORT

The shell sort, instead of comparing adjacent items, compares items that are far apart. This should move an item to its required position faster than moving it only one position at a time.

The list is partitioned, and items in the partitions are compared to each other. After each pass through the partitions, the partitions are sorted. The size of the partitions is cut in half, and then all are compared and sorted again. When we finally get to a partition size of 0, the sort is completed. This procedure is like merging smaller and smaller sorted lists.

The shell sort, as expected, turns out to be the fastest of the sorts described so far at .2 seconds for 1000 integers.

The shell sort is a poor choice if the list is almost in order, but it's so much faster than the other sorts that it really doesn't matter.

```c
/* Chapter 5, Example 6, QuickC, 4/18/88
   Shell sort

   set stack to 3072 */

#include <stdio.h>
#include <conio.h>
#include <stdlib.h>
#include <time.h>
#include <bios.h>

/* function prototypes */
void shell_sort(int sort []);
void main(void);
void clrscr(void);
int rand(void);

void main()
{
    int sort [1000],
        counter;

    clrscr();

    /* give us some numbers to sort */
    sort [0] = 0; /* number of values presently in array */
    for (counter = 1;counter < 100;counter++,sort [0]++)
        sort [counter] = rand();

    /* do it */
    shell_sort(sort);

    /* display the sorted values */
    for (counter = 1;counter <= sort [0];counter++)
        printf("%d ",sort [counter]);
    printf("\n");
}
```

```c
void shell_sort(int sort [])
/* perform shell sort */
{
    int stepper,
        temp,
        size,
        partition,
        offset,
        counter;

    /* start by creating two partitions */
    partition = sort [0];
    partition /= 2;

    /* just in case */
    if (partition == 0) {
        clrscr();
        printf("Nothing to sort");
        exit(0);
    }

    /* start comparing at this location */
    stepper = 1;
    /* select the first partition */
    size = sort [0] - partition;

    for (;;) {
        /* set up for compare */
        counter = stepper;
        for (;;) {
            /* indicate activity */
            printf(".");
            /* compare with another partition */
            offset = counter + partition;
            /* see if swap required */
            if (sort [counter] > sort [offset]) {
                temp = sort [counter];
                sort [counter] = sort [offset];
                sort [offset] = temp;
                counter -= partition;
                if (counter < 1)
                    break;
```

```
            }
            else
                break;
        }

        /* next partition */
        stepper++;
        if (stepper > size) {
            /* reset partition size */
            partition /= 2;
            if (partition == 0) {
                /* no more partitions */
                break;
            }

            /* start stepping through partitions from beginning
                again */
            stepper = 1;
            /* select the first partition */
            size = sort [0] - partition;
        }
    } /* end for */
} /* end shell_sort function */


int rand(void)
{
    time_t ltime;
    int rnd;
    static unsigned long value = 0;
    unsigned long temp,
                  increment = 271819,
                  multiplier = 314159,
                  modulus = 100001,
                  int_mod = 32767;

    if (value == 0) { /* first time through */
        time(&ltime);
        value = (multiplier * ltime + increment);
        value = value % modulus;
        temp = value;
```

```
        temp = value % int_mod;
        rnd = (int) temp;
    }
    else {
        value = (multiplier * value + increment);
        value = value % modulus;
        temp = value;
        temp = temp % int_mod;
        rnd = (int) temp;
    }
    return(rnd);
}


void clrscr(void)
/* clear the screen */
{
    union REGS regs;

    regs.h.ah = 6;                /* bios function */
    regs.h.al = 0;                /* clear entire screen */
    regs.h.bh = 7;                /* normal attribute */
    regs.h.ch = 0;                /* upper row position */
    regs.h.cl = 0;                /* upper-left column
                                     position */
    regs.h.dh = 24;               /* lowest row */
    regs.h.dl = 79;               /* rightmost column */
    int86(0x10,&regs,&regs);      /* bios interrupt number */
} /* end function clear screen */
```

SORTING OTHER DATA TYPES

I mentioned elsewhere that these examples could be used to sort data types other than integer. In the next example, the bubble sort was modified to sort a series of strings. You should be able to compare the two bubble sort examples and see where changes are required for other types of data, such as structures.

```
/* Chapter 5, Example 7, QuickC, 4/18/88
   Bubble sort for strings */

#include <stdio.h>
#include <conio.h>
#include <stdlib.h>
#include <string.h>
#include <bios.h>

#define STR_NUM 11 /* number of strings to sort plus
                      total */
#define STR_LEN 25 /* maximum string length + 1 */

/* function prototypes */
void bubble_sort(char sort [] [STR_LEN]);
void swap_string(char sort [] [STR_LEN],int counter);
void main(void);
void clrscr(void);


void main()
{
   char sort [STR_NUM] [STR_LEN];
   int counter;

   printf("\n"); /* so clrscr() will work in QC */
   clrscr();

   /* give us some strings to sort */
   strcpy(&sort [0] [0],"10"); /* number of values presently
                                  in array */
   strcpy(&sort [1] [0],"Pat");
   strcpy(&sort [2] [0],"Clyde");
   strcpy(&sort [3] [0],"Mary");
   strcpy(&sort [4] [0],"Fred");
   strcpy(&sort [5] [0],"Arlene");
   strcpy(&sort [6] [0],"Glenda");
   strcpy(&sort [7] [0],"Roberta");
```

```
          strcpy(&sort [8] [0],"Carol");
          strcpy(&sort [9] [0],"Linda");
          strcpy(&sort [10] [0],"Gerry");

          /* do it */
          bubble_sort(sort);

          /* display the sorted strings */
          for (counter = 1;counter <= atoi(sort [0]);counter++)
            printf("%s\n",sort [counter]);
   }


void bubble_sort(char sort [] [STR_LEN])
/* perform bubble sort */
{
   int done = 1,
       exchange = 1,
       counter;

   while (exchange != 0 && done < atoi(sort [0]) - 1) {
      exchange = 0; /* did we make an exchange? */

      /* compare elements with following element */
      for (counter = 1;counter <= atoi(sort [0]) - done;
                                          counter ++) {
         printf("."); /* indicate activity */
         if ((strcmp(&sort [counter] [0],
                        &sort [counter + 1] [0])) > 0) {
            swap_string(sort,counter); /* swap them */
            exchange = 1;
            }
         }
      done++;
   } /* end while */
   printf("\n");
} /* end bubble_sort function */


void swap_string(char sort [] [STR_LEN],int counter)
/* swap two strings */
{
   char temp [STR_LEN]; /* temporary string holder */
```

```
    strcpy(&temp [0],&sort [counter] [0]);
    strcpy(&sort [counter] [0],&sort [counter + 1] [0]);
    strcpy(&sort [counter + 1] [0],&temp [0]);
}


void clrscr(void)
/* clear the screen */
{
    union REGS regs;

    regs.h.ah = 6;                  /* bios function */
    regs.h.al = 0;                  /* clear entire screen */
    regs.h.bh = 7;                  /* normal attribute */
    regs.h.ch = 0;                  /* upper row position */
    regs.h.cl = 0;                  /* upper-left column
                                       position */
    regs.h.dh = 24;                 /* lowest row */
    regs.h.dl = 79;                 /* rightmost column */
    int86(0x10,&regs,&regs);        /* bios interrupt number */
} /* end function clear screen */
```

MORE SORTS

There are numerous other sorts. Some of them will be discussed in later chapters after a few new techniques are introduced.

6

Merging Arrays and Files

This chapter will discuss the merging of two ordered arrays or two ordered sequential files. Also discussed will be the merging of two unsorted arrays and placing the sorted result in an array.

MERGING TWO ARRAYS

This simple program is designed to merge two sorted arrays. The sorted result is placed in a third array. If you are curious, instead of the following program try copying one of the arrays to be merged into the third array; then use the insertion sort from Chapter 5 to add the other array to be merged. Time both methods. You'll probably need to use much larger arrays than the little ones provided in this program to get meaningful results. (Be sure the first array is in order.) I suspect the program supplied here will be the faster.

```
/* Chapter 6, Example 1, QuickC, 4/18/88
   A simple merge example, two arrays into a third */



#include <stdio.h>
#include <conio.h>
#include <bios.h>

#define MAX_1 15 /* number of items in first array */
#define MAX_2 15 /* number of items in second array */

int array_one [] = {1,3,5,8,56,78,112,115,200,300,320,
                    345,456,510,600},
    array_two [] = {2,6,9,11,27,65,79,83,92,310,321,
                    356,455,476,477};

/* function prototypes */
void merge(int sort [],int high_one,int high_two);
void main(void);
void clrscr(void);
```

```
void main()
{
    int sort [MAX_1 + MAX_2 + 1], /* Make room for both
                                     arrays + total count.
                                     The total count is
                                     stored in record 0. */
        high_one = MAX_1 - 1, /* position of last item in
                                 first array */
        high_two = MAX_2 - 1, /* position of last item in
                                 second array */
        counter;

    /* do it */
    merge(sort,high_one,high_two);

    /* display merged array */
    printf("\n"); /* so following clrscr will work */
    clrscr();
    for (counter = 1;counter <= (MAX_1 + MAX_2);counter++)
        printf("%d ",sort [counter]);
    printf("\n");
}



void merge(int sort [],int high_one,int high_two)
/* merge array_one and array_two into the sort array */
{
    int pos_one = 0, /* current position in array_one */
        pos_two = 0, /* current position in array_two */
        pos_sort = 1, /* current position in destination
                         array */
        true = -1, /* boolean variable */
        false = 0,
        exit_flag = false; /* flag */

    do {
        while (array_one [pos_one] <= array_two [pos_two]) {
            printf("."); /* indicate activity */

            /* add an item */
            sort [pos_sort] = array_one [pos_one];
```

```
      /* next position in destination array */
      pos_sort++;

      /* next position in current source array */
      pos_one++;

      if (pos_one > high_one) {
         /* end of current source array */
         exit_flag = true;
         break; /* leave secondary do loop */
      }
   }

   if (exit_flag == true)
      break; /* leave primary do loop */

   while (array_one [pos_one] > array_two [pos_two]) {
      printf("."); /* indicate activity */

      /* add an item */
      sort [pos_sort] = array_two [pos_two];

      /* next position in destination array */
      pos_sort++;

      /* next position in current source array */
      pos_two++;

      if (pos_two > high_two) {
         /* end of current source array */
         exit_flag = true;
         break; /* leave secondary do loop */
      }
   }

   if (exit_flag == true)
      break; /* leave primary do loop */
}
while (1); /* do forever */

/* copy array that is not empty to destination
   array */
```

```
        /* choose higher value */
        while (pos_one <= high_one) {
           printf("."); /* indicate activity */
           sort [pos_sort] = array_one [pos_one];
           pos_sort++;
           pos_one++;
        }

        /* choose higher value */
        while (pos_two <= high_two) {
           printf("."); /* indicate activity */
           sort [pos_sort] = array_two [pos_two];
           pos_sort++;
           pos_two++;
        }
        pos_sort--;
        sort [0] = pos_sort; /* number of items in
                                destination array */
}

void clrscr(void)
/* clear the screen */
{
   union REGS regs;

   regs.h.ah = 6;              /* bios function */
   regs.h.al = 0;              /* clear entire screen */
   regs.h.bh = 7;              /* normal attribute */
   regs.h.ch = 0;              /* upper row position */
   regs.h.cl = 0;              /* upper-left column
                                  position */
   regs.h.dh = 24;             /* lowest row */
   regs.h.dl = 79;             /* rightmost column */
   int86(0x10,&regs,&regs);    /* bios interrupt number */
} /* end function clear screen */
```

MERGING SEQUENTIAL FILES

This next program performs the same function as the previous program but works with sequential files instead of arrays.

Remember, the two files to be merged must be sorted, as they are in the example.

```
/* Chapter 6, Example 2, QuickC, 4/18/88
   A simple merge example, two files into a third */


#include <stdio.h>
#include <conio.h>
#include <stdio.h>
#include <process.h>
#include <io.h>
#include <bios.h>

int array_one [] = {1,3,5,8,56,78,112,115,200,300,320,
                    345,456,510,600},
    array_two [] = {2,6,9,11,27,65,79,83,92,310,321,
                    356,455,476,477};

#define MAX_1 15 /* number of items in first array */
#define MAX_2 15 /* number of items in second array */

/* function prototypes */
void merge(char data_one [],char data_two [],
           char sortfile [],int high_one,int high_two);
void main(void);
void clrscr(void);
void gotoxy(int x,int y);


void main()
{
   int high_one = MAX_1 - 1, /* position of last item in
                                 first array */
       high_two = MAX_2 - 1, /* position of last item in
                                 second array */
       data, /* data from file when displaying */
       counter;
   FILE *stream_one, /* datafile one */
        *stream_two; /* datafile two */
   size_t size = sizeof(int);
```

```
/* store first array to file */
if ((stream_one = fopen("ch6_2a.dat","w+b")) == NULL) {
   putch(7); /* beep */
   gotoxy(10,24);
   printf("Cannot open first data file\n");
   exit(1);
}
for (counter = 0;counter < MAX_1;counter++)
   fwrite(&array_one [counter],size,1,stream_one);
fclose(stream_one);

/* store second array to file */
if ((stream_two = fopen("ch6_2b.dat","w+b")) == NULL) {
   putch(7); /* beep */
   gotoxy(10,24);
   printf("Cannot open first data file\n");
   exit(1);
}
for (counter = 0;counter < MAX_2;counter++)
   fwrite(&array_two [counter],size,1,stream_two);
fclose(stream_two);

/* Do it. ch6_2.dat is destination file. */
merge("ch6_2a.dat","ch6_2b.dat","ch6_2.dat",
      high_one,high_two);

/* display merged file */
if ((stream_one = fopen("ch6_2.dat","rb")) == NULL) {
   putch(7); /* beep */
   gotoxy(10,24);
   printf("Cannot open destination file\n");
   exit(1);
}

printf("\n");
clrscr();
for (counter = 1;counter <= (MAX_1 + MAX_2);counter++) {
   fread(&data,size,1,stream_one);
   printf("%d ",data);
}
printf("\n");
}
```

```
void merge(char datafile_one [],char datafile_two [],
           char datafile [],int high_one,int high_two)
/* merge datafile_one and datafile_two into the destination
   file */
{
    int pos_one = 0, /* current file position in data file
                        one */
        pos_two = 0, /* current file position in data file
                        two */
        true = -1, /* boolean variable */
        false = 0,
        data_one, /* current data from datafile_one */
        data_two, /* current data from datafile_two */
        exit_flag = false; /* flag */
    FILE *stream, /* destination file */
         *stream_one, /* datafile_one */
         *stream_two; /* datafile_two */
    size_t size = sizeof(int);

    /* open destination file for writing */
    if ((stream = fopen(datafile,"wb")) == NULL) {
        putch(7); /* beep */
        gotoxy(10,24);
        printf("Cannot open destination file\n");
        exit(1);
    }

    /* open first data file for reading */
    if ((stream_one = fopen(datafile_one,"rb")) == NULL) {
        putch(7); /* beep */
        gotoxy(10,24);
        printf("Cannot open first data file\n");
        exit(1);
    }

    /* open second data file for reading */
    if ((stream_two = fopen(datafile_two,"rb")) == NULL) {
        putch(7); /* beep */
        gotoxy(10,24);
        printf("Cannot open second data file\n");
        exit(1);
    }
```

```
/* get starting values from each data file */
fread(&data_one,size,1,stream_one);
fread(&data_two,size,1,stream_two);

/* do merge */
do {
    while (data_one <= data_two) {
        printf("."); /* indicate activity */
        fwrite(&data_one,size,1,stream); /* add an item */
        pos_one++;
        if (pos_one > high_one) {
            /* end of current data file */
            exit_flag = true;
            break; /* leave secondary do loop */
        }
        /* next item in data file one */
        fread(&data_one,size,1,stream_one);
    }
    if (exit_flag == true)
        break; /* leave primary do loop */

    while (data_one > data_two) {
        printf("."); /* indicate activity */
        fwrite(&data_two,size,1,stream); /* add an item */
        pos_two++; /* next position in current data file */
        if (pos_two > high_two) {
            /* end of current data file */
            exit_flag = true;
            break; /* leave secondary do loop */
        }
        fread(&data_two,size,1,stream_two); /* next item in
                                            datafile_two */
    }
    if (exit_flag == true)
        break; /* leave primary do loop */
}
while (1); /* do forever */

/* copy file that is not empty to destination file */
while (pos_one <= high_one) {
    /* while records are still left */
```

```
            printf("."); /* indicate activity */
            /* store current record */
            fwrite(&data_one,size,1,stream);
            /* record counter */
            pos_one++;
            if (pos_one > high_one)
               break;
            else
               /* get next record */
               fread(&data_one,size,1,stream_one);
      }
      while (pos_two <= high_two) {
         printf("."); /* indicate activity */
         fwrite(&data_two,size,1,stream);
         pos_two++;
         if (pos_two > high_two)
            break;
         else
            fread(&data_two,size,1,stream_two);
      }
      fclose(stream);
      fclose(stream_one);
      fclose(stream_two);
}

void clrscr(void)
/* clear the screen */
{
   union REGS regs;

   regs.h.ah = 6;                  /* bios function */
   regs.h.al = 0;                  /* clear entire screen */
   regs.h.bh = 7;                  /* normal attribute */
   regs.h.ch = 0;                  /* upper row position */
   regs.h.cl = 0;                  /* upper-left column
                                       position */
   regs.h.dh = 24;                 /* lowest row */
   regs.h.dl = 79;                 /* rightmost column */
   int86(0x10,&regs,&regs);        /* bios interrupt number */
} /* end function clear screen */
```

```
void gotoxy(int x,int y)
/* position cursor */
{

    union REGS regs;


    regs.h.ah = 2;                  /* bios function */
    regs.h.dh = (char) y;           /* row */
    regs.h.dl = (char) x;           /* column */
    regs.h.bh = 0;                  /* video page number */
    int86(0x10,&regs,&regs);        /* bios interrupt number */
} /* end function gotoxy */
```

MERGING UNSORTED ARRAYS

The next example will merge two unsorted arrays. The program
is a combination of the simple merge from Example 1 in this chapter
and the insertion sort from Example 1 in Chapter 5. I believe the
algorithm is original with me (but probably not).

```
/* Chapter 6, Example 3, QuickC, 4/18/88
   A merge example, two unordered arrays into a third */


#include <stdio.h>
#include <conio.h>
#include <stdlib.h>
#include <time.h>
#include <bios.h>

#define MAX_1 15 /* number of items in first array */
#define MAX_2 15 /* number of items in second array */


/* function prototype */
void mergesort(int array_one [],int array_two [],
               int sort [],int high_one,int high_two);
```

```
void find(int num,int *position,int *found,int sort []);
void replace(int num,int position,int sort []);
void main(void);
void clrscr(void);
int rand(void);


void main()
{
    int array_one [MAX_1], /* first data array to merge */
        array_two [MAX_2], /* second data array to merge */
        sort [MAX_1 + MAX_2 + 1], /* Destination array. Make
                                     room for both arrays +
                                     total count. */
        high_one = MAX_1 - 1, /* position of last item in
                                 first array */
        high_two = MAX_2 - 1, /* position of last item in
                                 second array */
        counter;

    /* load source arrays */
    for (counter = 0;counter < MAX_1;counter++)
        array_one [counter] = rand();
    for (counter = 0;counter < MAX_2;counter++)
        array_two [counter] = rand();
    sort [0] = 0; /* number of items in array */

    /* do it */
    mergesort(array_one,array_two,sort,high_one,high_two);

    /* display merged array */
    clrscr();
    for (counter = 1;counter <= (MAX_1 + MAX_2);counter++)
        printf("%d ",sort [counter]);
    printf("\n");
}


void mergesort(int array_one [],int array_two [],
               int sort [],int high_one,int high_two)
```

```
/* merge array_one and array_two into the sort array */
{
    int false = 0, /* boolean variable */
        pos_one = 0, /* current position in array_one */
        pos_two = 0, /* current position in array_two */
        pos_sort = 1, /* current position in destination
                         array */
        temp, /* temporary holder for current sort value */
        position = 0, /* for binary search */
        found = false; /* for binary search */

    /* get lower value to begin merge */
    if (array_one [pos_one] <= array_two [pos_two]) {
        sort [pos_sort] = array_one [pos_one];
        pos_one++; /* array position */
    }
    else {
        sort [pos_sort] = array_two [pos_two];
        pos_two++; /* array position */
    }
    sort [0]++; /* update number of items in array */

    /* go until one source array is empty */
    while (1) { /* loop forever */
        printf("."); /* indicate activity */
        /* current value in destination array */
        temp = sort [pos_sort];
        /* find lower value */
        if (array_one [pos_one] >= sort [pos_sort] &&
                array_one [pos_one] < array_two [pos_two]) {
            /* array one item is smaller */
            /* add to top of destination array */
            /* next position in destination array */
            pos_sort++;
            /* total items in array for binary search */
            sort [0]++;
            /* add an item */
            sort [pos_sort] = array_one [pos_one];
            /* next position in current source array */
            pos_one++;
            if (pos_one > high_one) {
                /* end of current source array */
```

```
         break; /* leave do loop */
      }
   }
   if (array_two [pos_two] < temp) {
      /* temp is value at top of destination array */
      /* insert in destination array */
      find(array_two [pos_two],&position,&found,sort);
      replace(array_two [pos_two],position,sort);
      /* next position in destination array */
      pos_sort++;
      /* next position in current source array */
      pos_two++;
      if (pos_two > high_two) {
         /* end of current source array */
         break; /* leave do loop */
      }
   }
   if (array_two [pos_two] >= sort [pos_sort]) {
      /* put item at head of destination list */
      /* next position in destination array */
      pos_sort++;
      sort [0]++; /* total for binary search */
      /* add an item */
      sort [pos_sort] = array_two [pos_two];
      /* next position in current source array */
      pos_two++;
      if (pos_two > high_two) {
         /* end of current source array */
         break; /* leave do loop */
      }
   }
   if (array_one [pos_one] < temp) {
      /* temp is current value at top of destination
         array */
      /* insert new value via binary sort */
      find(array_one [pos_one],&position,&found,sort);
      replace(array_one [pos_one],position,sort);
      /* next position in destination array */
      pos_sort++;
      /* next position in current source array */
      pos_one++;
```

```
        if (pos_one > high_one) {
            /* end of current source array */
            break; /* leave do loop */
        }
    }
}


/* copy array that is not empty to destination array */
while (pos_one <= high_one) {
    printf("."); /* indicate activity */
    if (array_one [pos_one] > sort [pos_sort]) {
        /* add to top of destination array */
        pos_sort++; /* position in sort array */
        sort [0]++; /* for binary search */
        sort [pos_sort] = array_one [pos_one];
        /* next position in current source array */
        pos_one++;
    }
    else {
        /* insert in destination array */
        find(array_one [pos_one],&position,&found,sort);
        replace(array_one [pos_one],position,sort);
        /* next position in destination array */
        pos_sort++;
        /* next position in current source array */
        pos_one++;
    }
}

while (pos_two <= high_two) {
    if (array_two [pos_two] >= sort [pos_sort]) {
        /* add to end of destination array */
        printf("."); /* indicate activity */
        pos_sort++;
        sort [0]++;
        sort [pos_sort] = array_two [pos_two];
        pos_two++;
    }
    else {
        /* insert in destination array */
        find(array_two [pos_two],&position,&found,sort);
        replace(array_two [pos_two],position,sort);
```

```
                 /* next position in destination array */
                 pos_sort++;
                 /* next position in current source array */
                 pos_two++;
          }
      }
  }


void find(int num,int *position,int *found,int sort [])
/* binary search */
/* find location of a value or the largest value
   preceding it */
{
    int true = 1,
        false = 0,
        try,
        lowlimit = 1,
        highlimit = sort [0];

    *found = false;

    for (;;) {
       if (highlimit == 0) {
          /* empty list */
          break;
       }
       for (;;) {
          /* center of remainder of list */
          try = (lowlimit + highlimit) / 2;
          if (num > sort [try]) {
          /* take high half of remainder */
          lowlimit = try + 1;
       }
       else {
          if (num == sort [try]) {
             /* success! */
             *found = true;
             *position = try;
             break;
          }
          else {
             /* num < sort [try] */
```

```
                              /* take low half of remainder */
                              highlimit = try - 1;
                  }
            }
            /* no more remainder */
            if (lowlimit > highlimit)
                  break;
            }
            if (*found == false) {
                  /* highest value in array preceding num */
                  *position = highlimit;
            }
            break;
      }
} /* end find_index function */



void replace(int num,int position,int sort [])
/* move all the items in list above num up one notch */
{
      int counter;

      for (counter = sort [0];counter >= position + 1;counter--)
            sort [counter + 1] = sort [counter];

      /* plug new value into gap created */
      sort [position + 1] = num;
      /* increment array total */
      sort [0]++;
}

int rand(void)
/* random numbers to sort */{
      time_t ltime;
      int rnd;
      static unsigned long value = 0;
      unsigned long temp,
                  increment = 271819,
                  multiplier = 314159,
                  modulus = 100001,
                  int_mod = 32767;
```

```
        if (value == 0) { /* first time called */
            time(&ltime);
            value = (multiplier * ltime + increment);
            value = value % modulus;
            temp = value;
            temp = value % int_mod;
            rnd = (int) temp;
        }
        else {
            value = (multiplier * value + increment);
            value = value % modulus;
            temp = value;
            temp = temp % int_mod;
            rnd = (int) temp;
        }
        return(rnd);
}


void clrscr(void)
/* clear the screen */
{
    union REGS regs;

    regs.h.ah = 6;                      /* bios function */
    regs.h.al = 0;                      /* clear entire screen */
    regs.h.bh = 7;                      /* normal attribute */
    regs.h.ch = 0;                      /* upper row position */
    regs.h.cl = 0;                      /* upper-left column
                                           position */
    regs.h.dh = 24;                     /* lowest row */
    regs.h.dl = 79;                     /* rightmost column */
    int86(0x10,&regs,&regs);            /* bios interrupt number */
} /* end function clear screen */
```

The program merges the arrays array_one [ ] and array_two [ ], putting the sorted, merged result in the array sort [ ]. The concept is simple. If the next item in array_one [ ] and array_two [ ] are both larger than the last item in sort [ ], then the smaller is appended to sort [ ] first. If only one is larger, then it is appended to sort [ ]. If either the current array_one [ ] or array_two [ ] value is smaller than the last item in sort [ ], then it is inserted into sort [ ]. Finally, when you reach the end of array_one [ ] or array_two [ ], the remaining items in the other array are appended or inserted into sort [ ] as appropriate.

Because the program is frequently able to append a value to sort [ ] rather than inserting it, which is much faster, the program has to run faster than a straight insertion. In fact, you could probably speed up the insertion sort with this scheme.

You might wish to convert this to work with sequential or random access files. Look at Example 2 for a few ideas.

7

External Sorting

In this book, external sorting is considered to be the method to use on files that are too large to fit into memory.

Sorting large random access files is trivial; you can use any sort that works on arrays—things just happen a lot slower. A sample using the shell sort will be supplied as Example 3.

SORTING SEQUENTIAL FILES OF KNOWN LENGTH

Sorting sequential files is a bit more difficult. The first example is for sequential files when the number of records is known. This value must be accurate or the sort won't work properly; either you will lose some records or the program will crash with an input-past-end error.

```
/* Chapter 7, Example 1, QuickC, 4/18/88
   Sort an unordered sequential file to another file */

#include <stdio.h>
#include <stdlib.h>
#include <conio.h>
#include <io.h>
#include <string.h>
#include <bios.h>
#include <time.h>

#define INT 32767
#define TOTAL 100 /* supply this number of records to
                     sort */
#define SEGMENT 10 /* segment size */

/* function prototypes */
void disk_sort(char source_file [],char dest_file []);
void reverse_find(int num,int *position,int *found,
                  int sort []);
void reverse_replace(int num,int position,int sort []);
void main(void);
void clrscr(void);
int rand(void);
void gotoxy(int x,int y);
```

```
void main()
{
   FILE *stream;
   int counter,
       value; /* temporary holder */
   char source_file [13],
        dest_file [13];
   size_t size = sizeof(int); /* change for other data
                                    types */

   /* set data file names */
   /* source */
   strcpy(&source_file [0],"ch7_1s.dat");
   /* destination */
   strcpy(&dest_file [0],"ch7_1d.dat");

   printf("\n"); /* to make clrscr() work in QC environment *
   clrscr();

   /* open file to hold values to sort */
   if ((stream = fopen(dest_file,"w+b")) == NULL) {
      putch(7); /* beep */
      gotoxy(10,24);
      printf("Cannot open data file\n");
      exit(1);
   }

   /* supply numbers to sort */
   for (counter = 1;counter <= TOTAL;counter||) {
      printf("."); /* indicate activity */
      value = rand() % INT;
      fwrite(&value,size,1,stream);
   }

   fclose(stream);

   /* create second file */
   if ((stream = fopen(source_file,"w+b")) == NULL) {
      putch(7); /* beep */
      gotoxy(10,24);
      printf("Cannot open data file\n");
      exit(1);
   }
```

```
        fclose(stream);

        /* do it */
        disk_sort(source_file,dest_file);

        /* open file holding sorted values */
        if ((stream = fopen(dest_file,"rb")) == NULL) {
            putch(7); /* beep */
            gotoxy(10,24);
            printf("Cannot open data file\n");
            exit(1);
        }

        /* print the resulting sorted array */
        clrscr();

        for (counter = 1;counter <= TOTAL;counter++) {
            fread(&value,size,1,stream);
            printf("%d ",value);
        }
        printf("\n");

        fclose(stream);
    }


void disk_sort(char source_file [],char dest_file [])
/* sort numbers to destination file */
{
    FILE *stream_one,
         *stream_two;
    int sort [SEGMENT + 2],
        num, /* temporary holder */
        todo = TOTAL, /* remaining numbers to sort */
        counter,
        false = 0, /* boolean variable */
        found = false, /* used by binary search */
        position = 0; /* used by binary search */
    char temp [13];
    size_t size = sizeof(int); /* change for other data
                                  types */
```

```
sort [0] = 0; /* number of items in array */

while (todo >= SEGMENT) {

   /* swap file names */
   strcpy(temp,source_file);
   strcpy(source_file,dest_file);
   strcpy(dest_file,temp);

   /* open file to hold values to sort */
   if ((stream_one = fopen(source_file,"rb")) == NULL) {
      putch(7); /* beep */
      gotoxy(10,24);
      printf("Cannot open data file\n");
      exit(1);
   }

   /* open file to hold sorted values */
   if ((stream_two = fopen(dest_file,"r+b")) == NULL) {
      putch(7); /* beep */
      gotoxy(10,24);
      printf("Cannot open data file\n");
      exit(1);
   }

   printf("\n"); /* start new activity row */
   /* put next segment + 1 values in sort array using
      insertion sort */
   for (counter = 1;counter <= SEGMENT + 1;counter++) {
      fread(&num,size,1,stream_one);
      reverse_find(num,&position,&found,sort);
      reverse_replace(num,position,sort);
      printf(".");
   }
   /* get segment highest values remaining in file
      replacing items in array as required */
      printf("\n"); /* start new activity row */
      for (counter = SEGMENT + 2;counter <= todo;
                                    counter++) {
      printf("."); /* indicate activity */
      /* lowest value */
```

```
              fwrite(&sort [SEGMENT + 1],size,1,stream_two);
              /* make room for next item */
              sort [0]--;
              /* get next item to put into array */
              fread(&num,size,1,stream_one);
              if (num <= sort [sort [0]]) {
                 /* append to array */
                 sort [0]++;
                 sort [sort [0]] = num;
              }
              else {
                 /* insert into array */
                 reverse_find(num,&position,&found,sort);
                 reverse_replace(num,position,sort);
              }
          }
          printf("\n"); /* start new activity line */

          /* add new sorted records */
          for (counter = SEGMENT + 1;counter >= 1;counter--) {
             fwrite(&sort [counter],size,1,stream_two);
             printf(".");
          }
          /* add records sorted earlier */
          printf("\n");
          for (counter = 1;counter <= TOTAL - todo;counter++) {
             fread(&num,size,1,stream_one);
             fwrite(&num,size,1,stream_two);
             printf(".");
          }
          sort [0] = 0; /* empty array */
          fclose(stream_one);
          fclose(stream_two);
          todo -= SEGMENT; /* one less segment to go */

      }
}


void reverse_find(int num,int *position,int *found,
               int sort [])
```

```
/* find location of a value or the largest value
   preceding it */
{
    int true = -1,
        false = 0,
        try,
        lowlimit = 1,
        highlimit = sort [0];

    *found = false;

    for (;;) {
        if (highlimit == 0) {
            *position = 0;
            /* empty list */
            break;
        }

        for (;;) {
            /* center of remainder of list */
            try = (lowlimit + highlimit) / 2;

            if (num > sort [try]) {
                /* take high half of remainder */
                highlimit = try - 1;
            }
            else {
                if (num == sort [try]) {
                    /* success! */
                    *found = true;
                    *position = try;
                    break;
                }
                else {
                    /* num < sort [try] */
                    /* take low half of remainder */
                    lowlimit = try + 1;
                }
            }
            /* no more remainder */
            if (lowlimit > highlimit)
                break;
```

```
            }
         if (*found == false) {
            /* highest value in array preceding num */
            *position = highlimit + 1;
         }
         break;
      }
   } /* end find_index function */



void reverse_replace(int num,int position,int sort [])
/* move all the items in list above num up one notch */
{
   int counter;

   for (;;) {
      if (position == 0) {
         /* first item in list */
         sort [1] = num;
         sort [0]++; /* item counter */
         break;
      }

      /* move all items less than inserted item */
      for (counter = sort [0];counter >= position;counter--)
         sort [counter + 1] = sort [counter];
      /* add new item */
      sort [position] = num;
      /* new item count in array */
      sort [0]++;
      break;
   }
}



int rand(void)
/* random numbers to sort */
{
   time_t ltime;
   int rnd;
   static unsigned long value = 0;
```

```
        unsigned long temp,
                increment = 271819,
                multiplier = 314159,
                modulus = 100001,
                int_mod = 32767;

        if (value == 0) { /* first call to function */
            time(&ltime);
            value = (multiplier * ltime + increment);
            value = value % modulus;
            temp = value;
            temp = value % int_mod;
            rnd = (int) temp;
        }
        else {
            value = (multiplier * value + increment);
            value = value % modulus;
            temp = value;
            temp = temp % int_mod;
            rnd = (int) temp;
        }
        return(rnd);
    }



void clrscr(void)
/* clear the screen */
{
    union REGS regs;

    regs.h.ah = 6;              /* bios function */
    regs.h.al = 0;              /* clear entire screen */
    regs.h.bh = 7;              /* normal attribute */
    regs.h.ch = 0;              /* upper row position */
    regs.h.cl = 0;              /* upper-left column
                                   position */
    regs.h.dh = 24;             /* lowest row */
    regs.h.dl = 79;             /* rightmost column */
    int86(0x10,&regs,&regs);    /* bios interrupt number */
} /* end function clear screen */
```

```
void gotoxy(int x,int y)
/* position cursor */
{

   union REGS regs;


   regs.h.ah = 2;              /* bios function */
   regs.h.dh = (char) y;       /* row */
   regs.h.dl = (char) x;       /* column */
   regs.h.bh = 0;              /* video page number */
   int86(0x10,&regs,&regs);    /* bios interrupt number */
} /* end function gotoxy */
```

The example uses a small file of integers, but the program should work on any size file. Obviously, the larger the file the longer the sort will take. Make the segment size as large as you can fit into available memory, but it must be smaller than the number of records in the file. A good size is 30% or 40% of the file size, if you have the room. The larger the segment size the fewer the passes, which will speed up the sort. However, the other side of the coin is that the larger the segment size, the longer it takes to load them because the insertion sort used gets slow when the array gets very large and large numbers of array elements need moving.

This sort is actually a glorified bubble sort. In this case, instead of sinking single large values to the end of the array, we are sinking segments containing the largest values to the end of the target file.

Let's use an example here showing step by step how the program works. The source file will contain 10 records and the segment size will be 3.

todo = 10

The source file begins with

9 7 11 34 56 76 23 45 90 3

Put the first segment + 1 records into the array.

a(0) = 4, a(1) = 34, a(2) = 11, a(3) = 9, a(4) = 7

Go through the remaining records, retaining the highest values.

`a(0) = 4, a(1) = 90, a(2) = 76, a(3) = 56, a(4) = 45`

The target file contains

`7, 9, 23, 11, 34, 3`

Add the underlined array to the target file. These values will not be sorted in future passes.

`7, 9, 23, 11, 34, 3, 45, 56, 76, 90`

The todo variable now contains 7. Put the first segment + 1 records into the array.

`a(0) = 4, a(1) = 23, a(2) = 11, a(3) = 9, a(4) = 7`

Go through the remaining records, retaining the highest values.

`a(0) = 4, a(1) = 34, a(2) = 23, a(3) = 11, a(4) = 9`

The target file contains

`7, 3`

Add the underlined array to the target file. These values will not be sorted in future passes.

`7, 3, 9, 11, 23, 34`

Add the values beyond todo + 1.

`7, 3, 9, 11, 23, 34, 45, 56, 76, 90`

The todo variable now contains 4. Put the first segment + 1 records into the array.

`a(0) = 4, a(1) = 11, a(2) = 9, a(3) = 7, a(4) = 3`

No remaining records to check. The target file is empty. Add the underlined array to the target file.

`3, 7, 9, 11`

Add the values beyond todo + 1.

3, 7, 9, 11, 23, 34, 45, 56, 76, 90

The todo variable is now changed to 1, less than the segment of 3, so the sort is completed.

SORTING SEQUENTIAL FILES OF UNKNOWN LENGTH

This program will work even if you don't know how many records are in the file to be sorted. You must have a general idea since you must not set the segment size to a value greater than the total number of records. As mentioned concerning the previous program, there are several trade-offs when you choose the segment size.

Here is the program.

```
/* Chapter 7, Example 2, QuickC, 4/18/88
   Sort an unordered sequential file of
   any unknown length to another file */
/* Caution: The file length must be
   less than 32768 bytes. If you wish
   more you'll have to change some of
   the program's variable types and
   perhaps add some casts. Probably the
   simplest method would be to change all
   the integer variables to long and remove
   the (int) casts before the filelength()s
   and to add an 'L' to the #define constants.
   Don't forget data_size. */

#include <stdio.h>
#include <stdlib.h>
#include <conio.h>
#include <io.h>
#include <string.h>
#include <time.h>
#include <bios.h>

#define TOTAL 100 /* total numbers supplied for sort */
#define SEGMENT 10 /* segment size */
```

```
/* function prototypes */
void disk_sort(char source_file []);
void reverse_find(int num,int *position,int *found,
                  int sort []);
void reverse_replace(int num,int position,int sort []);
void main(void);
void clrscr(void);
void gotoxy(int x,int y);
int rand(void);


void main()
{
   FILE *stream;
   int handle,
       value, /* for loading & displaying file */
       file_length,
       counter;
   char source_file [13];
   size_t size = sizeof(int); /* change for other data
                                  types */

   /* file name */
   strcpy(&source_file [0],"ch7_2.dat");

   printf("\n");
   clrscr();

   /* open file to hold values to sort */
   if ((stream = fopen(source_file,"w+b")) == NULL) {
      putch(7); /* beep */
      gotoxy(10,24);
      printf("Cannot open data file\n");
      exit(1);
   }

   /* supply numbers to sort */
   for (counter = 1;counter <= TOTAL;counter++) {
      printf("."); /* indicate activity */
      value = rand();
      fwrite(&value,size,1,stream);
   }
```

```
            fclose(stream);

            /* do it */
            disk_sort(source_file);

            /* open file holding sorted values */
            if ((stream = fopen(source_file,"rb")) == NULL) {
               putch(7); /* beep */
               gotoxy(10,24);
               printf("Cannot open data file\n");
               exit(1);
            }

            handle = fileno(stream);
            file_length = (int) filelength(handle) / size;

            /* print the resulting sorted file */
            clrscr();
            for (counter = 1;counter <= file_length;counter++) {
               fread(&value,size,1,stream);
               printf("%d ",value);
            }
            printf("\n");

            fclose(stream);
         }


      void disk_sort(char source_file [])
      /* sort numbers to destination file */
      {
         FILE *stream_one,
              *stream_two,
              *stream_three;
         size_t data_size = sizeof(int); /* change for other
                                            data types */
         int sort [SEGMENT + 1],
             downcount = 0, /* total number of segments */
             firstfile, /* highest segment file number */
             handle_one, /* file handles for filelength() */
             handle_two,
             handle_three,
```

```
          num, /* temporary holder */
          num_two, /* value from file two */
          num_three, /* value from file three */
          counter,
          false = 0, /* boolean variable */
          found = false, /* used by binary search */
          position = 0, /* used by binary search */
          file_length, /* number of records in file */
          length_two, /* number of records in file two */
          length_three, /* number of records in file three */
          record_counter, /* number of records in file one */
          record_count_two, /* number of records read from and
                             written to file two */
          record_count_three; /* number of records read from
                                and written to file three */
  char temp [13], /* used for creating segment file
                    names */
       count [4]; /* used for generating segment file
                    names */
  /* open file holding values to sort */
  if ((stream_one = fopen(source_file,"rb")) == NULL) {
     putch(7); /* beep */
     gotoxy(10,24);
     printf("Cannot open data file\n");
     exit(1);
  }

  handle_one = fileno(stream_one);

  file_length = (int) filelength(handle_one) / data_size;

  record_counter = 0;
  while (record_counter < file_length) {

     /* sort each segment */
     sort [0] = 0; /* number of items in array */
     printf("\n"); /* start new activity row */
     while (record_counter < file_length &&
                              sort [0] < SEGMENT) {
        fread(&num,data_size,1,stream_one);
        if (sort [0] > 1 && num < sort [sort [0]]) {
```

```
                    /* append record */
                        sort [0]++;
                        sort [sort [0]] = num;
                    }
                    else {
                    /* insert record */
                        reverse_find(num,&position,&found,sort);
                        reverse_replace(num,position,sort);
                    }
                    printf(".");
                    record_counter++;
                }

                /* next segment */
                downcount++;
                /* create segment file to hold array */
                strcpy(&temp [0],"TEMP");
                itoa(downcount,count,10);
                strcat(temp,count);
                if ((stream_two = fopen(temp,"w+b")) == NULL) {
                    putch(7);  /* beep */
                    gotoxy(24,10);
                    printf("Cannot open data file\n");
                    exit(1);
                }

                /* store array to segment file */
                for (counter = sort [0];counter >= 1;counter--)
                    fwrite(&sort [counter],data_size,1,stream_two);
                fclose(stream_two);
            }
            fclose(stream_one);
            /* current file number */
            firstfile = downcount;
            /* one less segment */
            downcount--;

            /* merge segment files */
            do {
                /* target file */
                if ((stream_one = fopen(source_file,"r+b")) == NULL) {
                    putch(7);  /* beep */
```

```
      gotoxy(10,24);
      printf("Cannot open data file\n");
      exit(1);
   }

   /* select first segment file */
   strcpy(&temp [0],"TEMP");
   itoa(firstfile,count,10);
   strcat(temp,count);
   if ((stream_two = fopen(temp,"rb")) == NULL) {
      putch(7); /* beep */
      gotoxy(10,24);
      printf("Cannot open data file\n");
      exit(1);
   }

   handle_two = fileno(stream_two);

   /* get record count */
   length_two = (int) filelength(handle_two) / data_size;

   /* select second segment file */
   strcpy(&temp [0],"TEMP");
   itoa(downcount,count,10);
   strcat(temp,count);
   if ((stream_three = fopen(temp,"rb")) == NULL) {
      putch(7); /* beep */
      gotoxy(10,24);
      printf("Cannot open data file\n");
      exit(1);
   }

   handle_three = fileno(stream_three);

   length_three = (int) filelength(handle_three) /
                                          data_size;

   downcount--;

   /* proceed through two files */
   /* get the first two records from the files */
   fread(&num_two,data_size,1,stream_two);
   fread(&num_three,data_size,1,stream_three);
```

```
/* merge the two segment files */
printf("\n"); /* start new activity row */
record_count_two = 0;
record_count_three = 0;
/* merge until one of the segment files runs dry */
while (record_count_two < length_two &&
                record_count_three < length_three) {
    printf("."); /* indicate activity */
    if (num_two < num_three) {
        /* choose lower value */
        /* write chosen record to destination */
        fwrite(&num_two,data_size,1,stream_one);
        /* one more record transferred */
        record_count_two++;
        /* get next record if available */
        if (record_count_two < length_two) {
            fread(&num_two,data_size,1,stream_two);
        }
    }
    else {
        /* move other file's record to destination */
        fwrite(&num_three,data_size,1,stream_one);
        /* transferred another record */
        record_count_three++;
        /* get next record if available */
        if (record_count_three < length_three) {
            fread(&num_three,data_size,1,stream_three);
        }
    }
}

printf("\n"); /* start new activity row */
/* transfer remaining records from segment file, if
   any */
if (record_count_two < length_two) {
    /* some records remaining */
    printf("."); /* indicate activity */
    /* transfer record left over from previous loop */
    fwrite(&num_two,data_size,1,stream_one);
    /* transferred another record */
    record_count_two++;
```

```
      /* transfer remaining records if file not empty */
      while (record_count_two < length_two) {
         fread(&num_two,data_size,1,stream_two);
         fwrite(&num_two,data_size,1,stream_one);
         record_count_two++;
      }
   }


   printf("\n"); /* start new activity row */
   /* transfer remaining records from segment file, if
      any */
   if (record_count_three < length_three) {
      /* some records remain */
      printf("."); /* indicate activity */
      /* transfer record left over from previous loop */
      fwrite(&num_three,data_size,1,stream_one);
      /* transferred another record */
      record_count_three++;
      /* transfer remaining records if file not empty */
      while (record_count_three < length_three) {
         fread(&num_three,data_size,1,stream_three);
         fwrite(&num_three,data_size,1,stream_one);
         record_count_three++;
      }
   }


   printf("\n"); /* start new activity row */
   fclose(stream_one);
   fclose(stream_two);
   fclose(stream_three);
   if (downcount > 0) {
      /* there are unmerged remaining segment files */

      /* open file to hold values to sort */
      if ((stream_one = fopen(source_file,"rb")) == NULL)
{
         putch(7); /* beep */
         gotoxy(10,24);
         printf("Cannot open data file\n");
         exit(1);
      }
```

```
                          /* file presently containing records merged so
                             far */
                          strcpy(&temp [0],"TEMP");
                          itoa(firstfile,count,10);
                          strcat(temp,count);
                          if ((stream_two = fopen(temp,"r+b")) == NULL) {
                              putch(7); /* beep */
                              gotoxy(10,24);
                              printf("Cannot open data file\n");
                              exit(1);
                          }

                          /* transfer merged records to source file for next
                             pass */
                          for (counter = 1;counter <=
                                       (length_two + length_three);counter++) {
                              fread(&num,data_size,1,stream_one);
                              fwrite(&num,data_size,1,stream_two);
                          }
                          fclose(stream_one);
                          fclose(stream_two);
                      }
                  }
                  while (downcount > 0);

                  /* we're done with temporary files so remove them */
                  for (counter = 1;counter <= firstfile;counter++) {
                      strcpy(&temp [0],"TEMP");
                      itoa(counter,count,10);
                      strcat(temp,count);
                      remove(temp);
                  }
              }


      void reverse_find(int num,int *position,int *found,
                        int sort [])
      /* find location of a value or the largest value preceding
         it */
      {
          int true = -1,
              false = 0,
```

```
      try,
      lowlimit = 1,
      highlimit = sort [0];

*found = false;

for (;;) {
   if (highlimit == 0) {
      /* first record */
      *position = 0;
      /* empty list */
      break;
   }

   for (;;) {
      /* center of remainder of list */
      try = (lowlimit + highlimit) / 2;

      if (num > sort [try]) {
         /* take high half of remainder */
         highlimit = try - 1;
      }
      else {
         if (num == sort [try]) {
            /* success! */
            *found = true;
            *position = try;
            break;
         }
         else {
            /* num < sort [try] */
            /* take low half of remainder */
            lowlimit = try + 1;
         }
      }

      /* no more remainder */
      if (lowlimit > highlimit)
         break;
   }
   if (*found == false) {
      /* highest value in array preceding num */
```

```
                    *position = highlimit + 1;
            }
            break;
        }
    } /* end find_index function */



void reverse_replace(int num,int position,int sort [])
/* move all the items in list above num up one notch */
{
    int counter;

    for (;;) {
        if (position == 0) {
            /* first record */
            sort [1] = num;
            sort [0]++;
            break;
        }

        /* move all larger values up a position */
        for (counter = sort [0];counter >= position;counter--)
            sort [counter + 1] = sort [counter];
        /* new value */
        sort [position] = num;
        /* increment item count */
        sort [0]++;
        break;
    }
}



int rand(void)
/* random numbers to sort */
{
    time_t ltime;
    int rnd;
    static unsigned long value = 0;
```

```
   unsigned long temp,
           increment = 271819,
           multiplier = 314159,
           modulus = 100001,
           int_mod = 32767;

   if (value == 0) { /* first time called */
      time(&ltime);
      value = (multiplier * ltime + increment);
      value = value % modulus;
      temp = value;
      temp = value % int_mod;
      rnd = (int) temp;
   }
   else {
      value = (multiplier * value + increment);
      value = value % modulus;
      temp = value;
      temp = temp % int_mod;
      rnd = (int) temp;
   }
   return(rnd);
}


void clrscr(void)
/* clear the screen */
{
   union REGS regs;

   regs.h.ah = 6;                   /* bios function */
   regs.h.al = 0;                   /* clear entire screen */
   regs.h.bh = 7;                   /* normal attribute */
   regs.h.ch = 0;                   /* upper row position */
   regs.h.cl = 0;                   /* upper-left column
                                        position */
   regs.h.dh = 24;                  /* lowest row */
   regs.h.dl = 79;                  /* rightmost column */
   int86(0x10,&regs,&regs);         /* bios interrupt number */
} /* end function clear screen */
```

```
void gotoxy(int x,int y)
/* position cursor */
{

    union REGS regs;


    regs.h.ah = 2;                  /* bios function */
    regs.h.dh = (char) y;           /* row */
    regs.h.dl = (char) x;           /* column */
    regs.h.bh = 0;                  /* video page number */
    int86(0x10,&regs,&regs);        /* bios interrupt number */
} /* end function gotoxy */
```

Using an array for temporary storage (to permit an insertion sort to be used), a number of records equal to the segment size are insertion sorted into the segment array in descending order. Then the array is stored in a temporary segment file. This is repeated until we run out of records. We will end up with two or more segment files.

Next we set aside the last file created (for convenience in programming, actually any segment file would do). We'll call this the primary source file. Taking the next segment file in the list, we merge it, together with the primary source file, into the target file (formerly the original source file).

If there are still segment files to merge, we transfer the records from the target file to the primary source file and do it all again.

When completed, all the records are in sorted order in the target file.

SORTING RANDOM ACCESS FILES

As mentioned at the beginning of the chapter, sorting random access files is the same as sorting arrays, only slower. As an example of converting a program written to sort an array to one able to sort a random access file, the shell sort from Chapter 6 was chosen. For an explanation of how the sort works, see that chapter. A comparison of the two programs will reveal that only a few lines needed to be changed, and they were obvious.

```
/* Chapter 7, Example 3, QuickC, 4/19/88
   Shell sort */

#include <stdio.h>
#include <conio.h>
#include <stdlib.h>
#include <io.h>
#include <time.h>
#include <bios.h>
#include <string.h>

#define TOTAL 100L /* number of items to sort */

/* function prototypes */
void shell_rand_sort(char shell_file []);
void main(void);
void gotoxy(int x,int y);
int rand(void);
void clrscr(void);


void main()
{
    int value,
        num;
    long counter;
    FILE *stream;
    char shell_file [13];
    size_t size = sizeof(int); /* change for other types of
                                  data */

    /* data file */
    strcpy(&shell_file [0],"ch7_3.dat");

    printf("\n"); /* to make following clrscr() work */
    clrscr();

    /* give us some numbers to sort */
    /* open file to hold values to sort */
    if ((stream = fopen(shell_file,"w+b")) == NULL) {
        putch(7); /* beep */
        gotoxy(10,24);
```

```
            printf("Cannot open data file\n");
            exit(1);
        }

        /* supply numbers to sort */
        for (counter = 1L;counter <= TOTAL;counter++) {
            printf("."); /* indicate activity */
            value = rand();
            fwrite(&value,size,1,stream);
        }

        fclose(stream);

        /* do it */
        shell_rand_sort(shell_file);

        /* display the sorted values */
        /* open file holding values to sort */
        if ((stream = fopen(shell_file,"rb")) == NULL) {
            putch(7); /* beep */
            gotoxy(10,24);
            printf("Cannot open data file\n");
            exit(1);
        }

        for (counter = 1L;counter <= TOTAL;counter++) {
            fread(&num,size,1,stream);
            printf("%d ",num);
        }
        printf("\n");

        fclose(stream);
}


void shell_rand_sort(char shell_file [])
/* perform shell sort */
{
    long part_size,
         stepper,
         partition,
         offset,
```

```
      counter;
int value_one,
    value_two;
FILE *stream;
size_t size = sizeof(int);

/* open file holding values to sort */
if ((stream = fopen(shell_file,"r+b")) == NULL) {
   putch(7); /* beep */
   gotoxy(10,24);
   printf("Cannot open data file\n");
   exit(1);
}

 /* start by creating two partitions */
partition = TOTAL;
partition /= 2L;

/* just in case file is empty */
if (partition == 0L) {
   clrscr();
   printf("Nothing to sort");
   exit(0);
}

/* start comparing at this location */
stepper = 1L;
/* select the first partition */
part_size = TOTAL - partition;

for (;;) {
   /* set up for compare */
   counter = stepper;
   for (;;) {
      /* indicate activity */
      printf(".");
      /* compare with another partition */
      offset = counter + partition;

      /* see if swap required */
      if ((fseek(stream,(counter - 1L) *
                       (long) size,SEEK_SET)) != 0) {
```

```
            gotoxy(10,22);
            printf("Seek failed!");
            exit(1);
        }
        fread(&value_one,size,1,stream);

        /* get second value to test */
        if ((fseek(stream,(offset - 1L) *
                            (long) size,SEEK_SET)) != 0) {
            gotoxy(10,22);
            printf("Seek failed!");
            exit(1);
        }
        fread(&value_two,size,1,stream);

        /* test for correct order */
        if (value_one > value_two) {
            /* swap values on disk */
            if ((fseek(stream,(counter - 1L) *
                            (long) size,SEEK_SET)) != 0) {
                gotoxy(10,22);
                printf("Seek failed!");
                exit(1);
            }
            fwrite(&value_two,size,1,stream);
            if ((fseek(stream,(offset - 1L) *
                            (long) size,SEEK_SET)) != 0) {
                gotoxy(10,22);
                printf("Seek failed!");
                exit(1);
            }
            fwrite(&value_one,size,1,stream);
            counter -= partition;
            if (counter < 1L)
                break;
        }

        else
            break; /* next partition */
    }
```

```
      /* next partition */
      stepper++;
      if (stepper > part_size) {
         /* reset partition size */
         partition /= 2L;
         if (partition == 0L) {
            /* no more partitions */
            break;
         }
         /* start stepping through partitions from beginning
            again */
         stepper = 1L;
         /* select the first partition */
         part_size = TOTAL - partition;
      }
   } /* end for */
   fclose(stream);
} /* end shell_sort function */


int rand(void)
{
   time_t ltime;
   int rnd;
   static unsigned long value = 0;
   unsigned long temp,
          increment = 271819,
          multiplier = 314159,
          modulus = 100001,
          int_mod = 32767;

   if (value == 0) { /* first time called */
      time(&ltime);
      value = (multiplier * ltime + increment);
      value = value % modulus;
      temp = value;
      temp = value % int_mod;
      rnd = (int) temp;
   }
   else {
```

```
            value = (multiplier * value + increment);
            value = value % modulus;
            temp = value;
            temp = temp % int_mod;
            rnd = (int) temp;
        }
    return(rnd);
}


void clrscr(void)
/* clear the screen */
{
    union REGS regs;

    regs.h.ah = 6;                       /* bios function */
    regs.h.al = 0;                       /* clear entire screen */
    regs.h.bh = 7;                       /* normal attribute */
    regs.h.ch = 0;                       /* upper row position */
    regs.h.cl = 0;                       /* upper-left column
                                            position */
    regs.h.dh = 24;                      /* lowest row */
    regs.h.dl = 79;                      /* rightmost column */
    int86(0x10,&regs,&regs);             /* bios interrupt number */
} /* end function clear screen */


void gotoxy(int x,int y)
/* position cursor */
{

    union REGS regs;


    regs.h.ah = 2;                       /* bios function */
    regs.h.dh = (char) y;                /* row */
    regs.h.dl = (char) x;                /* column */
    regs.h.bh = 0;                       /* video page number */
    int86(0x10,&regs,&regs);             /* bios interrupt number */
} /* end function gotoxy */
```

The three programs in this chapter will get you started in external sorting. They all work, but there are quite a few other schemes you can use for this task; in fact, there are whole books written on sorting.

8

Linked Lists

Linked lists are used to arrange a list of items in sorted order. The process is probably closest to using the insertion sort to create a file or array of ordered values. However, linking the items in memory takes a little longer than the insertion sort. For 1000 numbers, the insertion sort took about 21 seconds; linking in an array takes 26 seconds. Linking takes longer because the list has to be read sequentially until the correct position is found, meaning that on the average half the list will have to be read each time a new item is added. As you'll remember, the insertion sort uses a binary search, which is much faster; if the item belongs at the end of the list, then no search at all is required, only one comparison. Linking does not require the items to be physically rearranged so that they remain in sequence, as they must be when the insertion sort is used, but this advantage does not offset the long search times.

A linked list functions by introducing an additional element to the array that contains a pointer to the next array element in the sequence. This pointer is simply the array subscript. Therefore, this version of a linked list works only in one direction.

CREATING A LINKED LIST

The first example is a simple linking program that orders items in ascending order as they are added to an array. The array is of type integer so you will be limited to a link pointer variable value of 32,767 and an array size of 32,767 elements. Using a long integer array normally won't help because the array size is usually limited to 64Kb. If you need more elements, use the huge memory model or the random access file version.

```
/* Chapter 8, Example 1, QuickC, 2/18/88
   Single linked list, ascending order */

#include <stdio.h>
#include <stdlib.h>
#include <conio.h>
#include <bios.h>
#include <time.h>

#define COUNT 100 /* number of records to link */
```

```
struct link {
   int item;
   int locator;
   };

/* function prototypes */
void single_link(int num,struct link link_list []);
void clrscr(void);
int rand(void);
void main(void);


void main()
{
   int num,
      counter;
   struct link link_list [COUNT + 1]; /* holds item and link
                                              locator */

   /* initialize array */
   for (counter = 0;counter <= COUNT;counter++) {
      link_list [counter].item = 0;
      link_list [counter].locator = 0;
   }

   /* number of items in list */
   link_list [0].item = 0;
   /* load numbers to link */
   for (counter = 1;counter <= COUNT;counter++)  {
      num = rand();
      single_link(num,link_list);
   }

   /* display the results */
   printf("\n"); /* so following clrscr() will work */
   clrscr();
   counter = link_list [0].locator; /* link locator to first
                                              item in list */
   while (counter != 0) {
      printf("%d ",link_list [counter].item);
```

```
          counter = link_list [counter].locator; /* next item */
      }
      printf("\n");
}


void single_link(int num,struct link link_list [])
/* link items in list in ascending order */
{
    int link_position = 0,
        previous = 0, /* previous link locator */
        remember; /* current link locator being replaced */
    do {
       /* previous locator */
       previous = link_position;
       /* current locator */
       link_position = link_list [link_position].locator;
    }
    while (link_list [link_position].item < num &&
                                    link_position != 0);

    printf("\n"); /* start new activity line */
    link_list [0].item++; /* new item */
    /* store current item */
    link_list [link_list [0].item].item = num;
    if (link_list [link_position].item >= num) {
       /* we didn't reach the end of the list so insert the
          new item */
       remember = link_position; /* save current locator */
       /* link previous item to current data */
       link_list [previous].locator = link_list [0].item;
       /* link current item to data that used to follow
          previous item */
       link_list [link_list [0].item].locator = remember;
    }
    else {
       /* append the new data to the end of the list */
       link_list [link_list [0].item].locator = 0;
       /* link the last item in the old list to the new
          data */
```

```
            link_list [previous].locator = link_list [0].item;
    }
}


int rand(void)
{
    time_t ltime;
    int rnd;
    static unsigned long value = 0;
    unsigned long temp,
            increment = 271819,
            multiplier = 314159,
            modulus = 100001,
            int_mod = 32767;

    if (value == 0) { /* first call to function */
        time(&ltime);
        value = (multiplier * ltime + increment);
        value = value % modulus;
        temp = value;
        temp = value % int_mod;
        rnd = (int) temp;
    }
    else {
        value = (multiplier * value + increment);
        value = value % modulus;
        temp = value;
        temp = temp % int_mod;
        rnd = (int) temp;
    }
    return(rnd);
}

void clrscr(void)
/* clear the screen */
{
    union REGS regs;

    regs.h.ah = 6;                      /* bios function */
    regs.h.al = 0;                      /* clear entire screen */
    regs.h.bh = 7;                      /* normal attribute */
```

```
        regs.h.ch = 0;                    /* upper row position */
        regs.h.cl = 0;                    /* upper-left column
                                              position */
        regs.h.dh = 24;                   /* lowest row */
        regs.h.dl = 79;                   /* rightmost column */
        int86(0x10,&regs,&regs);          /* bios interrupt number */
} /* end function clear screen */
```

FINDING A SPECIFIC RECORD

This next example shows how to locate an item in a linked list.

```
/* Chapter 8, Example 2, QuickC, 4/19/88
   Single linked list, ascending order.
   Find a record. */

#include <stdio.h>
#include <stdlib.h>
#include <conio.h>
#include <bios.h>

#define COUNT 10

struct link {
   int item;
   int locator;
   }; /* structure of linked record */

/* list of items to store */
int data [10] = {7,9,4,2,1,8,5,45,23,12},
   /* list of items to search for */
   search_for [5] = {8,1,10,50,5};

/* function prototypes */
void single_link(int num,struct link link_list []);
void findlink(int num,int *found,struct link link_list []);
void main(void);
void clrscr(void);
```

```
void main()
{
   int true = 1, /* boolean variable */
       false = 0,
       found, /* used when searching for item */
       counter;
   struct link link_list [COUNT + 1]; /* holds item and link
                                          locator */


   /* initialize array */
   for (counter = 0;counter <= COUNT;counter++) {
      link_list [counter].item = 0;
      link_list [counter].locator = 0;
   }

   link_list [0].item = 0; /* number of items in list */

   /* get numbers and link them */
   for (counter = 0;counter < COUNT;counter++)  {
      single_link(data [counter],link_list);
   }

   /* display the results */
   clrscr();
   counter = link_list [0].locator; /* link locator to first
                                        item in list */
   while (counter != 0) {
      printf("%d ",link_list [counter].item);
      counter = link_list [counter].locator; /* next item */
   }
   printf("\n");

   /* search for items */
   for (counter = 0;counter <= 4;counter++) {
      found = false; /* default */
      printf("Looking for %d\n",search_for [counter]);
      findlink(search_for [counter],&found,link_list);
      if (found == true) /* found it */
         printf("Found %d\n",search_for [counter]);
```

```
            else /* didn't find it */
                printf("Didn't find %d\n",search_for [counter]);
    }
}


void single_link(int num,struct link link_list [])
/* link items in list in ascending order */
{
    int link_position = 0,
        previous = 0, /* previous link locator */
        remember; /* current link locator being replaced */

    do {
        printf("."); /* indicate activity */
        previous = link_position; /* previous locator */
        /* current locator */
        link_position = link_list [link_position].locator;
    }
    while (link_list [link_position].item < num &&
                                    link_position != 0);


    printf("\n"); /* start new activity line */
    link_list [0].item++; /* new item */
    /* store current item */
    link_list [link_list [0].item].item = num;
    if (link_list [link_position].item >= num) {
        /* we didn't reach the end of the list so insert the
            new item */
        remember = link_position; /* save current locator */
        /* link previous item to current data */
        link_list [previous].locator = link_list [0].item;
        /* link current item to data that used to follow
            previous item */
        link_list [link_list [0].item].locator = remember;
    }
    else {
        /* append the new data to the end of the list */
        link_list [link_list [0].item].locator = 0;
```

```
                /* link the last item in the old list to the new
                    data */
                link_list [previous].locator = link_list [0].item;
            }
    }


    void findlink(int num,int *found,struct link link_list [])
    /* search for an item in a single linked list */
    {
        int true = 1, /* boolean variable */
            locate; /* link locator */

        /* start of chain */
        locate = link_list [0].locator;
        /* find item or next item */
        while (locate != 0 && link_list [locate].item < num)
            locate = link_list [locate].locator;
        if (link_list [locate].item == num)
            *found = true;
    }


    void clrscr(void)
    /* clear the screen */
    {
        union REGS regs;

        regs.h.ah = 6;                   /* bios function */
        regs.h.al = 0;                   /* clear entire screen */
        regs.h.bh = 7;                   /* normal attribute */
        regs.h.ch = 0;                   /* upper row position */
        regs.h.cl = 0;                   /* upper-left column
                                            position */
        regs.h.dh = 24;                  /* lowest row */
        regs.h.dl = 79;                  /* rightmost column */
        int86(0x10,&regs,&regs);         /* bios interrupt number */
    } /* end function clear screen */
```

DELETING AN ITEM FROM A LINKED LIST

The next example adds a subprogram to delete an item from a linked list.

```
/* Chapter 8, Example 3, QuickC, 4/19/88
   Single linked list, ascending order.
   Find a record and delete it. */

#include <stdio.h>
#include <stdlib.h>
#include <conio.h>
#include <bios.h>

#define COUNT 10

struct link {
   int item;
   int locator;
   }; /* structure of linked record */

/* list of items to search for */
int search_for [5] = {8,1,10,50,5},
   /* list of items to store */
   data [10] = {7,9,4,2,1,8,5,45,23,12};

/* function prototypes */
void single_link(int num,struct link link_list []);
void delete_slink(int num,int *found,
               struct link link_list []);
void main(void);
void clrscr(void);


void main()
{
   int true = 1, /* boolean variable */
      false = 0,
```

```
            found, /* used when searching for item */
            counter;
   struct link link_list [COUNT + 1]; /* holds item and link
                                         locator */


   /* initialize array */
   for (counter = 0;counter <= COUNT;counter++) {
      link_list [counter].item = 0;
      link_list [counter].locator = 0;
   }

   link_list [0].item = 0; /* number of items in list */

   /* get numbers and link them */
   for (counter = 0;counter < COUNT;counter++)  {
      single_link(data [counter],link_list);
   }

   /* display list of items */
   printf("\n"); /* to make following clrscr() work */
   clrscr();
   printf("The list is now\n");
   counter = link_list [0].locator; /* link locator to first
                                        item in list */


   while (counter != 0) {
      printf("%d ",link_list [counter].item);
      counter = link_list [counter].locator; /* next item */
   }
   printf("\n");

   /* search for items */
   for (counter = 0;counter <= 4;counter++) {
      found = false; /* default */
      printf("Looking for %d\n",search_for [counter]);
      delete_slink(search_for [counter],&found,link_list);
      if (found == true) /* found it */
         printf("Found and deleted %d\n",
                                     search_for [counter]);

      else /* didn't find it */
         printf("Didn't find %d\n",search_for [counter]);
   }
```

```
    /* display new list minus deleted items */
    printf("The list is now\n");
    counter = link_list [0].locator; /* link locator to first
                                         item in list */
    while (counter != 0) {
       printf("%d ",link_list [counter].item);
       counter = link_list [counter].locator; /* next item */
    }
    printf("\n");
}



void single_link(int num,struct link link_list [])
/* link items in list in ascending order */
{
    int link_position = 0,
        previous = 0, /* previous link locator */
        remember; /* current link locator being replaced */

    do {
       printf("."); /* indicate activity */
       previous = link_position; /* previous locator */
       /* current locator */
       link_position = link_list [link_position].locator;
    }
    while (link_list [link_position].item < num &&
                                     link_position != 0);

    printf("\n"); /* start new activity line */
    link_list [0].item++; /* new item */
    /* store current item */
    link_list [link_list [0].item].item = num;
    if (link_list [link_position].item >= num) {
       /* we didn't reach the end of the list so insert the
           new item */
       remember = link_position; /* save current locator */
       /* link previous item to current data */
       link_list [previous].locator = link_list [0].item;
       /* link current item to data that used to follow
           previous item */
       link_list [link_list [0].item].locator = remember;
    }
```

```
      else {
         /* append the new data to the end of the list */
         link_list [link_list [0].item].locator = 0;
         /* link the last item in the old list to the new
            data */
         link_list [previous].locator = link_list [0].item;
      }
   }


void delete_slink(int num,int *found,
                    struct link link_list [])
/* search for an item in a single linked list */
{
   int true = 1, /* boolean variable */
       previous = 0,
        locate = 0; /* link locator */

   /* start of chain */
   do {
      previous = locate;
      locate = link_list [locate].locator;
   }
   while (link_list [locate].item  < num && locate != 0);

   /* found? */
   if (link_list [locate].item == num) {
      link_list [locate].item = 0;
      link_list [previous].locator =
                                   link_list [locate].locator;
      *found = true;
   }
}



void clrscr(void)
/* clear the screen */
{
   union REGS regs;

   regs.h.ah = 6;                    /* bios function */
   regs.h.al = 0;                    /* clear entire screen */
   regs.h.bh = 7;                    /* normal attribute */
```

```
      regs.h.ch = 0;                    /* upper row position */
      regs.h.cl = 0;                    /* upper-left column
                                            position */

      regs.h.dh = 24;                   /* lowest row */
      regs.h.dl = 79;                   /* rightmost column */
      int86(0x10,&regs,&regs);          /* bios interrupt number */
} /* end function clear screen */
```

SAVING THE DELETED RECORD POSITION

This next example builds on those preceding by saving the position of the deleted records so that they can be used again.

```
/* Chapter 8, Example 4, QuickC, 4/19/88
   Single linked list, ascending order.
   Find a record and delete it. Then put the
   location of the deleted item in a list. */

#include <stdio.h>
#include <stdlib.h>
#include <conio.h>
#include <bios.h>

#define COUNT 10

struct link {
   int item;
   int locator;
   }; /* structure of linked record */

/* list of items to search for */
int search_for [5] = {8,1,10,50,5},
   /* list of items to store */
   data [10] = {7,9,4,2,1,8,5,45,23,12},
   /* list of items to replace deleted items */
   replace [5] = {14,15,16,17};

/* function prototypes */
void single_dlink(int num,int deleted [],
                  struct link link_list []);
```

```
void delete_sdlink(int num,int *found,int deleted [],
                   struct link link_list []);
void main(void);
void clrscr(void);


void main()
{
   int true = 1, /* boolean variable */
      false = 0,
      found, /* used when searching for item */
      counter,
      /* list of deleted items */
      deleted [COUNT];
   struct link link_list [COUNT + 1]; /* holds item and link
                                         locator */

   /* initialize array */
   for (counter = 0;counter <=COUNT;counter++) {
      link_list [counter].item = 0;
      link_list [counter].locator = 0;
   }

   link_list [0].item = 0; /* number of items in list */
   deleted [0] = 0; /* number of items in deleted list */

   /* get numbers and link them */
   for (counter = 0;counter < COUNT;counter++)  {
      single_dlink(data [counter],deleted,link_list);
   }

   /* display list of items */
   printf("\n"); /* to make following clrscr() work */
   clrscr();
   printf("The list is now\n");
   counter = link_list [0].locator; /* link locator to first
                                       item in list */
   while (counter != 0) {
      printf("%d ",link_list [counter].item);
      counter = link_list [counter].locator; /* next item */
   }
   printf("\n");
```

```
/* search for items */
for (counter = 0;counter <= 4;counter++) {
   found = false; /* default */
   printf("Looking for %d\n",search_for [counter]);
   delete_sdlink(search_for [counter],&found,deleted,
                                           link_list);
   if (found == true) /* found it */
   printf("Found and deleted %d\n",search_for [counter]);
   else /* didn't find it */
   printf("Didn't find %d\n",search_for [counter]);
}

/* display new list minus deleted items */
printf("The list is now\n");
counter = link_list [0].locator; /* link locator to first
                                     item in list */
while (counter != 0) {
   printf("%d ",link_list [counter].item);
   counter = link_list [counter].locator; /* next item */
}
printf("\n");

printf("now we add four items to replace deleted
items\n");
for (counter = 0;counter <= 3;counter++)  {
   printf("Adding item %d\n",replace [counter]);
   single_dlink(replace [counter],deleted,link_list);
}

/* new list with replaced items */
printf("The list is now\n");
counter = link_list [0].locator; /* link locator to first
                                     item in list */
while (counter != 0) {
   printf("%d ",link_list [counter].item);
   counter = link_list [counter].locator; /* next item */
}
printf("\n");
}


void single_dlink(int num,int deleted [],
                  struct link link_list [])
```

```
/* link items in list in ascending order */
{
    int link_position = 0,
        previous = 0, /* previous link locator */
        remember; /* current link locator being replaced */

    do {
        printf("."); /* indicate activity */
        previous = link_position; /* previous locator */
        /* current locator */
        link_position = link_list [link_position].locator;
    }
    while (link_list [link_position].item < num &&
                                    link_position != 0);

    printf("\n"); /* start new activity line */
    if (link_list [link_position].item >= num) {
        /* we didn't reach the end of the list so insert the
            new item */
        remember = link_position; /* save current locator */
        if (deleted [0] > 0) {
            /* replace last deleted item with new item */
            link_list [deleted [deleted [0]]].item = num;
            /* change previous pointer to point to new item */
            link_list [previous].locator =
                                    deleted [deleted [0]];
            /* link new item to data that used to follow
                previous item */
            link_list [deleted [deleted [0]]].locator =
                                                remember;
            /* one less deleted item */
            deleted [0]--;
        }
        else {
            /* link previous item to current data */
            link_list [0].item++;
            link_list [link_list [0].item].item = num;
            link_list [previous].locator = link_list [0].item;
            /* link current item to data that used to follow
                previous item */
```

```
                link_list [link_list [0].item].locator = remember;
            }
        }
        else {
            if (deleted [0] > 0) {
                /* replace last deleted item with new item */
                link_list [deleted [deleted [0]]].item = num;
                /* change previous item pointer to indicate new
                    item */
                link_list [previous].locator =
                                            deleted [deleted [0]];
                /* no items follow */
                link_list [deleted [deleted [0]]].locator = 0;
                /* one less deleted item */
                deleted [0]--;
            }
            else {
                /* append the new data to the end of the list */
                    link_list [0].item++;
                link_list [link_list [0].item].item = num;
                link_list [link_list [0].item].locator = 0;
                /* link the last item in the old list to the new
                    data */
                link_list [previous].locator = link_list [0].item;
            }
        }
    }


void delete_sdlink(int num,int *found,int deleted [],
                    struct link link_list [])
/* search for an item in a single linked list */
{
    int true = 1, /* boolean variable */
        previous = 0,
        locate = 0; /* link locator */

    /* start of chain */
    do {
        previous = locate;
```

```
      locate = link_list [locate].locator;
   }
   while (link_list [locate].item  < num && locate != 0);

   /* found? */
   if (link_list [locate].item == num) {
      link_list [locate].item = 0;
      link_list [previous].locator =
                           link_list [locate].locator;
      deleted [0]++;
      deleted [deleted [0]] = locate;
      *found = true;
   }
}


void clrscr(void)
/* clear the screen */
{
   union REGS regs;

   regs.h.ah = 6;                    /* bios function */
   regs.h.al = 0;                    /* clear entire screen */
   regs.h.bh = 7;                    /* normal attribute */
   regs.h.ch = 0;                    /* upper row position */
   regs.h.cl = 0;                    /* upper-left column
                                        position */
   regs.h.dh = 24;                   /* lowest row */
   regs.h.dl = 79;                   /* rightmost column */
   int86(0x10,&regs,&regs);          /* bios interrupt number */
} /* end function clear screen */
```

LINKING IN DESCENDING ORDER

This next example is like Example 1, but links in descending
alphabetical order.

```
/* Chapter 8, Example 5, QuickC, 4/19/88
   Single linked list, descending order */

#include <stdio.h>
#include <stdlib.h>
#include <conio.h>
#include <bios.h>
#include <time.h>

#define COUNT 50

struct link {
   int item;
   int locator;
   };

/* function prototypes */
void single_link(int num,struct link link_list []);
void main(void);
void clrscr(void);
int rand(void);


void main()
{
   int num,
       counter;
   struct link link_list [COUNT + 1]; /* holds item and link
locator */

   /* initialize array */
   for (counter = 0;counter <= COUNT;counter++) {
      link_list [counter].item = 0;
      link_list [counter].locator = 0;
   }

   link_list [0].item = 0; /* number of items in list */
```

```
/* load numbers to link */
for (counter = 1;counter <= COUNT;counter++)  {
   num = rand();
   single_link(num,link_list);
}

/* display the results */
printf("\n"); /* to make following clrscr() work */
clrscr();
counter = link_list [0].locator; /* link locator to first
                                     item in list */
while (counter != 0) {
   printf("%d ",link_list [counter].item);
   counter = link_list [counter].locator; /* next item */
}
printf("\n");
}


void single_link(int num,struct link link_list [])
/* link items in list in descending order */
{
   int link_position = 0,
       previous = 0, /* previous link locator */
       remember; /* current link locator being replaced */

   do {
      printf("."); /* indicate activity */
      previous = link_position; /* previous locator */
      /* current locator */
      link_position = link_list [link_position].locator;
   }
   while (link_list [link_position].item > num &&
                                   link_position != 0);

   printf("\n"); /* start new activity line */
   link_list [0].item++; /* new item */
   /* store current item */
   link_list [link_list [0].item].item = num;
   if (link_list [link_position].item <= num) {
      /* we didn't reach the end of the list so insert the
         new item */
```

```
         remember = link_position; /* save current locator */
         /* link previous item to current data */
         link_list [previous].locator = link_list [0].item;
         /* link current item to data that used to follow
            previous item */
         link_list [link_list [0].item].locator = remember;
      }
      else {
         /* append the new data to the end of the list */
         link_list [link_list [0].item].locator = 0;
         /* link the last item in the old list to the new
            data */
         link_list [previous].locator = link_list [0].item;
      }
   }
}


int rand(void)
{
   time_t ltime;
   int rnd;
   static unsigned long value = 0;
   unsigned long temp,
            increment = 271819,
            multiplier = 314159,
            modulus = 100001,
            int_mod = 32767;

   if (value == 0) {
      time(&ltime);
      value = (multiplier * ltime + increment);
      value = value % modulus;
      temp = value;
      temp = value % int_mod;
      rnd = (int) temp;
   }
   else {
      value = (multiplier * value + increment);
      value = value % modulus;
      temp = value;
      temp = temp % int_mod;
      rnd = (int) temp;
```

```
      }
      return(rnd);
   }

void clrscr(void)
/* clear the screen */
{
   union REGS regs;

   regs.h.ah = 6;                    /* bios function */
   regs.h.al = 0;                    /* clear entire screen */
   regs.h.bh = 7;                    /* normal attribute */
   regs.h.ch = 0;                    /* upper row position */
   regs.h.cl = 0;                    /* upper-left column
                                         position */

   regs.h.dh = 24;                   /* lowest row */
   regs.h.dl = 79;                   /* rightmost column */
   int86(0x10,&regs,&regs);          /* bios interrupt number */
} /* end function clear screen */
```

LINKING IN RANDOM ACCESS FILES

This next program is a modification of Example 1 that permits
linked lists to be used in random access files. The program looks
deceptively simple, but it took a great deal of time to get a version
that worked correctly. I'll leave it to you to add the subprograms
of Examples 2, 3, 4, and 5. I made the link pointer field an integer;
if you think your files will be larger than 32,767 records, then
you may wish to make it long integer instead.

```
/* Chapter 8, Example 6, QuickC, 2/20/88
   Single linked list, ascending order,
   random access file */

#include <stdio.h>
#include <stdlib.h>
#include <conio.h>
#include <string.h>
```

```c
#include <io.h>
#include <bios.h>
#include <time.h>

#define COUNT 100L

struct link {
   long item;
   long locator;
   };

/* function prototypes */
void single_ralink(long num,struct link *link_record,
                   FILE *stream);
void complain(void);
void main(void);
void clrscr(void);
int rand(void);
void gotoxy(int x,int y);


void main()
{
   size_t size = sizeof(struct link);
   FILE *stream;
   char dest_file [13];
   long num,
        counter;
   struct link link_record;

   strcpy(&dest_file [0],"ch8_6.dat");

   /* open the file to hold data */
   if ((stream = fopen(dest_file,"w+b")) == NULL) {
      putch(7); /* beep */
      gotoxy(10,24);
      printf("Cannot open file\n");
      exit(1);
   }

   link_record.item = 0L; /* number of items in list */
   link_record.locator = 0L;
```

```
        if ((fseek(stream,0L,SEEK_SET)) != 0)
            complain();
        fwrite(&link_record,size,1,stream);

        /* load numbers to link */
        for (counter = 1L;counter <= COUNT;counter++)  {
            num = (long) rand();
            single_ralink(num,&link_record,stream);
        }

        /* display the results */
        clrscr();
        if ((fseek(stream,0L,SEEK_SET)) != 0)
            complain();
        fread(&link_record,size,1,stream);
        counter = link_record.locator; /* link locator to first
                                             item in list */
        while (counter != 0L) {
            if ((fseek(stream,counter * (long) size,
                                         SEEK_SET)) != 0)
                complain();
            fread(&link_record,size,1,stream);
            printf("%ld ",link_record.item);
            counter = link_record.locator; /* next item */
        }
        printf("\n");

        fclose(stream);
}


void single_ralink(long num,struct link *link_record,
                    FILE *stream)
/* link items in list in descending order */
{
    size_t size = sizeof(struct link);
    long link_position = 0L,
         previous = 0L, /* previous link locator */
         current_size,
         remember; /* current link locator being replaced */
```

```
do {
   printf("."); /* indicate activity */
   previous = link_position; /* previous locator */
   if ((fseek(stream,link_position * (long) size,
                                      SEEK_SET)) != 0)
      complain();
   fread(link_record,size,1,stream);
   /* current locator */
   link_position = link_record->locator;
   /* read to previous item or end of list */
   if ((fseek(stream,link_position * (long) size,
                                      SEEK_SET)) != 0)
      complain();
   fread(link_record,size,1,stream);
}
while (link_record->item < num && link_position != 0L);

printf("\n"); /* start new activity line */
/* increment record count */
if ((fseek(stream,0L,SEEK_SET)) != 0)
   complain();
fread(link_record,size,1,stream);
link_record->item++; /* update record count */
current_size = link_record->item;
/* save new count */
if ((fseek(stream,0L,SEEK_SET)) != 0)
   complain();
fwrite(link_record,size,1,stream);

/* get new record from list */
if ((fseek(stream,current_size * (long) size,
                                   SEEK_SET)) != 0)
   complain();
fread(link_record,size,1,stream);

/* store current item */
link_record->item = num;
/* save new item */
if ((fseek(stream,current_size * (long) size,
                                   SEEK_SET)) != 0)
```

```
        complain();
    fwrite(link_record,size,1,stream);

    /* set the links */
    if ((fseek(stream,link_position * (long) size,
                                    SEEK_SET)) != 0)
        complain();
    fread(link_record,size,1,stream);
    if (link_record->item >= num) {
        /* we didn't reach the end of the list so insert the
            new item */
        remember = link_position; /* save current locator */
        /* link previous item to current data */
        if ((fseek(stream,previous * (long) size,
                                    SEEK_SET)) != 0)
            complain();
        fread(link_record,size,1,stream);
        link_record->locator = current_size;
        if ((fseek(stream,previous * (long) size,
                                    SEEK_SET)) != 0)
            complain();
        fwrite(link_record,size,1,stream);

        /* link current item to data that used to follow
            previous item */
        if ((fseek(stream,current_size * (long) size,
                                    SEEK_SET)) != 0)
            complain();
        fread(link_record,size,1,stream);
        link_record->locator = remember;
        if ((fseek(stream,current_size * (long) size,
                                    SEEK_SET)) != 0)
            complain();
        fwrite(link_record,size,1,stream);
    }
    else {
        /* append the new data to the end of the list */
        if ((fseek(stream,current_size * (long) size,
                                    SEEK_SET)) != 0)
            complain();
        fread(link_record,size,1,stream);
        link_record->locator = 0L;
```

```
         if ((fseek(stream,current_size * (long) size,
                                        SEEK_SET)) != 0)
            complain();
         fwrite(link_record,size,1,stream);

         /* link the last item in the old list to the new
            data */
         if ((fseek(stream,previous * (long) size,
                                        SEEK_SET)) != 0)
            complain();
         fread(link_record,size,1,stream);
         link_record->locator = current_size;
         if ((fseek(stream,previous * (long) size,
                                        SEEK_SET)) != 0)
            complain();
         fwrite(link_record,size,1,stream);
      }
}


void complain(void)
/* fseek didn't work */
{
   putch(7); /* beep */
   gotoxy(10,24);
   printf("Cannot position in file\n");
   exit(1);
}



int rand(void)
{
   time_t ltime;
   int rnd;
   static unsigned long value = 0;
   unsigned long temp,
           increment = 271819,
           multiplier = 314159,
           modulus = 100001,
           int_mod = 32767;

   if (value == 0) {
      time(&ltime);
```

```
            value = (multiplier * ltime + increment);
            value = value % modulus;
            temp = value;
            temp = value % int_mod;
            rnd = (int) temp;
        }
        else {
            value = (multiplier * value + increment);
            value = value % modulus;
            temp = value;
            temp = temp % int_mod;
            rnd = (int) temp;
        }
        return(rnd);
    }


    void clrscr(void)
    /* clear the screen */
    {
        union REGS regs;

        regs.h.ah = 6;                  /* bios function */
        regs.h.al = 0;                  /* clear entire screen */
        regs.h.bh = 7;                  /* normal attribute */
        regs.h.ch = 0;                  /* upper row position */
        regs.h.cl = 0;                  /* upper-left column
                                            position */
        regs.h.dh = 24;                 /* lowest row */
        regs.h.dl = 79;                 /* rightmost column */
        int86(0x10,&regs,&regs);        /* bios interrupt number */
    } /* end function clear screen */


    void gotoxy(int x,int y)
    /* position cursor */
    {

        union REGS regs;


        regs.h.ah = 2;                  /* bios function */
        regs.h.dh = (char) y;           /* row */
```

```
    regs.h.dl = (char) x;          /* column */
    regs.h.bh = 0;                 /* video page number */
    int86(0x10,&regs,&regs);       /* bios interrupt number */
} /* end function gotoxy */
```

This program took 33 minutes, 48 seconds to link 1000 records, about 60 times longer than linking in an array. Thus, it would seem logical to use arrays when linking if the number of records will fit in memory. Moreover, using the insertion sort is slightly faster than linking if you are using an array (21 seconds vs. 26 seconds), but much faster if you are using a random access file (344 seconds vs. 2009 seconds).

Incidentally, all the random access programs benchmarked so far ran totally in the 20 disk buffers assigned in my Config.sys file. If the disk had to be accessed for each fetch, comparison, and save, then the programs would have run a great deal slower. No disk cache was used.

DOUBLE LINKS

Sometimes it is useful to have a list of items that you can retrieve in either ascending or descending order. This is called a doubly linked list. The program follows.

```
/* Chapter 8, Example 7, QuickC, 4/19/88
   Double linked list, ascending order */

#include <stdio.h>
#include <stdlib.h>
#include <conio.h>
#include <bios.h>
#include <time.h>

#define COUNT 100 /* number of items in list */

struct link {
    int item; /* item in list */
    int forward; /* ascending pointer */
    int reverse; /* descending pointer */
    };
```

```
/* function prototypes */
void double_link(int num,struct link link_list []);
void main(void);
void clrscr(void);
int rand(void);

void main()
{
    int num,
        counter;
    struct link link_list [COUNT + 1]; /* holds item and link
                                            locator */

    /* initialize array */
    for (counter = 0;counter <= COUNT;counter++) {
        link_list [counter].item = 0;
        link_list [counter].forward = 0;
        link_list [counter].reverse = 0;
    }

    link_list [0].item = 0; /* number of items in list */

    /* load numbers to link */
    for (counter = 1;counter <= COUNT;counter++)   {
        num = rand();
        double_link(num,link_list);
    }

    /* display the results */
    clrscr();
    printf("Ascending\n");
    counter = link_list [0].forward; /* link locator to first
                                            item in list */

    while (counter != 0) {
        printf("%d ",link_list [counter].item);
        counter = link_list [counter].forward; /* next item */
    }
    printf("\n");

    printf("Descending\n");
    counter = link_list [0].reverse; /* link locator to last
                                            item in list */
```

```
   while (counter != 0) {
      printf("%d ",link_list [counter].item);
      counter = link_list [counter].reverse; /* next item */
   }
   printf("\n");
}


void double_link(int num,struct link link_list [])
/* link items in list in ascending and descending order */
{
   int link_position = 0,
       previous = 0, /* previous link locator */
       remember; /* current link locator being replaced */

   do {
      printf("."); /* indicate activity */
      previous = link_position; /* previous locator */
      /* current locator */
      link_position = link_list [link_position].forward;
   }
   while (link_list [link_position].item < num &&
                                  link_position != 0);


   printf("\n"); /* start new activity line */
   link_list [0].item++; /* new item */
   /* store current item */
   link_list [link_list [0].item].item = num;
   if (link_list [link_position].item >= num) {
      /* we didn't reach the end of the list so insert the
         new item */
      remember = link_position; /* save current locator */
      /* link previous item to current data */
      link_list [previous].forward = link_list [0].item;
      /* link current item to data that used to follow
         previous item */
      link_list [link_list [0].item].forward = remember;
      /* backlink from following item */
      link_list [remember].reverse = link_list [0].item;
      /* backlink to previous item */
      link_list [link_list [0].item].reverse = previous;
```

```
      }
      else {
         /* append the new data to the end of the list */
         link_list [link_list [0].item].forward = 0;
         /* link the last item in the old list to the new
            data */
         link_list [previous].forward = link_list [0].item;
         /* backlink to previous item */
         link_list [link_list [0].item].reverse = previous;
         /* provide a starting point */
         link_list [0].reverse = link_list [0].item;
      }
}


int rand(void)
/* random number generator */
{
   time_t ltime;
   int rnd;
   static unsigned long value = 0;
   unsigned long temp,
            increment = 271819,
            multiplier = 314159,
            modulus = 100001,
            int_mod = 32767;

   if (value == 0) {
      time(&ltime);
      value = (multiplier * ltime + increment);
      value = value % modulus;
      temp = value;
      temp = value % int_mod;
      rnd = (int) temp;
   }
   else {
      value = (multiplier * value + increment);
      value = value % modulus;
      temp = value;
```

```
        temp = temp % int_mod;
        rnd = (int) temp;
    }
    return(rnd);
}


void clrscr(void)
/* clear the screen */
{
    union REGS regs;

    regs.h.ah = 6;                  /* bios function */
    regs.h.al = 0;                  /* clear entire screen */
    regs.h.bh = 7;                  /* normal attribute */
    regs.h.ch = 0;                  /* upper row position */
    regs.h.cl = 0;                  /* upper-left column
                                       position */
    regs.h.dh = 24;                 /* lowest row */
    regs.h.dl = 79;                 /* rightmost column */
    int86(0x10,&regs,&regs);        /* bios interrupt number */
} /* end function clear screen */
```

DOUBLE LINKING IN A RANDOM ACCESS FILE

Here is the previous example modified to use a random access file.

```
/* Chapter 8, Example 8, QuickC, 4/20/88
   Double linked list, ascending and descending order,
   random access file */

#include <stdio.h>
#include <stdlib.h>
#include <conio.h>
#include <string.h>
#include <io.h>
```

```
#include <time.h>
#include <bios.h>
#include <string.h>

#define COUNT 50L

struct link {
    long item;
    long forward;
    long reverse;
    };

/* function prototypes */
void double_ralink(long num,struct link *link_record,
                   FILE *stream);
void complain(void);
void main(void);
void gotoxy(int x,int y);
void clrscr(void);
int rand(void);


void main()
{
    size_t size = sizeof(struct link);
    FILE *stream;
    char dest_file [13];
    long num,
        counter,
        var_size = (long) sizeof(struct link);
    struct link link_record;

    strcpy(&dest_file [0],"ch8_8.dat");

    /* open the file to hold data */
    if ((stream = fopen(dest_file,"w+b")) == NULL) {
        putch(7); /* beep */
        gotoxy(10,24);
        printf("Cannot open file\n");
        exit(1);
    }
```

```
link_record.item = 0L; /* number of items in list */
link_record.forward = 0L;
if ((fseek(stream,0L,SEEK_SET)) != 0)
   complain();
fwrite(&link_record,size,1,stream);

/* load numbers to link */
for (counter = 1L;counter <= COUNT;counter++)  {
   num = (long) rand();
   double_ralink(num,&link_record,stream);
}

/* display the results */
clrscr();
printf("Ascending\n");
if ((fseek(stream,0L,SEEK_SET)) != 0)
   complain();
fread(&link_record,size,1,stream);
counter = link_record.forward; /* link locator to first
                                        item in list */
while (counter != 0L) {
   if ((fseek(stream,counter * var_size,SEEK_SET)) != 0)
      complain();
   fread(&link_record,size,1,stream);
   printf("%ld ",link_record.item);
   counter = link_record.forward; /* next item */
}
printf("\n");

printf("Descending\n");
if ((fseek(stream,0L,SEEK_SET)) != 0)
   complain();
fread(&link_record,size,1,stream);
counter = link_record.reverse; /* counter to last item in
                                        list */
while (counter != 0L) {
   if ((fseek(stream,counter * var_size,SEEK_SET)) != 0)
      complain();
   fread(&link_record,size,1,stream);
   printf("%ld ",link_record.item);
```

```
        counter = link_record.reverse; /* previous item */
   }
   printf("\n");

   fclose(stream);
}


void double_ralink(long num,struct link *link_record,
                    FILE *stream)
/* link items in list in descending order */
{
   size_t size = sizeof(struct link);
   long var_size = (long) sizeof(struct link),
        link_position = 0L,
        previous = 0L, /* previous link locator */
        current_size,
        remember; /* current link locator being replaced */

   do {
      printf("."); /* indicate activity */
      previous = link_position; /* previous locator */
      if ((fseek(stream,link_position * var_size,
                                        SEEK_SET)) != 0)
         complain();
      fread(link_record,size,1,stream);
      /* current locator */
      link_position = link_record->forward;
      if ((fseek(stream,link_position * var_size,
                                        SEEK_SET)) != 0)
         complain();
      fread(link_record,size,1,stream);
   }
   while (link_record->item < num && link_position != 0L);

   printf("\n"); /* start new activity line */
   /* get current record count */
   if ((fseek(stream,0L,SEEK_SET)) != 0)
      complain();
   fread(link_record,size,1,stream);
```

```
link_record->item++; /* update count */
/* newly added record position */
current_size = link_record->item;
/* save new record count */
if ((fseek(stream,0L,SEEK_SET)) != 0)
   complain();
fwrite(link_record,size,1,stream);

/* get record to contain new item */
if ((fseek(stream,current_size * var_size,
                                  SEEK_SET)) != 0)
   complain();
fread(link_record,size,1,stream);

/* store current item */
link_record->item = num;
if ((fseek(stream,current_size * var_size,
                                  SEEK_SET)) != 0)
   complain();
fwrite(link_record,size,1,stream);

/* set new links */
if ((fseek(stream,link_position * var_size,
                                  SEEK_SET)) != 0)
   complain();
fread(link_record,size,1,stream);
if (link_record->item >= num) {
   /* we didn't reach the end of the list so insert the
      new item */
   remember = link_position; /* save current locator */

   /* link previous item to current data */
   if ((fseek(stream,previous * var_size,SEEK_SET)) != 0)
      complain();
   fread(link_record,size,1,stream);
   link_record->forward = current_size;
   if ((fseek(stream,previous * var_size,SEEK_SET)) != 0)
      complain();
   fwrite(link_record,size,1,stream);
```

```
            /* link current item to data that used to follow
               previous item */
            if ((fseek(stream,current_size * var_size,
                                                SEEK_SET)) != 0)
               complain();
            fread(link_record,size,1,stream);
            link_record->forward = remember;
            if ((fseek(stream,current_size * var_size,
                                                SEEK_SET)) != 0)
               complain();
            fwrite(link_record,size,1,stream);

            /* backlink from following record */
            if ((fseek(stream,remember * var_size,SEEK_SET)) != 0)
               complain();
            fread(link_record,size,1,stream);
            link_record->reverse = current_size;
            if ((fseek(stream,remember * var_size,SEEK_SET)) != 0)
               complain();
            fwrite(link_record,size,1,stream);

            /* backlink to previous item */
            if ((fseek(stream,current_size * var_size,
                                                SEEK_SET)) != 0)
               complain();
            fread(link_record,size,1,stream);
            link_record->reverse = previous;
            if ((fseek(stream,current_size * var_size,
                                            SEEK_SET)) != 0)
               complain();
            fwrite(link_record,size,1,stream);
         }
         else {
            /* append the new data to the end of the list */
            if ((fseek(stream,current_size * var_size,
                                            SEEK_SET)) != 0)
               complain();
            fread(link_record,size,1,stream);
```

```
link_record->forward = 0L;
if ((fseek(stream,current_size * var_size,
                                    SEEK_SET)) != 0)
    complain();
fwrite(link_record,size,1,stream);

/* link the last item in the old list to the new
   data */
if ((fseek(stream,previous * var_size,SEEK_SET)) != 0)
    complain();
fread(link_record,size,1,stream);
link_record->forward = current_size;
if ((fseek(stream,previous * var_size,SEEK_SET)) != 0)
    complain();
fwrite(link_record,size,1,stream);

/* backlink to previous item */
if ((fseek(stream,current_size * var_size,
                                    SEEK_SET)) != 0)
    complain();
fread(link_record,size,1,stream);
link_record->reverse = previous;
if ((fseek(stream,current_size * var_size,
                                    SEEK_SET)) != 0)
    complain();
fwrite(link_record,size,1,stream);

/* provide starting point */
if ((fseek(stream,0L,SEEK_SET)) != 0)
    complain();
fread(link_record,size,1,stream);
link_record->reverse = current_size;
if ((fseek(stream,0L,SEEK_SET)) != 0)
    complain();
fwrite(link_record,size,1,stream);
    }
}
```

```
void complain(void)
/* fseek didn't work */
{
   putch(7); /* beep */
   gotoxy(10,24);
   printf("Cannot position in file\n");
   exit(1);
}

int rand(void)
{
   time_t ltime;
   int rnd;
   static unsigned long value = 0;
   unsigned long temp,
           increment = 271819,
           multiplier = 314159,
           modulus = 100001,
           int_mod = 32767;

   if (value == 0) {
      time(&ltime);
      value = (multiplier * ltime + increment);
      value = value % modulus;
      temp = value;
      temp = value % int_mod;
      rnd = (int) temp;
   }
   else {
      value = (multiplier * value + increment);
      value = value % modulus;
      temp = value;
      temp = temp % int_mod;
      rnd = (int) temp;
   }
   return(rnd);
}


void clrscr(void)
/* clear the screen */
{
   union REGS regs;
```

```
        regs.h.ah = 6;                  /* bios function */
        regs.h.al = 0;                  /* clear entire screen */
        regs.h.bh = 7;                  /* normal attribute */
        regs.h.ch = 0;                  /* upper row position */
        regs.h.cl = 0;                  /* upper-left column
                                           position */
        regs.h.dh = 24;                 /* lowest row */
        regs.h.dl = 79;                 /* rightmost column */
        int86(0x10,&regs,&regs);        /* bios interrupt number */
} /* end function clear screen */


void gotoxy(int x,int y)
/* position cursor */
{

    union REGS regs;


        regs.h.ah = 2;                  /* bios function */
        regs.h.dh = (char) y;           /* row */
        regs.h.dl = (char) x;           /* column */
        regs.h.bh = 0;                  /* bios interrupt number */
        int86(0x10,&regs,&regs);        /* bios interrupt number */
} /* end function gotoxy */
```

USING POINTERS AND DYNAMIC ALLOCATION

This final version of the linked list uses pointers to dynamically allocate memory for each record. When a record is deleted, that memory is freed. This means you are not forced to determine an array size in advance and then be unable to exceed that chosen value. The random access versions shown in Examples 6 and 8 allocate disk space dynamically, but they do not release it. However, they could be converted to a version that keeps a list of deleted records such as Example 4. Also, the random access versions are much slower than this example.

```
/* Chapter 8, Example 9, QuickC, 3/24/88
   Single linked list, ascending order.
```

```
    Find a record and delete it.
    The list is allocated dynamically.*/

#include <stdio.h>
#include <stdlib.h>
#include <conio.h>
#include <bios.h>

#define COUNT 10

struct link {
    int item;
    struct link *locator;
    }; /* structure of linked record */

/* list of items to search for */
int search_for [5] = {8,1,10,50,5},
    /* list of items to store */
    data [10] = {7,9,4,2,1,8,5,45,23,12},
    /* list of items to replace deleted items */
    replace [5] = {14,15,16,17};

/* function prototypes */
void single_ddlink(int num,struct link *head);
void delete_ddlink(int num,int *found,struct link *head);
void main(void);
void clrscr(void);


void main()
{
    int size = sizeof(struct link),
        true = 1, /* boolean variable */
        false = 0,
        found, /* used when searching for item */
        counter;
    struct link *link_position, /* current link position */
                *head; /* first item in linked list */

    /* get memory for first record in list */
    if ((head = (void *) malloc((size_t) size)) == NULL) {
        putch(7);
```

```
      printf("Out of memory for list\n");
      exit(1);
}
head->item = 0; /* number of items in list */
head->locator = NULL; /* no next item */

/* get numbers and link them */
for (counter = 0;counter < COUNT;counter++)  {
   single_ddlink(data [counter],head);
}

/* display list of items */
clrscr();
printf("The list is now\n");
link_position = head->locator; /* link locator to first
                                     item in list */

/* now display list */
while (link_position != NULL) {
   printf("%d ",link_position->item);
   /* next item */
   link_position = link_position->locator;
}
printf("\n");

/* search for items */
for (counter = 0;counter <= 4;counter++) {
   found = false; /* default */
   printf("Looking for %d\n",search_for [counter]);
   delete_ddlink(search_for [counter],&found,head);
   if (found == true) /* found it */
      printf("Found and deleted %d",search_for
                                     [counter]);
   else /* didn't find it */
      printf("Didn't find %d\n",search_for [counter]);
}

/* display new list minus deleted items */
printf("The list is now\n");
link_position = head->locator; /* link locator to first
                                     item in list */
```

```
   /* display the list */
   while (link_position != NULL) {
      printf("%d ",link_position->item);
      /* next item */
      link_position = link_position->locator;
   }
   printf("\n");

   printf("now we add four items to replace deleted
items\n");
   for (counter = 0;counter <= 3;counter++)  {
      printf("Adding item %d\n",replace [counter]);
      single_ddlink(replace [counter],head);
   }

   /* new list with replaced items */
   printf("The list is now\n");
   link_position = head->locator; /* link locator to first
                                     item in list */

   /* display the list */
   while (link_position != NULL) {
      printf("%d ",link_position->item);
      /* next item */
      link_position = link_position->locator;
   }
   printf("\n");
}

void single_ddlink(int num,struct link *head)
/* link items in list in ascending order */
{
   struct link *link_position, /* current position */
               *current, /* new added position */
               *previous, /* previous link locator */
               *remember; /* current link locator being
                             replaced */
   int size = sizeof(struct link);

   /* set to head of list */
   link_position = head->locator;
   previous = head;
```

```
/* find insertion position in list */
/* always put the NULL check FIRST! */
while (link_position != NULL &&
                        link_position->item < num) {
    printf("."); /* indicate activity */
    previous = link_position; /* previous locator */
    /* current locator */
    link_position = link_position->locator;
}

printf("\n"); /* start new activity line */

/* add the new item to the list */
if (link_position != NULL) {
    /* we didn't reach the end of the list so insert the
        new item */
    remember = link_position; /* save current locator */

    /* increment record count */
    head->item++;

    /* get memory space for new item */
    if ((current = (void *) malloc((size_t) size)) ==
                                            NULL) {
        putch(7);
        printf("Out of memory for list\n");
        exit(1);
    }

    /* store new item */
    current->item = num;

    /* link previous item to current data */
    previous->locator = current;

    /* link current item to data that used to follow
        previous item */
    current->locator = remember;
}
else {
    /* append the new data to the end of the list */
```

```
                         /* increment record count */
                         head->item++;

                         /* get storage space for new item */
                         if ((current = (void *) malloc((size_t) size)) ==
                                                                       NULL) {
                            putch(7);
                            printf("Out of memory for list\n");
                            exit(1);
                         }

                         /* store new item and link */
                         current->item = num;
                         current->locator = NULL;

                         /* link the last item in the old list to the new
                            data */
                         previous->locator = current;
                   }
             }


       void delete_ddlink(int num,int *found,struct link *head)
       /* search for an item in a single linked list */
       {
          int true = 1, /* boolean variable */
              false = 0;
          struct link *previous,
                      *locate; /* link locator */

          *found = false;
          for (;;) {
             /* no records in list */
             if (head->locator == NULL)
                break;

             /* look for item to be deleted */
             previous = head;
             locate = head->locator; /* first item in list */
             while (locate != NULL && locate->item < num) {
                previous = locate;
                locate = locate->locator;
             }
```

```
        /* found? */
        if (locate != NULL && locate->item == num) {
            /* link previous record to following record */
            previous->locator = locate->locator;

            /* release storage space for deleted record */
                free(locate);
            *found = true;
        }
        break;
    }
}


void clrscr(void)
/* clear the screen */
{
    union REGS regs;

    regs.h.ah = 6;                      /* bios function */
    regs.h.al = 0;                      /* clear entire screen */
    regs.h.bh = 7;                      /* normal attribute */
    regs.h.ch = 0;                      /* upper row position */
    regs.h.cl = 0;                      /* upper-left column
                                           position */
    regs.h.dh = 24;                     /* lowest row */
    regs.h.dl = 79;                     /* rightmost column */
    int86(0x10,&regs,&regs);            /* bios interrupt number */
} /* end function clear screen */
```

Binary Trees

Binary trees are a great deal like linked lists, in that they have pointers to the following record. However, binary trees can be created much faster and searched for specific records very quickly, very much like a binary search. Binary trees can also be printed in order. In many cases, you could replace the insertion sort or linked list with a tree.

When left pointer and right pointer are discussed in this chapter, they mean array subscripts or record numbers, they are not pointers to addresses as the word pointer is usually understood in C. When a C-type pointer is meant, I will use the asterisk or explicitly call it an address pointer. The last example will use real C-type pointers.

Each record (or node) in a binary tree has two indicators to its two following nodes: a left pointer to nodes with a value less than itself and a right pointer for nodes with a value equal to greater than itself. An example of a binary tree can be seen in Figure 9-1. As you can see, to find a value in this tree start with the root or uppermost node (this tree is planted upside down!). If the value to be found is less than the node, follow the left pointer; otherwise, follow the right pointer. If the value is in the tree, you'll quickly find it; if not, you'll come to a zero pointer. If you are adding values to the tree, just make the appropriate zero pointer at that node point to the next available record location, store the value at that next available location, and set the new node's pointers to zero.

FIGURE 9-1   Binary Tree

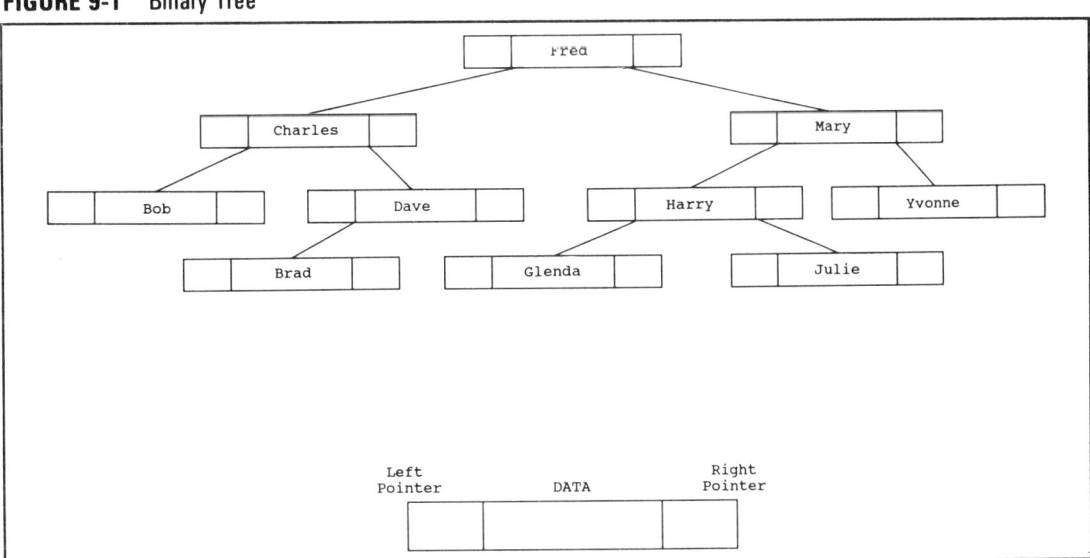

TRAVERSING A TREE

Reading and displaying the values in a tree in ascending order is far easier to describe than it is to program.

- Follow left pointers until you get to a zero pointer. You've reached the lowest value in the tree. Display it. Keep a list of the node numbers as you go.

- Using your list, back up one node. Display the value. If there is a right pointer, take it. Then look for a nonzero left pointer. If one is there, revert to the first step. Otherwise look for a nonzero right pointer. If one is there repeat this step.

- And so on.

Play computer with the example program Readtree subprogram to see how it works. As you'll see, there're a lot of repeated visits to nodes, but it works. This was a tough one for me to program.

Here's the first example. This program creates a binary tree in an array and reads it back in ascending order.

```
/* Chapter 9, Example 1, QuickC, 5/12/88
   Array binary tree

   set stack to 3072 */

#include <stdio.h>
#include <stdlib.h>
#include <bios.h>
#include <time.h>

#define COUNT 200

/* structure to contain tree elements */
struct tree {
    int item;
    int lpointer;
    int rpointer;
};

/* function prototypes */
void load_tree(int num,struct tree tree_array []);
```

```
void read_tree(struct tree tree_array []);
void main(void);
void clrscr(void);
int rand(void);
void write_node(struct tree tree_array [],int direction,
                int num,int prev_location,int location);


void main()
{
   int counter;
   struct tree tree_array [COUNT + 1];

   /* initialize array */
   for (counter = 0;counter <= COUNT;counter++) {
      tree_array [counter].item = 0;
      tree_array [counter].lpointer = 0;
      tree_array [counter].rpointer = 0;
   }

   /* number of items in tree */
   tree_array [0].item = 0;

   /* load items into tree */
   for (counter = 1;counter <= COUNT;counter++) {
      printf("."); /* show activity */
      load_tree(rand(),tree_array);
   }

   /* read and display tree contents */
   read_tree(tree_array);
}


void load_tree(int num,struct tree tree_array [])
/* create and load items into binary tree */
{
   int first_empty, /* first vacant tree location */
       counter,
       locator, /* tree node indicator */
       left = 1, /* current travel direction */
       right = 2, /* current travel direction */
       direction; /* last direction traveled */
```

```
            for (;;) {
               if (tree_array [0].item == 0) {
                  /* empty tree */
                  direction = 0;
                  write_node(tree_array,0,num,0,1);
                  break; /* leave function */
               }

               /* first empty row */
               first_empty = tree_array [0].item + 1;

               counter = 1; /* current array row */
               locator = 1; /* next array row */

               /* find highest value less than num */
               do {
                  counter = locator;
                  /* which direction? */
                  if (num < tree_array [counter].item) {
                     /* left pointer */
                     locator = tree_array [counter].lpointer;
                     direction = left;
                  }
                  else {
                     /* right pointer */
                     locator = tree_array [counter].rpointer;
                     direction = right;
                  }
               }
               while (locator != 0);

               /* set the tree pointer */
               write_node(tree_array,direction,num,counter,
                           first_empty);
               break;
            }
         }


void read_tree(struct tree tree_array [])
/* read the binary tree and display contents in ascending
   order */
```

```
{
    /* to keep track of position within tree */
    int back_count [COUNT],
        counter,
        locator, /* tree pointer */
        bcount; /* back_count array position */

    /* array row */
    counter = 1;
    /* back counter position */
    bcount = 0;
    /* value to test for completion */
    back_count [0] = 0;
    /* next row */
    locator = 1;

    for (;;) {
        /* back down through tree to get lowest value,
           keeping track of nodes visited in back_count
           array */

        while (locator > 0) {
            bcount++;
            back_count [bcount] = counter;
            /* left pointer */
            locator = tree_array [counter].lpointer;
            counter = locator;
        }

        /* lowest value */
        /* get latest node visited */
        counter = back_count [bcount];
        /* remove latest node from list */
        bcount--;

        if (counter == 0)
            /* end of list */
            break;

        /* display value */
        printf("%d ",tree_array [counter].item);
        /* look for next node */
```

```
        locator = tree_array [counter].rpointer;
        counter = locator;
    }
}


int rand(void)
/* produce a random number */
{
    time_t ltime;
    int rnd;
    static unsigned long value = 0;
    unsigned long temp,
                  increment = 271819,
                  multiplier = 314159,
                  modulus = 100001,
                  int_mod = 32767;

    if (value == 0) {
        time(&ltime);
        value = (multiplier * ltime + increment);
        value = value % modulus;
        temp = value;
        temp = value % int_mod;
        rnd = (int) temp;
    }
    else {
        value = (multiplier * value + increment);
        value = value % modulus;
        temp = value;
        temp = temp % int_mod;
        rnd = (int) temp;
    }
    return(rnd);
}


void clrscr(void)
/* clear the screen */
{
    union REGS regs;
```

```
        regs.h.ah = 6;              /* bios function */
        regs.h.al = 0;              /* clear entire screen */
        regs.h.bh = 7;              /* normal attribute */
        regs.h.ch = 0;              /* upper row position */
        regs.h.cl = 0;              /* upper-left column
                                        position */
        regs.h.dh = 24;            /* lowest row */
        regs.h.dl = 79;            /* rightmost column */
        int86(0x10,&regs,&regs);   /* bios interrupt number */
} /* end function clear screen */



void write_node(struct tree tree_array [],int direction,
                int num,int prev_location,int location)
/* add a node to the tree */
{
    int left = 1,
        right = 2;

    if (direction == 0) {
       tree_array [1].lpointer = 0;
       tree_array [1].rpointer = 0;
    }
    else {
       if (direction == left)
          tree_array [prev_location].lpointer = location;
       else
          tree_array [prev_location].rpointer = location;
    }
    tree_array [location].item = num; /* store value */
    tree_array [0].item++; /* another item stored */
}
```

This program added 1000 numbers to the tree in .3 seconds. The insertion sort took 21 and the linked list took 26 for the same number of records. You can see that a binary tree could often advantageously replace either.

RANDOM ACCESS BINARY TREE

The next program uses the same techniques but stores the nodes in a random access file instead of an array.

```
/* Chapter 9, Example 2, QuickC, 5/10/88
   Random access binary tree */

#include <stdio.h>
#include <stdlib.h>
#include <conio.h>
#include <io.h>
#include <time.h>
#include <bios.h>
#include <string.h>

#define COUNT 100L

/* structure to contain tree elements */
struct tree {
    long item;
    long lpointer;
    long rpointer;
};

/* function prototypes */
void load_ratree(long num,struct tree *tree_record,
                 FILE *stream);
void read_ratree(struct tree *tree_record,FILE *stream);
void complain(void);
void main(void);
void clrscr(void);
int rand(void);
void gotoxy(int x,int y);
void write_node(struct tree *tree_record,int direction,
                long num,long prev_location,
                long location,long var_size,int size,
                FILE *stream);
```

```
void main()
{
   size_t size = sizeof(struct tree);
   long var_size = (long) sizeof(struct tree), /* for
                                                  fseek() */
         num,
         counter;
   char dest_file [13];
   FILE *stream;
   struct tree tree_record; /* record structure */

   /* data file name */
   strcpy(&dest_file [0],"ch9_2.dat");

   /* open file to contain tree */
   if ((stream = fopen(dest_file,"w+b")) == NULL) {
      putch(7); /* beep */
      gotoxy(10,24);
      printf("Unable to open file\n");
      exit(1);
   }

   /* number of items in tree */
   tree_record.item = 0L;
   if ((fseek(stream,0L,SEEK_SET)) != 0)
      complain();
   fwrite(&tree_record,size,1,stream); /* store record
                                          zero */

   /* load items into tree */
   for (counter = 1L;counter <= COUNT;counter++) {
      printf("."); /* show activity */
      num = (long) rand();
      load_ratree(num,&tree_record,stream); /* do it! */
   }

   printf("\n"); /* end dot line */
   read_ratree(&tree_record,stream); /* read and display
                                        tree contents */

   fclose(stream);
}
```

```
void load_ratree(long num,struct tree *tree_record,
                 FILE *stream)
/* create and load items into random access binary tree */
{
    long var_size = (long) sizeof(struct tree), /* for
                                                 fseek() */
         first_empty, /* first vacant tree location */
         counter,
         locator; /* tree node indicator */
    size_t size = sizeof(struct tree); /* for fread() &
                                        fwrite () */
    int left = 1, /* current travel direction */
        right = 2, /* current travel direction */
        direction; /* last direction traveled */

    for (;;) {
        /* get number of records in tree */
        if ((fseek(stream,0L,SEEK_SET)) != 0)
            complain();
        fread(tree_record,size,1,stream);
        if (tree_record->item == 0L) {
            /* empty tree */

            direction = 0;
            write_node(tree_record,direction,num,0L,1L,
                       var_size,size,stream);
            break; /* leave function */
        }

        /* first empty record */
        first_empty = tree_record->item + 1L;

        locator = 1L; /* first record (tree root) */

        /* find highest value less than num */
        do {
            counter = locator; /* current array row */
            /* which direction? */
            if ((fseek(stream,counter * var_size,
                                    SEEK_SET)) != 0)
                complain();
            fread(tree_record,size,1,stream);
```

```
            if (num < tree_record->item) {
               /* left pointer */
               locator = tree_record->lpointer;
               direction = left;
            }
            else {
               /* right pointer */
               locator = tree_record->rpointer;
               direction = right;
             }
         }
         while (locator != 0);

         /* store current record */
         write_node(tree_record,direction,num,counter,
                    first_empty,var_size,size,stream);
         break;
      }
   }
}


void read_ratree(struct tree *tree_record,FILE *stream)
/* read the binary tree and display contents in ascending
   order */
{
   /* to keep track of position within tree */
   long var_size = (long) sizeof(struct tree), /* for
                                                 fseek() */
        counter,
        locator, /* tree pointer */
        bcount; /* back_count array position */
   size_t size = sizeof(struct tree); /* for fread() &
                                         fwrite() */
   int back_handle; /* for visited node file */
   char back_file [13]; /* name of visited node file */
   FILE *back_stream; /* for visited node file */

   strcpy(&back_file [0],"ch9_2b.dat");

   /* open file to contain back-list */
   if ((back_stream = fopen(back_file,"w+b")) == NULL) {
      putch(7); /* beep */
```

```
            gotoxy(10,24);
            printf("Unable to open file\n");
            exit(1);
        }

        /* record number */
        counter = 1L;
        /* back counter position */
        bcount = 0L;
        /* value to test for completion */
        if ((fseek(back_stream,0L,SEEK_SET)) != 0)
            complain();
        fwrite(0L,(size_t) sizeof(long),1,back_stream);
        /* next record */
        locator = 1L;

        for (;;) {
            /* back down through tree to get lowest value,
               keeping track of nodes visited in back_list file */
            while (locator > 0L) {
                /* read next lower item */
                if ((fseek(stream,counter * var_size,
                                            SEEK_SET)) != 0)
                    complain();
                fread(tree_record,size,1,stream);

                /* save next back-list item */
                bcount++;
                if ((fseek(back_stream,bcount *
                            (long) sizeof(long),SEEK_SET)) != 0)
                    complain();
                fwrite(&counter,(size_t) sizeof(long),1,
                                            back_stream);


                /* left pointer */
                locator = tree_record->lpointer; /* next lower
                                                    item */
                counter = locator;
            }
            /* lowest value */
```

```
         /* get latest node visited */
         if ((fseek(back_stream,bcount *
                         (long) sizeof(long),SEEK_SET)) != 0)
            complain();
         fread(&counter,(size_t) sizeof(long),1,back_stream);

         /* remove latest node from list */
         bcount--;
         if (counter == 0L)
            /* end of list */
            break;

         /* display value */
         if ((fseek(stream,counter * var_size,SEEK_SET)) != 0)
            complain();
         fread(tree_record,size,1,stream);
         printf("%d ",tree_record->item);

         /* look for next node */
         locator = tree_record->rpointer;
         counter = locator;
      }
   fclose(back_stream);
   remove(back_file);
}


void complain(void)
{
   putch(7); /* beep */
   gotoxy(10,24);
   printf("Unable to position file\n");
   exit(1);
}
void complain(void); /* bug fix */


int rand(void)
/* generate random number */
{
   time_t ltime;
   int rnd;
```

```
        static unsigned long value = 0;
        unsigned long temp,
                    increment = 271819,
                    multiplier = 314159,
                    modulus = 100001,
                    int_mod = 32767;

    if (value == 0) {
        time(&ltime);
        value = (multiplier * ltime + increment);
        value = value % modulus;
        temp = value;
        temp = value % int_mod;
        rnd = (int) temp;
    }
    else {
        value = (multiplier * value + increment);
        value = value % modulus;
        temp = value;
        temp = temp % int_mod;
        rnd = (int) temp;
    }
    return(rnd);
}


void clrscr(void)
/* clear the screen */
{
    union REGS regs;

    regs.h.ah = 6;              /* bios function */
    regs.h.al = 0;              /* clear entire screen */
    regs.h.bh = 7;              /* normal attribute */
    regs.h.ch = 0;              /* upper row position */
    regs.h.cl = 0;              /* upper-left column
                                   position */
    regs.h.dh = 24;             /* lowest row */
    regs.h.dl = 79;             /* rightmost column */
    int86(0x10,&regs,&regs);    /* bios interrupt number */
} /* end function clear screen */
```

```
void gotoxy(int x,int y)
/* position cursor */
{

   union REGS regs;


   regs.h.ah = 2;              /* bios function */
   regs.h.dh = (char) y;       /* row */
   regs.h.dl = (char) x;       /* column */
   regs.h.bh = 0;              /* video page number */
   int86(0x10,&regs,&regs);    /* bios interrupt number */
} /* end function gotoxy */



void write_node(struct tree *tree_record,int direction,
                long num,long prev_location,
                long location,long var_size,int size,
                FILE *stream)
/* write a node to disk */
{
   int left = 1, /* pointer direction values */
       right = 2;

   if (direction != 0) {
      /* not first record */
      /* save pointer to new record */
      if ((fseek(stream,prev_location * var_size,
                                     SEEK_SET)) != 0)
         complain();
      fread(tree_record,size,1,stream);
      if (direction == left)
         tree_record->lpointer = location;
      else
         tree_record->rpointer = location;
      if ((fseek(stream,prev_location * var_size,
                                     SEEK_SET)) != 0)
         complain();
      fwrite(tree_record,size,1,stream);
   }
```

```
/* update record count */
if ((fseek(stream,0L,SEEK_SET)) != 0)
    complain();
fread(tree_record,size,1,stream);
tree_record->item++; /* another item stored */
if ((fseek(stream,0L,SEEK_SET)) != 0)
    complain();
fwrite(tree_record,size,1,stream);

/* save new record */
if ((fseek(stream,location * var_size,SEEK_SET)) != 0)
    complain();
fread(tree_record,size,1,stream);
tree_record->item = num;
tree_record->lpointer = 0L;
tree_record->rpointer = 0L;
if ((fseek(stream,location * var_size,SEEK_SET)) != 0)
    complain();
fwrite(tree_record,size,1,stream);
}
```

Integer variables are used throughout. If your file will contain more than 32,767 records, then you must make the backcount array and the counter and pointer variables long integer. Also adjust the field sizes of the left and right pointers to sizeof(long).

This program created a tree with 1000 nodes in 39 seconds. The linked list took 2008 seconds and the insertion sort 344 seconds. Not bad, huh?

DELETING NODES FROM A TREE

Here are two more programs. The first stores the tree in an array, the second in a random access file.

These programs have an added subprogram to delete nodes from a tree. This was also rather tricky to program. The locations of the deleted nodes are stored in an array, deleted [ ], and these positions are used when new nodes are added to a tree.

The deleted array was arbitrarily set to 50. You may wish to increase this value if you expect to do a lot of deleting and not much subsequent addition of nodes.

The demonstration program creates a tree, deletes a few records, then adds a few. You are shown the state of the deleted array after each deletion and addition so you can see that it is operating correctly.

In a real program similar to Example 3, you'd save the deleted array in a sequential file for use the next time you use the ch9_3.dat file or include it in that file as will be seen in Chapter 11.

Here is the array version.

```
/* Chapter 9, Example 3, QuickC, 4/20/88
   Array binary tree including saving
   deleted locations in another array */

#include <stdio.h>
#include <stdlib.h>
#include <conio.h>
#include <time.h>
#include <bios.h>

#define COUNT 30

/* structure to contain tree elements */
struct tree {
    int item;
    int lpointer;
    int rpointer;
};

/* function prototypes */
void load_dtree(int num,struct tree tree_array [],
                int deleted []);
void read_tree(struct tree tree_array []);
void delete_tree(int num,int *found,
                struct tree tree_array [],int deleted []);
void pause(void);
void main(void);
void clrscr(void);
int rand(void);
void write_dnode(struct tree tree_array [],int direction,
                int num,int prev_location,int location);
void move_node(struct tree tree_array [],int num,
                int location,int lpointer,int rpointer);
```

```
void main()
{
   int counter,
       counter2,
       value,
       delete_count,
       true = 1, /* boolean variable */
       found = true, /* used by delete routine */
       to_delete [5], /* used only by demo program */
       num, /* temporary holder */
       deleted [COUNT + 1]; /* array containing deleted
                              nodes for reuse */
   struct tree tree_array [COUNT + 1]; /* main database
                                         array */

   /* initialize array */
   for (counter = 0;counter <= COUNT;counter++) {
      tree_array [counter].item = 0;
      tree_array [counter].lpointer = 0;
      tree_array [counter].rpointer = 0;
   }

   /* number of items in tree */
   tree_array [0].item = 0;

   /* initialize deleted array */
   deleted [0] = 0; /* number of items in array */

   /* load items into tree */
   /* put a few numbers in delete list that probably
      do not appear in the file */
   delete_count = 0;
   to_delete [delete_count] = 555;
   delete_count++;
   to_delete [delete_count] = 666;

   for (counter = 1;counter <= (COUNT - 10);counter++) {
      printf("."); /* show activity */
      value = rand();
      load_dtree(value,tree_array,deleted);
      /* put a few numbers in delete list that do appear in
         file */
```

```
      if (counter % 2 == 0 && counter < 7) {
         delete_count++;
         to_delete [delete_count] = value;
      }
}

/* read and display tree contents */
read_tree(tree_array);
printf("\n");

/* delete some records */

for (counter = 0;counter < 5;counter++) {
   num = to_delete [counter];
   printf("\nDeleting record %d\n",num);
   delete_tree(num,&found,tree_array,deleted);
   if (found == true) {
      printf("Successfully deleted record %d\n",num);
      printf("Here is the new list\n");
      read_tree(tree_array); /* show new tree */
      printf("\nHere is the deleted node list\n");
      for (counter2 = 1;counter2 <=
                                deleted [0];counter2++)
         printf("%d ",deleted [counter2]);
      printf("\n");
   }
   else
      printf("Record with %d not found\n",num);
   pause();
}

/* now add a few records */
printf("\n");
for (counter = 1;counter <= 5;counter++) {
   num = rand();
   printf("Adding record %d\n",num);
   load_dtree(num,tree_array,deleted);
   printf("Here is the new list\n");
   read_tree(tree_array);
   printf("\nHere is the deleted node list\n");
   for (counter2 = 1;counter2 <= deleted [0];counter2++)
      printf("%d ",deleted [counter2]);
```

```
            printf("\n");
            pause();
    }
}


void load_dtree(int num,struct tree tree_array [],
                int deleted [])
/* create and load items into binary tree */
{
    int first_empty, /* first vacant tree location */
        counter,
        locator, /* tree node indicator */
        left = 1, /* current travel direction */
        right = 2, /* current travel direction */
        direction; /* last direction traveled */

    for (;;) {
        if (tree_array [0].item == 0) {
            /* empty tree */
            direction = 0;
            write_dnode(tree_array,direction,num,0,1);
            tree_array [0].item++;
            break; /* leave function */
        }

        if (deleted [0] > 0) {
            first_empty = deleted [deleted [0]];
            deleted [0]--;
        }
        else {
            tree_array [0].item++;
            /* first empty row */
            first_empty = tree_array [0].item;
        }

        counter = 1; /* current array row */
        locator = 1; /* next array row */

        /* find highest value less than num */
        do {
            counter = locator;
            /* which direction? */
```

```
            if (num < tree_array [counter].item) {
                /* left pointer */
                locator = tree_array [counter].lpointer;
                direction = left;
            }
            else {
                /* right pointer */
                locator = tree_array [counter].rpointer;
                direction = right;
            }
        }
        while (locator != 0);

        /* save new record */
        write_dnode(tree_array,direction,num,counter,
                    first_empty);
        break;
    }
}


void read_tree(struct tree tree_array [])
/* read the binary tree and display contents in ascending
   order */
{

    /* to keep track of position within tree */
    int back_count [COUNT2], /* visited nodes array */
        counter,
        locator, /* tree pointer */
        bcount; /* back_count (visited nodes) array
                    position */

    /* array row */
    counter = 1;
    /* back_counter position */
    bcount = 0;
    /* value to test for completion */
    back_count [0] = 0;
    /* next row */
    locator = 1;
```

```
            for(;;) {
                /* back down through tree to get lowest value,
                keeping track of nodes visited in back_count array */
                while (locator > 0) {
                    bcount++;
                    back_count [bcount] = counter;
                    /* left_pointer */
                    locator = tree_array [counter].lpointer;
                    counter = locator;
                }
                /* lowest value */

                /* get latest node visited */
                counter = back_count [bcount];

                /* remove latest node from list */
                bcount--;
                if (counter == 0)
                    /* end of list */
                    break;

                /* display value */
                printf("%d ",tree_array [counter].item);

                /* look for next node */
                locator = tree_array [counter].rpointer;
                counter = locator;
            }
        }


void delete_tree(int num,int *found,
                    struct tree tree_array [],int deleted [])
/* delete a node from the tree and store the node location
    in an array */
{
    int back_pointer, /* a previous position in the tree */
        locator, /* another tree position */
        old_locator, /* another previous position */
        counter, /* another tree position */
```

```
         save_place,  /* deleted node number */
         true = 1,  /* boolean */
         false = 0;

*found = false;
back_pointer = 0;

for (;;) {
   if (tree_array [0].item == 0)
      /* empty tree */
      break;

   if (tree_array [1].item == num) {
      /* special case of deletion of root node */
      *found = true;
      if (tree_array [1].lpointer == 0 ||
                           tree_array [1].rpointer == 0) {
         /* at least one pointer null, select the
            other */
         if (tree_array [1].lpointer == 0)
            locator = tree_array [1].rpointer;
         else
            locator = tree_array [1].lpointer;
         if (locator == 0) {
            /* both pointers null */
            tree_array [0].item = 0;
            break;
         }
      }
      else {
         /* both pointers in use */
         locator = tree_array [1].rpointer;

         /* find first free lpointer in right half of
            tree */
         do {
            back_pointer = locator;
            locator = tree_array [locator].lpointer;
         }
         while (locator != 0);
```

```
                    /* add left half of tree to that pointer */
                    tree_array [back_pointer].lpointer =
                                            tree_array [1].lpointer;

                    /* get first node in right half of tree */
                    locator = tree_array [1].rpointer;
                }

                /* move node to root node */
                move_node(tree_array,tree_array [locator].item,1,
                        tree_array [locator].lpointer,
                        tree_array [locator].rpointer);

                /* delete moved node */
                move_node(tree_array,0,locator,0,0);

                /* add deleted node to deleted node list */
                if (deleted [0] < COUNT) { /* room in array? */
                    /* increment node count */
                    deleted [0]++;
                    /* add the node */
                    deleted [deleted [0]] = locator;
                    break; /* done */
                }
                else {
                    printf("Out of deleted array space\n");
                    putch(7); /* beep */
                    break;
                }
            }

            /* not root node */
            /* next tree node */
            counter = 1;

            /* tree node */
            locator = 1;

            /* find the value to be deleted from the tree */
            do {
                counter = locator; /* previous node */
                if (num < tree_array [counter].item) {
```

```
        /* left pointer */
        back_pointer = locator;
        locator = tree_array [counter].lpointer;
    }
    else {
        if (num > tree_array [counter].item) {
            /* right pointer */
            back_pointer = locator;
            locator = tree_array [counter].rpointer;
        }
        else {
            *found = true;
            break;
        }
    }
}
while (locator != 0);

if (*found == false)
    /* record not found */
    break;

if (tree_array [counter].rpointer == 0) {
    /* rpointer free */
    /* delete record */
    tree_array [counter].item = 0;

    /* remember deleted node */
    save_place = counter;

    /* move tree pointer */
    if (tree_array [back_pointer].lpointer == counter)
        tree_array [back_pointer].lpointer =
                        tree_array [counter].lpointer;
    else
        tree_array [back_pointer].rpointer =
                        tree_array [counter].lpointer;

    /* delete other tree pointer */
    tree_array [counter].lpointer = 0;
}
else {
```

```
      if (tree_array [counter].lpointer == 0) {
         /* lpointer free */
         /* delete record */
         tree_array [counter].item = 0;

         /* remember deleted node */
         save_place = counter;

         /* move tree pointer */
         if (tree_array [back_pointer].lpointer ==
                                           counter)
            tree_array [back_pointer].lpointer =
                       tree_array [counter].rpointer;
         else
            tree_array [back_pointer].rpointer =
                       tree_array [counter].rpointer;

         /* delete other pointer */
         tree_array [counter].rpointer = 0;
      }
      else {
         /* neither pointer free */
         if (tree_array [back_pointer].rpointer ==
                                           counter) {
            /* move tree pointer back one node */
            tree_array [back_pointer].rpointer =
                       tree_array [counter].rpointer;

            /* save tree pointer */
            locator = tree_array [counter].rpointer;

            /* delete old tree pointer */
            tree_array [counter].rpointer = 0;

            /* find first free lpointer */
            do {
               old_locator = locator;
               locator = tree_array [locator].lpointer;
            }
            while (locator != 0);
```

```
/* move tree pointer */
tree_array [old_locator].lpointer =
                tree_array [counter].lpointer;

/* delete pointer */
tree_array [counter].lpointer = 0;

/* delete tree value */
tree_array [counter].item = 0;

/* remember deleted node */
save_place = counter;
}
else {
    /* move pointer back one node */
    tree_array [back_pointer].lpointer =
                    tree_array [counter].lpointer;

    /* save tree pointer */
    locator = tree_array [counter].lpointer;

    /* delete old tree pointer */
    tree_array [counter].lpointer = 0;

    /* find first free rpointer */
    do {
        old_locator = locator;
        locator = tree_array [locator].rpointer;
    }
    while (locator != 0);

    /* move pointer */
    tree_array [old_locator].rpointer =
                    tree_array [counter].rpointer;
    /* delete pointer */
    tree_array [counter].rpointer = 0;

    /* delete tree value */
    tree_array [counter].item = 0;
```

```
                              /* remember deleted node */
                              save_place = counter;
                    }
              }
        }

        /* add deleted node to deleted list */
        if (deleted [0] < COUNT) {
           deleted [0]++;
           deleted [deleted [0]] = save_place;
        }
        else {
           printf("Out of deleted array space\n");
           putch(7); /* beep */
        }
        break;
    } /* end for(;;) */
} /* end function */


void pause(void)
/* wait for keypress */
{
   printf("Press any key to continue\n");
   getch();
}


int rand(void)
/* generate random number */
{
   time_t ltime;
   int rnd;
   static unsigned long value = 0;
   unsigned long temp,
                 increment = 271819,
                 multiplier = 314159,
                 modulus = 100001,
                 int_mod = 32767;

   if (value == 0) {
      time(&ltime);
```

```
        value = (multiplier * ltime + increment);
        value = value % modulus;
        temp = value;
        temp = value % int_mod;
        rnd = (int) temp;
    }
    else {
        value = (multiplier * value + increment);
        value = value % modulus;
        temp = value;
        temp = temp % int_mod;
        rnd = (int) temp;
    }
    return(rnd);
}

void clrscr(void)
/* clear the screen */
{
    union REGS regs;

    regs.h.ah = 6;                  /* bios function */
    regs.h.al = 0;                  /* clear entire screen */
    regs.h.bh = 7;                  /* normal attribute */
    regs.h.ch = 0;                  /* upper row position */
    regs.h.cl = 0;                  /* upper-left column
                                       position */
    regs.h.dh = 24;                 /* lowest row */
    regs.h.dl = 79;                 /* rightmost column */
    int86(0x10,&regs,&regs);        /* bios interrupt number */
} /* end function clear screen */



void write_dnode(struct tree tree_array [],int direction,
                 int num,int prev_location,int location)
/* save a record to a new node */
{
    int left = 1, /* pointer direction values */
        right = 2;

    if (direction == 0) {
        /* record 0 */
```

```
            tree_array [1].lpointer = 0;
            tree_array [1].rpointer = 0;
    }
    else {
        /* other record */
        if (direction == left)
            tree_array [prev_location].lpointer = location;
        else
            tree_array [prev_location].rpointer = location;
    }
    tree_array [location].item = num;
}


void move_node(struct tree tree_array [],int num,
                int location,int lpointer,int rpointer)
/* move a record to a new node during deletion */
{
    tree_array [location].lpointer = lpointer;
    tree_array [location].rpointer = rpointer;
    tree_array [location].item = num;
}
```

RANDOM ACCESS FILE VERSION OF BINARY TREE WITH DELETION

Here's the random access file version of Example 3.

```
/* Chapter 9, Example 4, QuickC, 5/12/88
   Random access binary tree with record deletion */

#include <stdio.h>
#include <stdlib.h>
#include <conio.h>
#include <io.h>
#include <bios.h>
#include <time.h>
#include <string.h>

#define COUNT 50L
```

```
/* structure to contain tree elements */
struct tree {
   long item;
   long lpointer;
   long rpointer;
};

/* function prototypes */
void load_radtree(long num,struct tree *tree_record,
               FILE *stream,char delete_file []);
void read_ratree(struct tree *tree_record,FILE *stream);
void complain(void);
void delete_ratree(long num,int *found,FILE *stream,
                  char delete_file []);
void pause(void);
void main(void);
void clrscr(void);
int rand(void);
void gotoxy(int x,int y);
void write_node(struct tree *tree_record,int direction,
             long num,long prev_location,
             long location,long var_size,int size,
             FILE *stream);
void delete_record(struct tree *tree_record,long counter,
                  long back_pointer,long var_size,
                  long *save_place,int size,
                  int direction,FILE *stream);
void move_record(struct tree *tree_record,long counter,
             long back_pointer,long var_size,
             long *save_place,int size,int direction,
              FILE *stream);


void main()
{
   size_t size = sizeof(struct tree); /* for fread() &
                                     fwrite() */
   int delete_count,
       true = 1,
       found = true; /* used when deleting a record */
   long var_size = (long) sizeof(struct tree), /* for
                                          fseek() */
```

```
        num,
        to_delete [5], /* numbers to delete for demo */
        del_len, /* number of deleted nodes in delete
                     file */
        counter,
        counter2;
char dest_file [13], /* destination file name */
     delete_file [13]; /* delete file name */
FILE *stream, /* for tree file */
     *dstream; /* for delete file */
struct tree_record; /* record structure */
/* set file names */
strcpy(&dest_file [0],"ch9_4.dat");
strcpy(&delete_file [0],"ch9_4.del");

/* open file to contain tree */
if ((stream = fopen(dest_file,"w+b")) == NULL) {
   putch(7); /* beep */
   gotoxy(10,24);
   printf("Unable to open file\n");
   exit(1);
}

/* open file to contain deleted nodes */
if ((dstream = fopen(delete_file,"w+b")) == NULL) {
   putch(7); /* beep */
   gotoxy(10,24);
   printf("Unable to open file\n");
   exit(1);
}

/* number of deleted nodes to start */
if ((fseek(dstream,0L,SEEK_SET)) != 0)
   complain();
/* store record zero */
fwrite(0L,(size_t) sizeof(long),1,dstream);

fclose(dstream);

/* number of items in tree to start */
tree_record.item = 0L;
if ((fseek(stream,0L,SEEK_SET)) != 0)
   complain();
```

```
/* store record zero */
fwrite(&tree_record,size,1,stream);

/* put a few numbers in delete list that probably
   do not appear in the file */
delete_count = 0;
to_delete [delete_count] = 555;
delete_count++;
to_delete [delete_count] = 666;

/* load items into tree */
for (counter = 1L;counter <= COUNT;counter++) {
   printf("."); /* show activity */
   num = (long) rand();
   /* do it! */
   load_radtree(num,&tree_record,stream,delete_file);
   /* put a few numbers in delete list that do appear in
      the file */
   if (counter % 2 == 0 && counter < 7) {
      delete_count++;
      to_delete [delete_count] = (long) num;
   }
}

printf("\n"); /* end dot line */
/* read and display tree contents */
read_ratree(&tree_record,stream);

/* delete some records */
for (counter = 0L;counter < 5L;counter++) {
   /* number to delete */
   num = to_delete [(int) counter];
   printf("\nDeleting record %ld\n",num);
   /* do it */
   delete_ratree(num,&found,stream,delete_file);
   if (found == true) {
      printf("Successfully deleted record %ld\n",num);
      printf("Here is the new list\n");

      /* show new tree */
      read_ratree(&tree_record,stream);
      printf("\nHere is the deleted node list\n");
```

```
        /* open file containing deleted nodes */
        if ((dstream = fopen(delete_file,"r+b")) == NULL) {
           putch(7); /* beep */
           gotoxy(10,24);
           printf("Unable to open file\n");
           exit(1);
        }

        /* number of deleted nodes*/
        if ((fseek(dstream,0L,SEEK_SET)) != 0)
           complain();

        /* fetch record zero */
        fread(&del_len,(size_t) sizeof(long),1,dstream);

        /* display deleted nodes */
        for (counter2 = 1L;counter2 <= del_len;counter2++){
           if ((fseek(dstream,counter2 *
                       (long) sizeof(long),SEEK_SET)) != 0)
              complain();
           /* fetch deleted node number */
           fread(&num,(size_t) sizeof(long),1,dstream);
           printf("%ld ",num);
        }
        printf("\n");
        fclose(dstream);
     }

     else
        printf("Record with %ld not found\n",num);
     pause();
  }

  /* now add a few records */
  for (counter = 1;counter <= 5;counter++) {
     num = (long) rand();
     printf("Adding record %ld\n",num);
     /* do it! */
     load_radtree(num,&tree_record,stream,delete_file);
  }

  printf("Here is the new list\n");
  /* read and display tree contents */
```

```
        read_ratree(&tree_record,stream);
        printf("\nHere is the deleted node list\n");

        /* open file to contain deleted nodes */
        if ((dstream = fopen(delete_file,"r+b")) == NULL) {
            putch(7); /* beep */
            gotoxy(10,24);
            printf("Unable to open file\n");
            exit(1);
        }


        /* number of deleted nodes*/
        if ((fseek(dstream,0L,SEEK_SET)) != 0)
            complain();
        /* show deleted node list */
        /* get record count */
        fread(&del_len,(size_t) sizeof(long),1,dstream);
        for (counter = 1L;counter <= del_len;counter++) {
            if ((fseek(dstream,counter2 *
                            (long) sizeof(long),SEEK_SET)) != 0)
                complain();
            /* fetch deleted node list */
            fread(&num,(size_t) sizeof(long),1,dstream);
            printf("%ld ",num);
        }
        printf("\n");
        fclose(dstream);

        fclose(stream);
}


void load_radtree(long num,struct tree *tree_record,
                    FILE *stream,char delete_file [])
/* create and load items into random access binary tree */
{

    long first_empty, /* first vacant tree location */
        var_size = (long) sizeof(struct tree), /* for
                                                    fseek() */
        del_len, /* number of deleted nodes */
        counter,
        locator; /* tree node indicator */
```

```
size_t size = sizeof(struct tree); /* for fread &
                                        fwrite */
int left = 1, /* current travel direction */
    right = 2, /* current travel direction */
    direction; /* last direction traveled */
FILE *dstream;

for (;;) {
    /* get number of records in tree */
    if ((fseek(stream,0L,SEEK_SET)) != 0)
        complain();
    fread(tree_record,size,1,stream);
    if (tree_record->item == 0L) {
        /* empty tree */

        /* update record count */
        tree_record->item++;
        if ((fseek(stream,0L,SEEK_SET)) != 0)
            complain();
        fwrite(tree_record,size,1,stream);

        /* first record */
        direction = 0;
        /* load it into the tree */
        write_node(tree_record,direction,num,0L,1L,
                    var_size,size,stream);

        break; /* leave function */
    }

    /* open file containing deleted nodes */
    if ((dstream = fopen(delete_file,"r+b")) == NULL) {
        putch(7); /* beep */
        gotoxy(10,24);
        printf("Unable to open file\n");
        exit(1);
    }

    /* number of deleted nodes*/
    if ((fseek(dstream,0L,SEEK_SET)) != 0)
        complain();
    /* get deleted record count */
    fread(&del_len,(size_t) sizeof(long),1,dstream);
```

```
if (del_len > 0L) {
   /* reuse a deleted node */
   if ((fseek(dstream,del_len *
                 (long) sizeof(long),SEEK_SET)) != 0)
      complain();
   fread(&first_empty,(size_t) sizeof(long),1,
        dstream);
   del_len--; /* don't use this node next time */
   if ((fseek(dstream,0L,SEEK_SET)) != 0)
      complain();
   /* save new node count */
   fwrite(&del_len,(size_t) sizeof(long),1,dstream);
}
else {
   /* no nodes in deleted list */
   tree_record->item++; /* next unused node */
   /* first empty record */
   first_empty = tree_record->item;
   if ((fseek(stream,0L,SEEK_SET)) != 0)
      complain();
   /* save new record count */
   fwrite(tree_record,size,1,stream);
}
fclose(dstream);

locator = 1L; /* first record (tree root) */

/* find highest value less than num */
do {
   counter = locator; /* current array row */
   /* which direction? */
   if ((fseek(stream,counter * var_size,
                              SEEK_SET)) != 0)
      complain();
   fread(tree_record,size,1,stream);
   if (num < tree_record->item) {
      /* left pointer */
      locator = tree_record->lpointer;
      direction = left;
   }
   else {
      /* right pointer */
```

```
                       locator = tree_record->rpointer;
                       direction = right;
                   }
               }
           while (locator != 0);


           /* save new record & pointer info */
           write_node(tree_record,direction,num,counter,
                       first_empty,var_size,size,stream);

           break; /* leave function */
       }
   }



void read_ratree(struct tree *tree_record,FILE *stream)
/* read the binary tree and display contents in ascending
   order */
{
   /* to keep track of position within tree */
   long counter,
       var_size = (long) sizeof(struct tree), /* for
                                                  fseek() */
       locator, /* tree pointer */
       bcount; /* back_count array position */
   size_t size = sizeof(struct tree); /* for fread &
                                          fwrite */
   char back_file [13];
   FILE *back_stream; /* keeps track of visited nodes */

   strcpy(&back_file [0],"ch9_2b.dat");

   /* open file to contain back-list */
   if ((back_stream = fopen(back_file,"w+b")) == NULL) {
       putch(7); /* beep */
       gotoxy(10,24);
       printf("Unable to open file\n");
       exit(1);
   }

   /* record number */
   counter = 1L;
```

```c
/* back counter position */
bcount = 0L;
/* value to test for completion */
if ((fseek(back_stream,0L,SEEK_SET)) != 0)
   complain();
fwrite(0L,(size_t) sizeof(long),1,back_stream);
/* next record */
locator = 1L;

for (;;) {
   /* back down through tree to get lowest value,
   keeping track of nodes visited in back_list file */
   while (locator > 0L) {
      /* read next lower item */
      if ((fseek(stream,counter * var_size,
                                       SEEK_SET)) != 0)
         complain();
      fread(tree_record,size,1,stream);

      /* save next back-list item */
      bcount++;
      if ((fseek(back_stream,bcount *
                   (long) sizeof(long),SEEK_SET)) != 0)
         complain();
      fwrite(&counter,(size_t) sizeof(long),1,
            back_stream);

      /* left pointer */
      /* next lower item */
      locator = tree_record->lpointer;
      counter = locator;
   }
   /* lowest value */

   /* get latest node visited */
   if ((fseek(back_stream,bcount *
                   (long) sizeof(long),SEEK_SET)) != 0)
      complain();
   fread(&counter,(size_t) sizeof(long),1,back_stream);

   /* remove latest node from list */
   bcount--;
```

```
                     if (counter == 0L)
                        /* end of list */
                        break; /* leave function */

                     /* display value */
                     if ((fseek(stream,counter * var_size,SEEK_SET)) != 0)
                        complain();
                     fread(tree_record,size,1,stream);
                     printf("%d ",tree_record->item);

                     /* look for next node */
                     locator = tree_record->rpointer;
                     counter = locator;
                  }
                  fclose(back_stream);
                  remove(back_file);
               }


   void complain(void)
   /* fseek failed */
   {
      putch(7); /* beep */
      gotoxy(10,24);
      printf("Unable to position file\n");
      exit(1);
   }
   void complain(void); /* bug fix */


   void delete_ratree(long num,int *found,FILE *stream,
                      char delete_file [])
   /* delete a node from the tree and store the node location
      in a file */
   {
      int direction, /* use left or right pointer */
         left = 1, /* directions */
         right = 2,
         true = 1, /* boolean */
         false = 0;
      size_t size = sizeof(struct tree); /* for fread &
                                            fwrite */
```

```
FILE *dstream;
long var_size = (long) sizeof(struct tree),
     temp_item, /* temporary structure holders */
     temp_lpointer, /* temporary pointer holders */
     temp_rpointer,
     back_pointer, /* a previous position in the tree */
     locator, /* another tree position */
     counter, /* another tree position */
     del_len, /* length of deleted node file */
     save_place; /* deleted node number */
struct tree tree_record; /* record structure */

*found = false;
back_pointer = 0L;

for (;;) {
   if ((fseek(stream,0L,SEEK_SET)) != 0)
      complain();
   fread(&tree_record,size,1,stream);
   if (tree_record.item == 0L) /* node 0 */
      /* empty tree */
      break;

   /* is it in root node? */
   if ((fseek(stream,1L * var_size,SEEK_SET)) != 0)
      complain();
   fread(&tree_record,size,1,stream);
   if (tree_record.item == num) { /* node 1 */
      /* special case of deletion of root node */
      *found = true;
      if (tree_record.lpointer == 0L ||
                          tree_record.rpointer == 0L) {
         /* at least one pointer null in root node,
            select the other */
         if (tree_record.lpointer == 0L)
            locator = tree_record.rpointer;
         else
            locator = tree_record.lpointer;
         if (locator == 0L) {
            /* both pointers in root node are null */
            /* set record count to zero */
```

```
                        if ((fseek(stream,0L,SEEK_SET)) != 0)
                           complain();
                        fread(&tree_record,size,1,stream);
                        tree_record.item = 0L;
                        if ((fseek(stream,0L,SEEK_SET)) != 0)
                           complain();
                        fwrite(&tree_record,size,1,stream);
                        break;
                  }
            }
            else {
               /* both root node pointers in use */
               locator = tree_record.rpointer;

               /* find first free lpointer in right half of
                  tree */
               do {
                  back_pointer = locator;
                  if ((fseek(stream,locator * var_size,
                                          SEEK_SET)) != 0)
                     complain();
                  fread(&tree_record,size,1,stream);
                  /* node locator */
                  locator = tree_record.lpointer;
               }
               while (locator != 0L);

               /* add left half of tree to that pointer */
               /* get root record */
               if ((fseek(stream,1L * var_size,SEEK_SET)) != 0)
                  complain();
               fread(&tree_record,size,1,stream);
               /* copy root node pointers */
               temp_lpointer = tree_record.lpointer;
               temp_rpointer = tree_record.rpointer;
               /* get previous record to deleted record */
               if ((fseek(stream,back_pointer * var_size,
                                          SEEK_SET)) != 0)
                  complain();
               fread(&tree_record,size,1,stream);
```

```
    /* point to left half of tree with old root node
       lpointer */
    tree_record.lpointer = temp_lpointer;
    /* save new pointer in previous node record */
    if ((fseek(stream,back_pointer *
                          var_size,SEEK_SET)) != 0)
        complain();
    fwrite(&tree_record,size,1,stream);

    /* get first node in right half of tree */
    locator = temp_rpointer; /* node 1 */
}


/* move pointer to right half of tree to root
   node */
if ((fseek(stream,locator * var_size,
                            SEEK_SET)) != 0)
    complain();
fread(&tree_record,size,1,stream);
/* save all data from first node in right half of
   tree */
temp_item = tree_record.item; /* node locator */
temp_lpointer = tree_record.lpointer;
temp_rpointer = tree_record.rpointer;

/* blank above node */
tree_record.item = 0l ;
tree_record.lpointer = 0L;
tree_record.rpointer = 0L;
if ((fseek(stream,locator * var_size,
                            SEEK_SET)) != 0)
    complain();
fwrite(&tree_record,size,1,stream);

/* put data from deleted node in root node,
   effectively deleting the root node */
tree_record.item = temp_item;
tree_record.lpointer = temp_lpointer;
tree_record.rpointer = temp_rpointer;
```

```c
            if ((fseek(stream,1L * var_size,SEEK_SET)) != 0)
               complain();
            fwrite(&tree_record,size,1,stream);

            /* add moved node to deleted node list */
            /* open file containing deleted nodes */
            if ((dstream = fopen(delete_file,"r+b")) == NULL) {
               putch(7); /* beep */
               gotoxy(10,24);
               printf("Unable to open file\n");
               exit(1);
            }

            /* number of deleted nodes*/
            if ((fseek(dstream,0L,SEEK_SET)) != 0)
               complain();
            fread(&del_len,(size_t) sizeof(long),1,dstream);

            /* update node count */
            del_len++;
            if ((fseek(dstream,0L,SEEK_SET)) != 0)
               complain();
            fwrite(&del_len,(size_t) sizeof(long),1,dstream);

            /* store deleted node value in first available
               record */
            if ((fseek(dstream,del_len *
                       (long) sizeof(long),SEEK_SET)) != 0)
               complain();
            fwrite(&locator,(size_t) sizeof(long),1,dstream);

            fclose(dstream); /* deleted node file */
            break;
        }

        /* not root node */
        /* next tree node */
        counter = 1L;
        /* tree node */
        locator = 1L;
```

```
/* find the value to be deleted from the tree
   or a null tree pointer */
do {
   counter = locator; /* previous node */
   if ((fseek(stream,counter * var_size,
                                 SEEK_SET)) != 0)
      complain();
   /* get record to test */
   fread(&tree_record,size,1,stream);

   /* what to do */
   if (num < tree_record.item) {
      /* left pointer */
      back_pointer = locator;
      locator = tree_record.lpointer;
   }
   else {
      if (num > tree_record.item) {
         /* right pointer */
         back_pointer = locator;
         locator = tree_record.rpointer;
      }
      else {
         *found = true;
         break;
      }
   }
}
while (locator != 0L);

if (*found == false)
   /* record not found, null found first */
   break; /* leave function */

if (tree_record.rpointer == 0L) { /* rpointer free */

   /* delete record and adjust pointers */
   direction = left;
   delete_record(&tree_record,counter,back_pointer,
                 var_size,&save_place,size,direction,
                 stream);
```

```
            }
            else {
               if ((fseek(stream,counter * var_size,
                                           SEEK_SET)) != 0)
                  complain();
               fread(&tree_record,size,1,stream);
               if (tree_record.lpointer == 0L) {
                  /* counter node lpointer free */

                  /* delete record and adjust pointers */
                  direction = right;
                  delete_record(&tree_record,counter,back_pointer,
                             var_size,&save_place,size,
                             direction,stream);
               }
               else {
                  /* neither pointer free */
                  if ((fseek(stream,back_pointer *
                                     var_size,SEEK_SET)) != 0)
                     complain();
                  fread(&tree_record,size,1,stream);
                  if (tree_record.rpointer == counter) {
                     /* back_pointer node */
                     direction = right;
                     move_record(&tree_record,counter,
                                  back_pointer,var_size,
                                  &save_place,size,
                                  direction,stream);
                  }
                  else {
                     direction = left;
                     move_record(&tree_record,counter,
                                  back_pointer,var_size,
                                  &save_place,size,
                                  direction,stream);

                  }
               }
            }

         /* add deleted node to deleted list */
         /* open file containing deleted nodes */
         if ((dstream = fopen(delete_file,"r+b")) == NULL) {
            putch(7); /* beep */
```

```
            gotoxy(10,24);
            printf("Unable to open file\n");
            exit(1);
        }

        /* number of deleted nodes*/
        if ((fseek(dstream,0L,SEEK_SET)) != 0)
            complain();
        fread(&del_len,(size_t) sizeof(long),1,dstream);

        /* update node count */
        del_len++;
        if ((fseek(dstream,0L,SEEK_SET)) != 0)
            complain();
        fwrite(&del_len,(size_t) sizeof(long),1,dstream);

        /* store deleted node in first available record */
        if ((fseek(dstream,del_len *
                        (long) sizeof(long),SEEK_SET)) != 0)
            complain();
        fwrite(&save_place,(size_t) sizeof(long),1,dstream);

        fclose(dstream); /* deleted node file */
        break;
    } /* end for(;;) */
} /* end function */

void pause(void)
/* wait for keypress */
{
    printf("Press any key to continue\n");
    getch();
}


int rand(void)
{
    time_t ltime;
    int rnd;
    static unsigned long value = 0;
    unsigned long temp,
                increment = 271819,
                multiplier = 314159,
```

```
                        modulus = 100001,
                        int_mod = 32767;

        if (value == 0) {
           time(&ltime);
           value = (multiplier * ltime + increment);
           value = value % modulus;
           temp = value;
           temp = value % int_mod;
           rnd = (int) temp;
        }
        else {
           value = (multiplier * value + increment);
           value = value % modulus;
           temp = value;
           temp = temp % int_mod;
           rnd = (int) temp;
        }
        return(rnd);
}


void clrscr(void)
/* clear the screen */
{
   union REGS regs;

   regs.h.ah = 6;                  /* bios function */
   regs.h.al = 0;                  /* clear entire screen */
   regs.h.bh = 7;                  /* normal attribute */
   regs.h.ch = 0;                  /* upper row position */
   regs.h.cl = 0;                  /* upper-left column
                                      position */
   regs.h.dh = 24;                 /* lowest row */
   regs.h.dl = 79;                 /* rightmost column */
   int86(0x10,&regs,&regs);        /* bios interrupt number */
} /* end function clear screen */


void gotoxy(int x,int y)
/* position cursor */
{
```

```
    union REGS regs;


    regs.h.ah = 2;            /* bios function */
    regs.h.dh = (char) y;     /* row */
    regs.h.dl = (char) x;     /* column */
    regs.h.bh = 0;            /* video page number */
    int86(0x10,&regs,&regs);  /* bios interrupt number */
} /* end function gotoxy */


void write_node(struct tree *tree_record,int direction,
                long num,long prev_location,
                long location,long var_size,int size,
                FILE *stream)
/* save the new node */
{
    int left = 1, /* pointer direction values */
        right = 2;

    if (direction != 0) {
        /* not first record */
        /* save pointer to new record */
        if ((fseek(stream,prev_location * var_size,
                                        SEEK_SET)) != 0)
            complain();
        fread(tree_record,size,1,stream);
        if (direction == left)
            tree_record->lpointer = location;
        else
            tree_record->rpointer = location;
        if ((fseek(stream,prev_location * var_size,
                                        SEEK_SET)) != 0)
            complain();
        fwrite(tree_record,size,1,stream);
    }

    /* save new record */
    if ((fseek(stream,location * var_size,SEEK_SET)) != 0)
        complain();
    fread(tree_record,size,1,stream);
    tree_record->item = num;
    tree_record->lpointer = 0L;
```

```
        tree_record->rpointer = 0L;
        if ((fseek(stream,location * var_size,SEEK_SET)) != 0)
           complain();
        fwrite(tree_record,size,1,stream);
}


void delete_record(struct tree *tree_record,
                   long counter,long back_pointer,
                   long var_size,long *save_place,
                   int size,int direction,FILE *stream)
/* delete a record and adjust the pointers */
{
    int left = 1; /* pointer selection */
    long temp_pointer; /* temporary tree pointer */

    /* deleted record node */
    /* delete stored value */
    tree_record->item = 0L;
    /* get deleted record's active pointer */
    if (direction == left)
       temp_pointer = tree_record->lpointer;
    else
       temp_pointer = tree_record->rpointer;
    /* save deleted record, we'll need other pointer later */
    if ((fseek(stream,counter * var_size,SEEK_SET)) != 0)
       complain();
    fwrite(tree_record,size,1,stream);

    /* remember deleted node */
    *save_place = counter;

    /* move tree pointer */
    /* get node previous to deleted node */
    if ((fseek(stream,back_pointer * var_size,
                                    SEEK_SET)) != 0)
       complain();
    fread(tree_record,size,1,stream);
    /* point to record deleted record used to point to */
    if (tree_record->lpointer == counter)
       tree_record->lpointer = temp_pointer;
```

```
      else
         tree_record->rpointer = temp_pointer;
      /* save previous node with new pointer */
      if ((fseek(stream,back_pointer * var_size,
                                          SEEK_SET)) != 0)
         complain();
      fwrite(tree_record,size,1,stream);

      /* delete other deleted record pointer */
      if ((fseek(stream,counter * var_size,SEEK_SET)) != 0)
         complain();
      fread(tree_record,size,1,stream);
      /* set pointer to null */
      if (direction == left)
         tree_record->lpointer = 0L;
      else
         tree_record->rpointer = 0L;
      /* save deleted record with all nulls */
      if ((fseek(stream,counter * var_size,SEEK_SET)) != 0)
         complain();
      fwrite(tree_record,size,1,stream);
}


void move_record(struct tree *tree_record,long counter,
                 long back_pointer,long var_size,
                 long *save_place,int size,int direction,
                 FILE *stream)
/* move a record and insert a record when no pointers are
   free */
{
   int left = 1; /* pointer direction */
   long temp_pointer, /* temporary pointer holders */
        locator,
        old_locator;

   /* move tree pointer back one node */
   /* get record to be deleted */
   if ((fseek(stream,counter * var_size,SEEK_SET)) != 0)
      complain();
   fread(tree_record,size,1,stream);
```

```
/* save active pointer */
if (direction == left)
   temp_pointer = tree_record->lpointer;
else
   temp_pointer = tree_record->rpointer;

/* get node previous to deleted node */
if ((fseek(stream,back_pointer * var_size,
                                  SEEK_SET)) != 0)
   complain();
fread(tree_record,size,1,stream);

/* point previous node to record that was pointed to by
   deleted record */
if (direction == left)
   tree_record->lpointer = temp_pointer;
else
   tree_record->rpointer = temp_pointer;

/* save new pointer in previous node */
if ((fseek(stream,back_pointer * var_size,
                                  SEEK_SET)) != 0)
   complain();
fwrite(tree_record,size,1,stream);

/* get deleted record's active pointer */
if ((fseek(stream,counter * var_size,SEEK_SET)) != 0)
   complain();
fread(tree_record,size,1,stream);

/* get active pointer and save */
if (direction == left)
   locator = tree_record->lpointer; /* counter node */
else
   locator = tree_record->rpointer; /* counter node */

/* null active pointer in deleted node */
if (direction == left)
   tree_record->lpointer = 0L;
else
   tree_record->rpointer = 0L;
```

```
/* save deleted record */
if ((fseek(stream,counter * var_size,SEEK_SET)) != 0)
   complain();
fwrite(tree_record,size,1,stream);

/* find first null lpointer or rpointer*/
do {
   old_locator = locator;
   if ((fseek(stream,locator * var_size,SEEK_SET)) != 0)
      complain();
   fread(tree_record,size,1,stream);
   if (direction == left)
      locator = tree_record->rpointer; /* locator node */
   else
      locator = tree_record->lpointer; /* locator node */
}
while (locator != 0L);

/* retrieve deleted node again */
if ((fseek(stream,counter * var_size,SEEK_SET)) != 0)
   complain();
/* current node */
fread(tree_record,size,1,stream);

/* get other pointer to be changed */
if (direction == left)
   temp_pointer = tree_record->rpointer;
else
   temp_pointer = tree_record->lpointer;

/* other pointer will go here */
if ((fseek(stream,old_locator * var_size,SEEK_SET)) != 0)
   complain();
fread(tree_record,size,1,stream);

/* replace which pointer? */
if (direction == left)
   tree_record->rpointer = temp_pointer;
else
   tree_record->lpointer = temp_pointer;
```

```
/* save with new pointer */
if ((fseek(stream,old_locator * var_size,SEEK_SET)) != 0)
   complain();
/* save other pointer */
fwrite(tree_record,size,1,stream);

/* delete other current pointer */
if ((fseek(stream,counter * var_size,SEEK_SET)) != 0)
   complain();
fread(tree_record,size,1,stream);

/* which pointer? */
if (direction == left)
   tree_record->rpointer = 0L; /* counter node */
else
   tree_record->lpointer = 0L; /* counter node */

/* null deleted node's other pointer */
tree_record->item = 0L; /* counter node */
/* save blank record */
if ((fseek(stream,counter * var_size,SEEK_SET)) != 0)
   complain();
fwrite(tree_record,size,1,stream);

/* remember deleted node */
*save_place = counter;
}
```

If you intend to use these programs in one of yours, you might go through them and do a little fine-tuning to make the programs a little shorter and faster, especially the random access versions. For example, when you are jumping back and forth between two nodes, you might be able to change the order of the commands (and perhaps use a few additional temporary variables) to cut down the number of fseeks, reads, and writes. I suspect the algorithm used in the subprogram that deletes nodes could be refined a bit too.

Also, be sure not to enter data into a tree in alphabetical or numerical order; if you do, you'll end up with the linked equivalent of a sequential file, which will greatly increase the search times.

USING ADDRESS POINTERS AND
DYNAMICALLY ALLOCATED MEMORY

This final example uses pointers to the beginning of areas of allocated memory for each record structure. In this example, pointers are really C-type pointers.

```
/* Chapter 9, Example 5, QuickC, 4/22/88
   Binary tree using allocated memory */

#include <stdio.h>
#include <stdlib.h>
#include <conio.h>
#include <bios.h>
#include <time.h>

#define COUNT 200
#define SENTINAL -9999 /* in first record designates
                          empty tree */

/* structure to contain tree elements */
struct tree {
   int item;
   struct tree *lpointer; /* pointer to structure with next
                             lower item */
   struct tree *rpointer; /* pointer to structure with next
                             higher item */
};

/* function prototypes */
void load_tree(int num,struct tree *head);
void read_tree(struct tree *head);
void main(void);
void clrscr(void);
int rand(void);

void main()
{
   int counter;
   size_t size = sizeof(struct tree); /* for malloc() */
   struct tree *head;
```

```
      /* initialize tree */
      if ((head = (void *) malloc(size)) == NULL) {
         putch(7);
         printf("\nOut of memory for list\n");
         exit(1);
      }
      head->item = SENTINAL; /* mark first item as unused */

      /* load items into tree */
      for (counter = 1;counter <= COUNT;counter++) {
         printf("."); /* show activity */
         load_tree(rand(),head); /* add record to tree */
      }
      printf("\n");

      read_tree(head); /* read and display tree contents */

      printf("\n");
}


void load_tree(int num,struct tree *head)
/* load items into binary tree */
{
   size_t size = sizeof(struct tree);
   int left = 1, /* current travel direction */
       right = 2, /* current travel direction */
       direction; /* last direction traveled */
   struct tree *first_empty, /* pointer to next tree
                                     record */
              *counter, /* pointer to active tree record */
              *locator; /* pointer to active tree record */

   for (;;) {
      if (head->item == SENTINAL) {
         /* empty tree */
         head->item = num; /* store first record */
         head->lpointer = NULL;
         head->rpointer = NULL;
         break; /* leave function */
      }
      counter = NULL; /* current record pointer */
      locator = head; /* next record pointer*/
```

```
        /* find highest value less than num */
        do {
           counter = locator;
           /* which direction? */
           if (num < counter->item) {
              /* left pointer */
              locator = counter->lpointer;
              direction = left;
           }
           else {
              /* right pointer */
              locator = counter->rpointer;
              direction = right;
           }
        }
        while (locator != NULL);

        /* set the tree pointer to available memory */
        if ((first_empty = (void *) malloc(size)) == NULL) {
           putch(7);
           printf("\nOut of memory for list\n");
           exit(1);
        }
        if (direction == left)
           counter->lpointer = first_empty;
        else
           counter->rpointer = first_empty;
        first_empty->item = num; /* store value */
        first_empty->lpointer = NULL;
        first_empty->rpointer = NULL;
        break;
    }
}


void read_tree(struct tree *head)
/* read the binary tree and display contents in ascending
order */
{
    /* to keep track of position within tree */
    struct tree *back_count [COUNT / 2]; /* array of pointers
                                          to structure */

    int bcount; /* back_count array position */
```

```
struct tree *locator, /* pointer to active record */
            *counter; /* pointer to active record */

/* starting record */
counter = head;

/* back counter position */
bcount = 0;

/* value to test for completion */
back_count [0] = NULL;

/* next record pointer */
locator = head;

for (;;) {
   /* back down through tree to get lowest value,
   keeping track of nodes visited in back_count array */

   /* while pointer not NULL */
   while (locator != NULL) {
      bcount++;

      /* save current position */
      back_count [bcount] = counter;

      /* left pointer */
      locator = counter->lpointer;
      counter = locator;
   }
   /* lowest value */
   /* get pointer to latest node visited */
   counter = back_count [bcount];

   /* remove latest node from list */
   bcount--;

   if (counter == NULL)
      /* end of list */
      break;
```

```
    /* display value */
    printf("%d ",counter->item);

    /* look for next node */
    locator = counter->rpointer;
    counter = locator;
  }
}


int rand(void)
{
  time_t ltime;
  int rnd;
  static unsigned long value = 0;
  unsigned long temp,
                increment = 271819,
                multiplier = 314159,
                modulus = 100001,
                int_mod = 32767;


  if (value == 0) {
    time(&ltime);
    value = (multiplier * ltime + increment);
    value = value % modulus;
    temp = value;
    temp = value % int_mod;
    rnd = (int) temp;
  }
  else {
    value = (multiplier * value + increment);
    value = value % modulus;
    temp = value;
    temp = temp % int_mod;
    rnd = (int) temp;
  }
  return(rnd);
}
```

```
void clrscr(void)
/* clear the screen */
{
   union REGS regs;

   regs.h.ah = 6;                       /* bios function */
   regs.h.al = 0;                       /* clear entire screen */
   regs.h.bh = 7;                       /* normal attribute */
   regs.h.ch = 0;                       /* upper row position */
   regs.h.cl = 0;                       /* upper-left column
                                           position */
   regs.h.dh = 24;                      /* lowest row */
   regs.h.dl = 79;                      /* rightmost column */
   int86(0x10,&regs,&regs);             /* bios interrupt number */
} /* end function clear screen */
```

I'll leave it as an exercise to the reader to remove no longer needed tree records. See Example 3 in this chapter and Example 9 in Chapter 8 for some ideas.

10

Hash Tables

Hashing is yet another method of storing strings or numbers so that they can be easily and quickly retrieved. In this way, it is like using a linked list. Unfortunately, unlike using the insertion sort or linked lists, hashing does not provide any built-in method to retrieve the list of items in ascending (or descending) order.

Insofar as storing and retrieving are concerned, hashing usually is the quickest method available. But if the table size and/or coding scheme are incorrectly chosen, hashing can be almost as bad as sequential searching. Unfortunately, there are no hard and fast rules for choosing the table size and coding method—but there are a few rules of thumb that usually work fairly well.

When using hashing, you must know (or be able to make a good guess) how many items will need to be stored in the table.

In the discussion to follow, the following abbreviations will be used.

- Item_count   The total number of items to be placed in the table.
- Table_size   The size of the hash table.
- Key   The key to be converted to a hash code; the item to be stored and retrieved.
- Key_code   The hash code resulting from converting the key.

ABOUT HASHING

First you need a structure to hold the list of items to be stored. This is usually an array but could be a random access file. In this chapter, we'll assume it is an array of names. The size of this array is Table_size. In a real hash table, the array usually contains a structure with room for both the name and a record indicator associated with each item. This indicator references the record and its data in the file that the item, name, or key stored in the hash table represents. (See Chapter 11 for more information about keys and record indicators.)

Let's say we are going to store a key. The first step is to convert the key to be stored to a hash code. The method, or hash function, is usually

```
Key_code = Key MOD Table_size
```

This of course assumes the item (Key) is an integer or has been converted to an integer.

The table position designated by Key_code is checked to see if it is empty (or null). If so, the item is stored there. If not, an empty location for the key must be found. This is called a collision. Two methods are commonly used to handle collisions: double-hashing and buckets.

DOUBLE-HASHING

The double-hashing method is the easiest to implement. The first thing to remember is that the hash table must be larger than the number of items to be stored, usually about 25%, at least 10%. Thus,

```
Table_size = Item_count * 1.25
```

or at the minimum

```
Table_size = Item_count * 1.1.
```

When a collision occurs, the Key is hashed again, this time using a different hash function. One common double-hash function is

```
Key_code = (Key_code + 1) MOD Table_size
```

Essentially, all this does is advance to the next position in the table. Since MOD Table_size is used, it will automatically wrap around to the beginning of the table if necessary. Continue to use this function until an empty table location is reached. Obviously, this is the reason that the table (Table_size) must be larger than the number of keys (Item_count) to be contained within it. If Table_size were smaller than Item_count, this double-hashing method would eventually result in an infinite loop as soon as all the table positions were filled. An alternate double-hashing function could be

```
Key_code = abs(Table_size - 2 - Key_code) MOD (Table_size - 2)
```

This function works best when Table_size is a prime number.

Each visit to the hash table with its resulting position test is called a probe.

Here is a program using double-hashing to store string values. As mentioned earlier, in a real hash program a structure containing both the name and a record number would be stored in the hash table. In this case, it would be redundant, but in real-life the record would contain more than just the key: It would contain the data associated with that key as well. The average number of probes for each key entry is displayed.

```
/* Chapter 10, Example 1, QuickC, 4/22/88
   Hash table */
#include <stdlib.h>
#include <string.h>
#include <conio.h>
#include <stdio.h>
#include <bios.h>

#define TABLE_SIZE 25 /* number of table slots */
#define ADD_SIZE 20 /* number of strings to add to table */
#define SEARCH_SIZE 6 /* number of strings to search for */
#define NAME_SIZE 10 /* size of string */

char name_list [ADD_SIZE] [NAME_SIZE] =
                       {"Fred","Mary","Linda","Carol",
                        "John","Zepherine","Harold",
                        "Nancy","Bob","Ray","Betty",
                        "Frank","Elmer","Al","Tom",
                        "Diane","Glenda","Bernard",
                        "Clarence","Joe"},
     search_list [SEARCH_SIZE] [NAME_SIZE] =
                        {"Mary","Fred","Tom",
                         "Diahn","Irene","Yvonne"};

/* function prototypes */
void dhash(char firstname [],int *probes,
           unsigned int *code,char hash [] [NAME_SIZE],
           int *test);
void readdhash(char firstname [],unsigned int code,
               int *found,char hash [][NAME_SIZE],
               int *test);
void main(void);
void clrscr(void);
```

```
void main()
{
    unsigned int code = 0; /* hash code */
    int totalprobes = 0, /* total number of probes */
        probes = 0, /* probes for storing one item */
        test, /* valid data? */
        true = 1,
        false = 0,
        found = true, /* successful search? */
        counter;
    char hash [TABLE_SIZE] [NAME_SIZE], /* hash table */
        firstname [NAME_SIZE]; /* name to search for */

    /* initialize array */
    for (counter = 0;counter < TABLE_SIZE;counter++)
        hash [counter] [0] = '\0';

    /* store names in hash table */
    printf("\n");
    clrscr();
    for (counter = 0;counter < ADD_SIZE;counter++) {
        printf("."); /* indicate activity */

        /* put name in store variable */
        strcpy(firstname,name_list [counter]);

        /* convert name to key code */
        dhash(firstname,&probes,&code,hash,&test);
        if (test== false) {
            /* zero length name to store */
            putch(7);
            printf("Attempt to store zero length string");
            exit(1);
        }

        /* add on latest number of probes */
        totalprobes += probes;

        /* store name in array */
        strcpy(hash [code],firstname);
        printf("\n");
    }
```

```
    clrscr();
    printf("Average number of probes %d\n\n",totalprobes/
ADD_SIZE);

    /* search for some names */
    for (counter = 0;counter < SEARCH_SIZE;counter++) {
       strcpy(firstname,search_list [counter]);
       readdhash(firstname,code,&found,hash,&test);
       if (found == false)
          printf("The name %s was not found\n\n",firstname);
    }
}


void dhash(char firstname [],int *probes,
           unsigned int *code,char hash [] [NAME_SIZE],
           int *test)
/* store a string in a double hash-coded table */
{
    int stringcode, /* temporary code holder */
        length, /* length of string being stored */
        true = 1,
        false = 0,
        counter;

    length = strlen(firstname); /* length of string being
                                         stored */
    *test = true;

    /* be sure there is a string to code */
    if (length != 0) {
       /* create code */
       stringcode = firstname [0];
       for (counter = 1;counter < length;counter++)
          /* use XOR operator for conversion */
          stringcode = stringcode ^ firstname [counter];
       *code = stringcode % TABLE_SIZE;

       *probes = 1;

       /* find an empty slot in the table */
       while (hash [*code] [0] != '\0') {
```

```
            /* count the probes */
            *probes += 1;

            /* next table position */
            /* double-hashing */
            *code = (*code + 1) % TABLE_SIZE;
        }
    }
    else
        /* zero length string */
        *test = false;
}


void readdhash(char firstname [],unsigned int code,
               int *found,char hash [] [NAME_SIZE],int *test)
/* search hash array */
{
    int true = 1,
        false = 0,
        stringcode, /* temporary code holder */
        length, /* length of string being searched for */
        counter;

    /* default */
    *found = true;
    *test = true;

    /* test for zero length string */
    length = strlen(firstname);
    if (length != 0) {
        /* create a code */
        stringcode = firstname [0];
        for (counter = 1;counter < length;counter++)
            /* use XOR operator for unhashing */
            stringcode = stringcode ^ firstname [counter];
        code = stringcode % TABLE_SIZE;

        /* search the table */
        while (strcmp(firstname,hash [code]) != 0) {
            if (hash [code] [0] == '\0') {
                /* no more names */
                *found = false;
```

```
                        break;
                }

            /* next position in table */
            code = (code + 1) % TABLE_SIZE;
        }
    }
    else
        /* zero length string */
        *test = false;
}


void clrscr(void)
/* clear the screen */
{
    union REGS regs;

    regs.h.ah = 6;              /* bios function */
    regs.h.al = 0;              /* clear entire screen */
    regs.h.bh = 7;              /* normal attribute */
    regs.h.ch = 0;              /* upper row position */
    regs.h.cl = 0;              /* upper-left column
                                   position */
    regs.h.dh = 24;             /* lowest row */
    regs.h.dl = 79;             /* rightmost column */
    int86(0x10,&regs,&regs);    /* bios interrupt number */
} /* end function clear screen */
```

You can see the method I used to create the hash key from the string key. I XORed the ASCII value of each character in the string, in turn, with the result of the preceding XOR operation. The result is guaranteed to be an integer in the range 0–255. There are many other possible methods that could be used to create a hash key. Another possibility is to use squaring, multiplying, or some other arithmetic operation on the key to create a large number. Then use some specific number of digits from some specific area, usually the center, of the resulting numeric string as the hash key. This method is called midsquare. Using multiplication instead of squaring:

```
long Key_code;
char Key [10],
     code [10],
     temp [4];

...

/* multiply ASCII values of Key's characters together */
Key_code = Key [0];
for (x = 1;x < strlen(Key);x++)
   Key_code *= Key [x];

/* convert product to string so center can be
   extracted */
ultoa(Key_code,code,10);
/* erase contents of string variable */
temp [0] = '\0';
/* move 4th, 5th, and 6th digits to temp variable */
for (x = 3;x < 6;x++) {
   strcat(temp,&code [x]);
/* terminate string */
temp [3] = '\0';
/* convert back to a numeric value */
Key_code = atol(temp);

...
```

Another possibility might be to use the last few digits of a unique regularly distributed number, such as a social security number. or a serial number.

As you can see in the program example, to retrieve an item from the table use the same first hash function to create a code and check that table position. If it contains the item, then you are done. If it is empty, the item is not in the table. If the position is not empty and does not contain the item, then use the second hash function until the item is located or an empty table position is reached.

PUTTING THE HASH TABLE IN A FILE

This next example is the same as the first except that the table is kept in a random access file instead of an array in memory. Obviously, this permits you to have a potentially much larger hash table.

```
/* Chapter 10, Example 2, QuickC, 4/22/88
   Double-hashing in a random access file*/
#include <stdlib.h>
#include <string.h>
#include <conio.h>
#include <stdio.h>
#include <io.h>
#include <bios.h>

#define TABLE_SIZE 25  /* number of potential storage
                              slots */
#define ADD_SIZE 20 /* number of items to store */
#define SEARCH_SIZE 6 /* number of items to search for */
#define NAME_SIZE 10 /* size of items being stored */

char name_list [ADD_SIZE] [NAME_SIZE] =
                        {"Fred","Mary","Linda","Carol",
                         "John","Zepherine","Harold",
                         "Nancy","Bob","Ray","Betty",
                         "Frank","Elmer","Al","Tom",
                         "Diane","Glenda","Bernard",
                         "Clarence","Joe"},
      search_list [SEARCH_SIZE] [NAME_SIZE] =
                            {"Mary","Fred","Tom",
                             "Diahn","Irene","Yvonne"};


/* function prototypes */
void dhash(char firstname [],int *probes,
           unsigned int *code,FILE *stream,int *test);
void readdhash(char firstname [],unsigned int code,
               int *found,FILE *stream,int *test);
void complain(char string [15]);
void main(void);
void clrscr(void);
```

```
void main()
{
   unsigned int code = 0; /* hash code */
   int totalprobes = 0, /* total number of probes */
       test, /* invalid code? */
       probes = 0, /* probes for storing one item */
       handle, /* data file handle */
       true = 1,
       false = 0,
       found = true,
       counter;
   char firstname [NAME_SIZE], /* name to search for */
        deleted [8], /* used to mark unused slots */
        filename [13]; /* name of hash (data) file */
   FILE *stream; /* for data file */

   strcpy(&deleted [0],"DELETED");
   strcpy(&filename [0],"ch10_2.dat");

   /* open file */
   if ((stream = fopen(filename,"w+b")) == NULL)
      complain("open file");

   /* initialize file with "DELETED" in every position */
   for (counter = 0;counter < TABLE_SIZE;counter++) {
      if ((fseek(stream,(long) counter *
                         (long) NAME_SIZE,SEEK_SET)) != 0)
         complain("find record");
      fwrite(deleted,(size_t) NAME_SIZE,1,stream);
   }

   /* store names in hash file */
   clrscr();
   for (counter = 0;counter < ADD_SIZE;counter++) {
      printf(".");

      /* put name in store variable */
      strcpy(firstname,name_list [counter]);
      dhash(firstname,&probes,&code,stream,&test);
      if (test == false) {
         /* zero length name to store */
         putch(7);
```

```
              printf("Attempt to store zero length string");
              exit(1);
         }

         /* add on latest number of probes */
         totalprobes += probes;

         /* store name in file */
         if ((fseek(stream,(long) code *
                              (long) NAME_SIZE,SEEK_SET)) != 0)
            complain("find record");
         fwrite(firstname,(size_t) NAME_SIZE,1,stream);
         printf("\n");
    }

    clrscr();
    printf("Average number of probles %d\n\n",
                                        totalprobes/ADD_SIZE);

    /* search for some names */
    for (counter = 0;counter < SEARCH_SIZE;counter++) {
       strcpy(firstname,search_list [counter]);
       /* look in file */
       readdhash(firstname,code,&found,stream,&test);
       if (found == false)
          printf("The name %s was not found\n\n",firstname);
    }

}

void dhash(char firstname [],int *probes,
           unsigned int *code,FILE *stream,int *test)
/* store a string in a double hash-coded table */
{
    int handle, /* for data file */
        stringcode, /* temporary hash code holder */
        length, /* length of string being stored */
        true = 1,
        false = 0,
        counter;
    char hashname [NAME_SIZE]; /* string retrieved from
                                  file */
```

```
handle = fileno(stream);
length = strlen(firstname);
*test = true;

/* be sure there is a string to code */
if (length != 0) {
   /* create code */
   stringcode = firstname [0];
   for (counter = 1;counter < length;counter++)
      /* use XOR operator for hashing */
      stringcode = stringcode ^ firstname [counter];
   *code = stringcode % TABLE_SIZE;

   *probes = 1;

   /* find an empty slot in the table */
   if ((fseek(stream,(long) *code *
                     (long) NAME_SIZE,SEEK_SET)) != 0)
      complain("find record");
   fread(hashname,(size_t) NAME_SIZE,1,stream);
   while (strcmp(hashname,"DELETED") != 0) {

      /* next table position */
      *code = (*code + 1) % TABLE_SIZE;

      /* retrieve string at code position */
      if ((fseek(stream,(long) *code *
                        (long) NAME_SIZE,SEEK_SET)) != 0)
         complain("find record");
      fread(hashname,(size_t) NAME_SIZE,1,stream);

      /* count the probes */
      *probes += 1;
   }
}
else
   /* zero length string */
   *test = false;
}


void readdhash(char firstname [],unsigned int code,
            int *found,FILE *stream,int *test)
```

```
/* search hash array */
{
   int true = 1,
       false = 0,
       handle, /* for data file */
       stringcode, /* temporary hash code holder */
       length, /* length of string being stored */
       counter;
   char hashname [NAME_SIZE]; /* string retrieved from
                                        file */


   /* default */
   *found = true;
   *test = true;

   /* test for zero length string */
   length = strlen(firstname);
   if (length != 0) {
      /* create a code */
      stringcode = firstname [0];
      for (counter = 1;counter < length;counter++)
         stringcode = stringcode ^ firstname [counter];
      code = stringcode % TABLE_SIZE;

      /* search table */
      if ((fseek(stream,(long) code *
                        (long) NAME_SIZE,SEEK_SET)) != 0)
         complain("find record");
      /* fetch data at that code */
      fread(hashname,(size_t) NAME_SIZE,1,stream);
      /* keep searching if necessary */
      while (strcmp(firstname,hashname) != 0) {
         /* next position in table */
         code = (code + 1) % TABLE_SIZE;

         /* next string */
         if ((fseek(stream,(long) code *
                           (long) NAME_SIZE,SEEK_SET)) != 0)
            complain("find record");
```

```
            /* get data at new position */
            fread(hashname,(size_t) NAME_SIZE,1,stream);

            if (strcmp(hashname,"DELETED") == 0) {
                /* no more names */
                *found = false;
                break;
            }
        }
    }
    else
        /* zero length string */
        *test = false;
}


void complain(char string [])
/* error message */
{
    putch(7);
    printf("Error! Can't %s\n",string);
    exit(1);
}


void clrscr(void)
/* clear the screen */
{
    union REGS regs;

    regs.h.ah = 6;                  /* bios function */
    regs.h.al = 0;                  /* clear entire screen */
    regs.h.bh = 7;                  /* normal attribute */
    regs.h.ch = 0;                  /* upper row position */
    regs.h.cl = 0;                  /* upper-left column
                                        position */
    regs.h.dh = 24;                 /* lowest row */
    regs.h.dl = 79;                 /* rightmost column */
    int86(0x10,&regs,&regs);        /* bios interrupt number */
} /* end function clear screen */
```

BUCKETS

The bucket method keeps a list (bucket) of every key that codes to each position in the hash table. Collisions are added to the appropriate list instead of being placed elsewhere in the table.

You can use a separate array for each list, or use a separate dimension of an array for each list. In the example to follow, I used a separate dimension for each list. In this method, Table_size does not need to exceed Item_count; in fact, Table_size is usually smaller than Item_count. The next step is to calculate the size of the lists. A rule of thumb is that the list size should be no less than Item_count / Table_size. In my example I used Item_count / Table_size * 2.5. (Item_count is 20, Table_size is 10, and the list [bucket] size is 5.)

The lists are searched sequentially. You could use the insertion sort to order the lists and a binary search to retrieve a key, but the extra code and time required would probably not be worthwhile. A better plan is to use more table positions, smaller lists, and carefully craft your coding function to avoid collisions.

Here is an example to give you an idea of how the system works.

```
/* Chapter 10, Example 3, QuickC, 4/22/88
   Hash table, buckets */
#include <stdlib.h>
#include <string.h>
#include <conio.h>
#include <stdio.h>
#include <bios.h>

#define BUCKET_SIZE 5 /* size of each bucket */
#define TABLE_SIZE 10 /* size of the table */
#define ADD_SIZE 20 /* number of items to add to table */
#define SEARCH_SIZE 6 /* number of items to search for */
#define NAME_SIZE 10 /* size of string */

char name_list [ADD_SIZE] [NAME_SIZE] =
                    {"Fred","Mary","Linda","Carol",
                    "John","Zepherine","Harold",
                    "Nancy","Bob","Ray","Betty",
                    "Frank","Elmer","Al","Tom",
```

```
                              "Diane","Glenda","Bernard",
                              "Clarence","Joe"},
        search_list [SEARCH_SIZE] [NAME_SIZE] =
                                {"Mary","Fred","Tom",
                                "Diahn","Irene","Yvonne"};


/* function prototypes */
void bhash(char firstname [],int *probes,
           int *position,unsigned int *code,
           char hash [] [TABLE_SIZE] [NAME_SIZE],int *test);
void readhash(char firstname [],unsigned int code,
              int *found,char hash [] [TABLE_SIZE]
              [NAME_SIZE],int *test);
void main(void);
void clrscr(void);


void main()
{
   unsigned int code = 0; /* hash code */
   int totalprobes = 0, /* total number of probes */
       probes = 0, /* probes for storing one item */
       position = 0, /* position within bucket */
       test, /* valid code? */
       true = 1,
       false = 0,
       found = true,
       counter,
       counter1;
   char hash [BUCKET_SIZE] [TABLE_SIZE] [NAME_SIZE], /* hash
                                                      table */
        firstname [NAME_SIZE]; /* name to search for */

   /* initialize array */
   for (counter = 0;counter < BUCKET_SIZE;counter++) {
      for (counter1 = 0;counter1 < TABLE_SIZE;counter1++)
         hash [counter] [counter1] [0] = '\0';
   }

   /* store names in hash table */
   clrscr();
   for (counter = 0;counter < ADD_SIZE;counter++) {
      printf(".");
```

```
                  /* put name in store variable */
                  strcpy(firstname,name_list [counter]);
                  /* store name */
                  bhash(firstname,&probes,&position,&code,hash,&test);
                  if (test == false) {
                     /* zero length name to store */
                     putch(7);
                     printf("Attempt to store zero length string");
                     exit(1);
                  }

                  /* add on latest number of probes */
                  totalprobes += probes;

                  /* store name in array */
                  strcpy(hash [position] [code],firstname);
                  printf("\n");
               }

               clrscr();
               printf("Average number of probes %d\n\n",
                                              totalprobes/ADD_SIZE);

               /* search for some names */
               for (counter = 0;counter < SEARCH_SIZE;counter++) {
                  strcpy(firstname,search_list [counter]);
                  readhash(firstname,code,&found,hash,&test);
                  if (found == false)
                     printf("The name %s was not found\n\n",firstname);
               }
            }


void bhash(char firstname [],int *probes,
              int *position,unsigned int *code,
              char hash [] [TABLE_SIZE] [NAME_SIZE],int *test)
/* store a string in a hash-coded table with buckets */
{
    int stringcode, /* temporary holder for code */
        length, /* length of string to store */
        true = 1,
        false = 0,
        counter;
```

```
        length = strlen(firstname);
        *test = true;

        /* be sure there is a string to code */
        if (length != 0) {
            /* create code */
            stringcode = firstname [0];
            for (counter = 1;counter < length;counter++)
                stringcode = stringcode ^ firstname [counter];
            *code = stringcode % TABLE_SIZE; /* table position */
            *probes = 1;
            *position = 1; /* bucket position */

            /* find an empty slot in the table */
            while (hash [*position] [*code] [0] != '\0') {
                /* count the probes */
                *probes += 1;

                /* move within bucket */
                *position += 1;
            }
        }
    else
        /* zero length string */
        *test = false;
}


void readhash(char firstname [],unsigned int code,
              int *found,char hash [] [TABLE_SIZE]
              [NAME_SIZE],int *test)
/* search hash array */
{
    int true = 1,
        false = 0,
        stringcode, /* temporary holder for code */
        length, /* length of string being searched for */
        position, /* position within bucket */
        counter;

    /* default */
    *found = true;
    *test = true;
```

```
                /* test for zero length string */
                length = strlen(firstname);
                if (length != 0) {
                   /* not zero, create a code */
                   stringcode = firstname [0];
                   for (counter = 1;counter < length;counter++)
                      /* use XOR operator */
                      stringcode = stringcode ^ firstname [counter];
                   code = stringcode % TABLE_SIZE; /* table position */
                   position = 1; /* bucket position */

                   /* search table */
                   while (strcmp(firstname,hash [position] [code]) != 0){
                      if (hash [position] [code] [0] == '\0') {
                         /* no more names */
                         *found = false;
                         break;
                      }
                   position++; /* next bucket position */
                   }
                }
                else
                   /* zero length string */
                   *test = false;
        }


        void clrscr(void)
        /* clear the screen */
        {
           union REGS regs;

           regs.h.ah = 6;                /* bios function */
           regs.h.al = 0;                /* clear entire screen */
           regs.h.bh = 7;                /* normal attribute */
           regs.h.ch = 0;                /* upper row position */
           regs.h.cl = 0;                /* upper-left column
                                            position */

           regs.h.dh = 24;              /* lowest row */
           regs.h.dl = 79;              /* rightmost column */
           int86(0x10,&regs,&regs);     /* bios interrupt number */
        } /* end function clear screen */
```

The bhash( ) and readhash( ) functions do not test for the end of the bucket list. This should be added to a real version of the program.

DELETING TABLE ENTRIES

When you delete a table entry, you must not set it back to null or you will interfere with future searches. Remember, when a null entry is reached in the course of a search the search stops. In the example program, the string "DELETED" is used in place of the key to indicate it has been deleted. The next time a new key is added to the table, it is placed in the first position where a null or "DELETED" is found. Searches ignore the "DELETED" string and move on to the next position.

Here is a double-hash program example using deletion.

```
/* Chapter 10, Example 4, QuickC, 4/22/88
   Hash table with deletions */
#include <stdlib.h>
#include <string.h>
#include <conio.h>
#include <stdio.h>
#include <bios.h>

#define TABLE_SIZE 25 /* number of table slots */
#define ADD_SIZE 20 /* number of strings to add to table */
#define SEARCH_SIZE 6 /* number of strings to search for */
#define NAME_SIZE 10 /* size of string */
#define DELETE_SIZE 5 /* number of strings to delete */

char name_list [ADD_SIZE] [NAME_SIZE] =
                    {"Fred","Mary","Linda","Carol",
                     "John","Zepherine","Harold",
                     "Nancy","Bob","Ray","Betty",
                     "Frank","Elmer","Al","Tom",
                     "Diane","Glenda","Bernard",
                     "Clarence","Joe"},
      delete_list [DELETE_SIZE] [NAME_SIZE] =
                      {"Linda","Carol","Robert",
                       "John","Fred"},
```

```
                    search_list [SEARCH_SIZE] [NAME_SIZE] =
                                        {"Mary","Fred","Tom",
                                        "Diahn","Irene","Yvonne"};


        /* function prototypes */
        void dhash(char firstname [],int *probes,
                    unsigned int *code,char hash [] [NAME_SIZE],
                    int *test);
        void readdhash(char firstname [],unsigned int *code,
                        int *found,char hash [][NAME_SIZE],
                        int *test);
        void clrscr(void);
        void main(void);


        void main()
        {
            unsigned int code = 0; /* hash code */
            int totalprobes = 0, /* total number of probes */
                probes = 0, /* probes for storing one item */
                test, /* valid code? */
                true = 1,
                false = 0,
                found = true,
                counter;
            char hash [TABLE_SIZE] [NAME_SIZE], /* hash table */
                firstname [NAME_SIZE]; /* name to search for */

            /* initialize array */
            for (counter = 0;counter < TABLE_SIZE;counter++)
                hash [counter] [0] = '\0';

            /* store names in hash table */
            clrscr();
            for (counter = 0;counter < ADD_SIZE;counter++) {
                printf(".");

                /* put name in store variable */
                strcpy(firstname,name_list [counter]);
                dhash(firstname,&probes,&code,hash,&test);
                if (test == false) {
                    /* zero length name to store */
```

```
        putch(7);
        printf("Attempt to store zero length string");
        exit(1);
    }

    /* add on latest number of probes */
    totalprobes += probes;

    /* store name in array */
    strcpy(hash [code],firstname);
    printf("\n");
}

clrscr();
printf("Average number of probes %d\n\n",
                            totalprobes/ADD_SIZE);

/* delete a few strings */
for (counter = 0;counter < DELETE_SIZE;counter++) {
    strcpy(firstname,delete_list [counter]);
    readdhash(firstname,&code,&found,hash,&test);
    if (found == true)
        strcpy(hash [code],"DELETED");
}

/* search for some names */
for (counter = 0;counter < SEARCH_SIZE;counter++) {
    strcpy(firstname,search_list [counter]);
    readdhash(firstname,&code,&found,hash,&test);
    if (found == false)
        printf("The name %s was not found\n\n",firstname);
}
}


void dhash(char firstname [],int *probes,
        unsigned int *code,char hash [] [NAME_SIZE],
        int *test)
/* store a string in a double hash-coded table */
{
    int stringcode, /* temporary code holder */
        length, /* length of string being stored */
```

```
          true = 1,
          false = 0,
          counter;

      length = strlen(firstname); /* length of string being
                                          stored */
      *test = true;

      /* be sure there is a string to code */
      if (length != 0) {
         /* create code */
         stringcode = firstname [0];
         for (counter = 1;counter < length;counter++)
            /* use XOR operator for hashing */
            stringcode = stringcode ^ firstname [counter];
         *code = stringcode % TABLE_SIZE;

         *probes = 1;
         /* find an empty slot in the table */
         while (hash [*code] [0] != '\0' &&
                      strcmp("DELETED",hash [*code]) != 0) {

            /* count the probes */
            *probes += 1;

            /* next table position */
            *code = (*code + 1) % TABLE_SIZE;
         }
      }
      else
         /* zero length string */
         *test = false;
}


void readdhash(char firstname [],unsigned int *code,
                int *found,char hash [] [NAME_SIZE],
                int *test)
/* search hash array */
{
   int true = 1,
       false = 0,
```

```
            stringcode, /* temporary code holder */
            length, /* length of string being searched for */
            counter;

    /* default */
    *found = true;
    *test = false;

    /* test for zero length string */
    length = strlen(firstname);
    if (length != 0) {
        /* create a code */
        stringcode = firstname [0];
        for (counter = 1;counter < length;counter++)
            stringcode = stringcode ^ firstname [counter];
        *code = stringcode % TABLE_SIZE;

        /* search table */
        while (strcmp(firstname,hash [*code]) != 0) {
            if (hash [*code] [0] == '\0') {
                /* no more names */
                *found = false;
                break;
            }

            /* next position in table */
            *code = (*code + 1) % TABLE_SIZE;
        }
    }
    else
        /* zero length string */
        *test = false;
}

void clrscr(void)
/* clear the screen */
{
    union REGS regs;

    regs.h.ah = 6;                      /* bios function */
    regs.h.al = 0;                      /* clear entire screen */
    regs.h.bh = 7;                      /* normal attribute */
```

```
        regs.h.ch = 0;              /* upper row position */
        regs.h.cl = 0;              /* upper-left column
                                       position */
        regs.h.dh = 24;            /* lowest row */
        regs.h.dl = 79;            /* rightmost column */
        int86(0x10,&regs,&regs);   /* bios interrupt number */
    } /* end function clear screen */
```

PRINTING THE TABLE

As mentioned at the beginning of the chapter, hash tables do not lend themselves to printing the list of keys or records in order. You must use a supplementary method to keep a list of the ordered items or sort the table.

UNIQUE KEYS

The keys must be unique or you won't be able to tell when you reach the correct one when searching. See Chapter 11 for more information about unique keys.

11

Indexing

When you have a data file containing a large number of records, each with a large number of fields, index files can be useful.

Let's say you have a mailing list containing a list of customers. The fields are:

- Name
- Company
- Address
- City
- State
- ZIP

Normally you access the customers by name. In that case, you could sort the file on the name field and look up specific names with a binary search. This would work fine. But when you print the mailing labels for a bulk mailing, you would wish to print them in ZIP code order. You could then easily bundle the letters by ZIP code, get faster service from the post office, and save a little money. You could re-sort the list in ZIP code order, but if it was very large all this sorting and re-sorting would waste a lot of time. You could keep two versions of the file, but this would use up a lot of disk space, as well as making changes to the files a lot of extra work with new possibilities for error. The answer is to use one file and two indexes.

An index file is simply the contents of an array loaded with a list of index entries. Each index entry is the contents of the field or fields you wish to index and an indicator, usually the random access record number, to the record containing those field contents. Since an array can normally occupy 64Kb, if the pointer is an integer (2 bytes) and the field content is a string of 10 bytes, you can put approximately 5400 entries in an array. If you have more records or a larger index key, you'll have to put the index list in a random access file instead of an array.

There are four ways you can organize the index:

1. You can use an insertion sort and binary search.
2. You can use a binary tree.
3. You can use a hash table.
4. You can use a linked list.

Material was previously supplied explaining each of these options.

The insertion sort would take up the least memory and disk space but would require the most time to search, add, and delete records. However, if your list is short, a few hundred items, then the insertion sort uses a great deal less code.

The hash table would be the fastest for searching for specific entries but would also take up the most room. Also, if you chose a poor hash function then the hash table would perform poorly as well. Besides which, a convenient method of printing the table contents in order was not discussed. This would require a much more complex program than any of those listed in Chapter 10.

The linked list has about the same performance as the insertion sort but requires more program code. Therefore, the insertion sort is the preference here, especially if the index is read much more than it is changed. If it is changed much more than it is read, then perhaps the linked list might be the better choice.

If speed is important, and it usually is, the binary tree would be the best choice, even though the required supporting subprograms are the longest.

The program examples in this chapter will organize the index as a binary tree and an insertion sorted list. However, you could substitute any scheme that permitted reading the index list in ascending order, quickly finding any specific entry in that list, as well as being capable of rapidly adding new entries and deleting old ones.

MULTIFIELD INDEXES

Sometimes an index is not unique, such as a ZIP code. But there are also times when you wish to index on that field anyway. This will work fine when you add your records and when you print the list. But how would you then delete the nonunique index entry and be sure you got the right one? You could examine each matching record until you located the correct one, but that would be tedious. A better scheme would be to combine another field with the ZIP code field, which combination would be unique. In the mailing list program that follows, I could have combined the ZIP with the customer name. This is not an especially good choice, because it still might be duplicated. If you are writing a real-world version of such a program, you'd need a better plan, such as a computer-generated unique customer number. To make the program simple, it uses the name as the key. This can easily be changed. As an exercise, you might wish to change the program to use a concatenation of the name and ZIP code as mentioned earlier. Customer numbers are frequently generated by using a few characters from the last name, a few from the ZIP, and a few from the city. Use enough characters from the beginning of the last name to make sure the index is in alphabetical order by last name. You might want to try this.

A MAILING LIST USING A BINARY TREE INDEX

The first example will handle the mailing list previously mentioned. I will not use formatted data entry screens or fancy menus as described in earlier chapters since the programs would then take up far too much space in the book. Also, the error checking and user-friendliness will be minimal; the object of the programs is to illustrate the use of an index. The programs make the rather rash assumption that there are no duplicate names. Unique index entries were discussed in the previous section and Chapter 10.

This version of the binary tree program is a bit different from Example 4 in Chapter 9. In that example, separate files were used for the tree and the deleted node list. In this example, I use one big structure containing the binary tree key and its left and right pointers to the next key (the total is stored in the left pointer field in record zero), another field, delete, for the deleted list (the list total is stored in that field in record zero), and the record information such as name, address, etc. The program uses the name field for the key but you could easily change this in the lines where I store the name field to tree_record.key. The key and its associated name, address, etc., are stored in the same record.

```
/* Chapter 11, Example 1, QuickC, 5/14/88
   Mailing list database using random access
   binary tree with record deletion */

#include <stdio.h>
#include <stdlib.h>
```

```c
#include <conio.h>
#include <io.h>
#include <string.h>
#include <bios.h>

#define KEY_LEN 25
#define NAME_LEN 25
#define ADR_LEN 25
#define CITY_LEN 15
#define STATE_LEN 3
#define ZIP_LEN 6

/* structure to contain tree elements */
struct tree {
    long lpointer; /* left pointer except record count in
                        record zero */
    long rpointer; /* right pointer */
    long delete; /* deleted node (if any) except delete count
                    in record zero */
    char key [KEY_LEN]; /* index key data */
    char name [NAME_LEN];
    char address [ADR_LEN];
    char city [CITY_LEN];
    char state [STATE_LEN];
    char zip [ZIP_LEN];
};

/* function prototypes */
void load_radtree(struct tree *tree_record,FILE *stream);
void read_ratree(struct tree *tree_record,FILE *stream);
void complain(void);
void delete_ratree(char key [],int *found,FILE *stream);
void pause(void);
void add(void);
void change(void);
void delete(void);
void print(void);
void get_info(int col,int row,char entry [],int length);
void clrscr(void);
void gotoxy(int x,int y);
void main(void);
void blank_tree(struct tree *empty_tree);
```

```
void main()
{
   size_t size = sizeof(struct tree); /* for fread & fwrite
                                                functions */
   char dest_file [13]; /* file name */
   FILE *stream; /* for tree file */
   struct tree tree_record; /* for record data */
   int choice; /* menu choice */

   /* set file name */
   strcpy(&dest_file [0],"ch11_1.dat");


   /* see if file exists */
   if (access(dest_file,0) != 0) {
      /* create file to contain tree if not */
      if ((stream = fopen(dest_file,"wb")) == NULL) {
         putch(7); /* beep */
         gotoxy(10,24);
         printf("Unable to open file\n");
         exit(1);
      }

      /* number of deleted nodes to start */
      tree_record.delete = 0L;

      /* number of items in tree to start */
      tree_record.lpointer = 0L; /* use lpointer in record
                                    zero to contain total of
                                    records */
      if ((fseek(stream,0L,SEEK_SET)) != 0)
         complain();
      fwrite(&tree_record,size,1,stream); /* store record
                                             zero */

      fclose(stream);
   }

   printf("\n"); /* so clrscr() works in QC environment */
```

```
/* menu */
for (;;) {
   clrscr();
   gotoxy(20,10);
   printf("Menu");
   gotoxy(10,12);
   printf("Add a name");
   gotoxy(10,13);
   printf("Change a name");
   gotoxy(10,14);
   printf("Delete a name");
   gotoxy(10,15);
   printf("Print names");
   gotoxy(10,17);
   printf("End program");

   gotoxy(10,19);
   printf("Your choice by first letter ");
   choice = getche();

   switch (choice) {
      case 'A':
      case 'a':
         add();
         break;
      case 'C':
      case 'c':
         change();
         break;
      case 'D':
      case 'd':
         delete();
         break;
      case 'P':
      case 'p':
         print();
         break;
      case 'E':
      case 'e':
         break;
```

```
                default:
                    putch(7);
                    break;
                }
                if (choice == 'E' || choice == 'e')
                break;
            } /* end for */
        } /* end main */


void add(void)
/* add a record */
{
    char dest_file [13]; /* file name */
    FILE *stream; /* for tree file */
    struct tree tree_record; /* record structure */
    int answer; /* reply to prompt */

    /* set file name */
    strcpy(&dest_file [0],"ch11_1.dat");

    /* open file containing mailing list */
    if ((stream = fopen(dest_file,"r+b")) == NULL) {
        putch(7); /* beep */
        gotoxy(10,24);
        printf("Unable to open file\n");
        exit(1);
    }

    /* get data */
    for (;;) {
        clrscr();

        gotoxy(10,10);
        /* prompt */
        printf("Name? ");
        /* erase any data in variable */
        tree_record.name [0] = '\0';
        /* get the name data */
        get_info(16,10,tree_record.name,NAME_LEN - 1);

        gotoxy(10,11);
        printf("Address? ");
```

```
        tree_record.address [0] = '\0';
        get_info(19,11,tree_record.address,ADR_LEN - 1);

        gotoxy(10,12);
        printf("City? ");
        tree_record.city [0] = '\0';
        get_info(16,12,tree_record.city,CITY_LEN - 1);

        gotoxy(10,13);
        printf("State? ");
        tree_record.state [0] = '\0';
        get_info(17,13,tree_record.state,STATE_LEN - 1);

        gotoxy(10,14);
        printf("Zip? ");
        tree_record.zip [0] = '\0';
        get_info(15,14,tree_record.zip,ZIP_LEN - 1);

        if (strlen(tree_record.name) == 0) {
            putch(7);
            gotoxy(10,20);
            printf("No name entered\n");
            pause();
            break;
        }

        /* save record */
        strcpy(tree_record.key,tree_record.name);
        load_radtree(&tree_record,stream);

        /* more? */
        gotoxy(10,16);
        printf("Another? ");
        answer = getch();
        if (answer == 'N' || answer == 'n')
            break;
    } /* end for */
    fclose(stream);
}


void get_info(int col,int row,char entry [],int length)
/* get the operator's data input */
```

```
{
    int counter;
    char ch;

    gotoxy(col,row);
    /* get characters up to length of variable or
       return key */
    for (counter = 0;counter < length;counter++) {
        ch = (char) getche();
        if (ch == 13) /* carriage return */
            break;
        if (ch == 8) { /* backspace */
            col --;
            gotoxy(col,row);
            putch(32);
            col--;
            counter -= 2;
        }
        else
            entry [counter] = ch; /* store character entered */
        col++; /* next character */
        gotoxy(col,row);
    }
    putch(7); /* tell operator field is completed */
    entry [counter] = '\0';
}


void change(void)
/* change a record */
{
    long locator, /* record node */
         var_size = (long) sizeof(struct tree); /* for
                                                    fseek() */
    size_t size = sizeof(struct tree); /* for fread & fwrite
                                          functions */
    int true = 1,
        false = 0,
        found, /* for key search */
        answer; /* reply to prompt */
    char dest_file [13], /* file name */
         old_key [KEY_LEN], /* temporary variable for key
                               value */
```

```
      name [NAME_LEN], /* for record data */
      address [ADR_LEN],
      city [CITY_LEN],
      state [STATE_LEN],
      zip [ZIP_LEN];
FILE *stream; /* for tree file */
struct tree tree_record; /* record structure */

/* set file name */
strcpy(&dest_file [0],"ch11_1.dat");

/* open file containing mailing list */
if ((stream = fopen(dest_file,"r+b")) == NULL) {
   putch(7); /* beep */
   gotoxy(10,24);
   printf("Unable to open file\n");
   exit(1);
}

/* show old data, get new data */
for (;;) {
   /* start with blank fields */
   name [0] = '\0';
   address [0] = '\0';
   city [0] = '\0';
   state [0] = '\0';
   zip [0] = '\0';

   clrscr();
   gotoxy(10,1);
   /* prompt */
   printf("Name to change? ");
   /* get key of record to change */
   get_info(26,1,old_key,NAME_LEN - 1);

   /* see if name entered */
   if (strlen(old_key) == 0) {
      putch(7);
      gotoxy(10,20);
      printf("No name entered");
      pause();
      break;
   }
```

```
/* look for record */
found = false;
locator = 1L;
while (found == false && locator != 0L) {
   if ((fseek(stream,locator * var_size,
                                 SEEK_SET)) != 0)
      complain();
   fread(&tree_record,size,1,stream);
   if (strcmp(old_key,tree_record.key) == 0)
      found = true; /* success */
   else {
      /* if locator comes up 0 we couldn't find the
         record */
      if (strcmp(old_key,tree_record.key) < 0)
         locator = tree_record.lpointer;
      else
         locator = tree_record.rpointer;
   }
}

/* get changed data if record found */
if (found == true) {
   gotoxy(10,2);
   /* show original data */
   printf("Name is %s\n",tree_record.name);
   gotoxy(10,3);
   /* get new data */
   printf("New name? Press return to skip\n");
   get_info(10,4,name,NAME_LEN - 1);
   if (strlen(name) != 0)
      /* something was entered */
      strcpy(tree_record.name,name);

   gotoxy(10,5);
   printf("Address is %s\n",tree_record.address);
   gotoxy(10,6);
   printf("New address? Press return to skip\n");
   get_info(10,7,address,ADR_LEN - 1);
   if (strlen(address) != 0)
      strcpy(tree_record.address,address);

   gotoxy(10,8);
   printf("City is %s\n",tree_record.city);
```

```c
        gotoxy(10,9);
        printf("New city? Press return to skip\n");
        get_info(10,10,city,CITY_LEN - 1);
        if (strlen(city) != 0)
           strcpy(tree_record.city,city);

        gotoxy(10,11);
        printf("State is %s\n",tree_record.state);
        gotoxy(10,12);
        printf("New state? Press return to skip\n");
        get_info(10,13,state,STATE_LEN - 1);
        if (strlen(state) != 0)
           strcpy(tree_record.state,state);
        gotoxy(10,14);

        printf("Zip is %s\n",tree_record.zip);
        gotoxy(10,15);
        printf("New zip? Press return to skip\n");
        get_info(10,16,zip,ZIP_LEN - 1);
        if (strlen(zip) != 0)
           strcpy(tree_record.zip,zip);

        /* use name for key */
        strcpy(tree_record.key,tree_record.name);

        /* delete the old version */
        delete_ratree(old_key,&found,stream);

        /* replace with new version */
        load_radtree(&tree_record,stream);
      }

      else {
         gotoxy(10,18);
         printf("Name not found\n");
      }

      /* more? */
      gotoxy(10,20);
      printf("Another? ");
      answer = getch();
      if (answer == 'N' || answer == 'n')
         break;
```

```
      } /* end for */
      fclose(stream);
   }


void delete(void)
/* delete a record */
{
   int true = 1,
       false = 0,
       found, /* for record search */
       answer; /* reply to prompt */
   char dest_file [13], /* for file name */
        key [KEY_LEN]; /* for key to record to be deleted */
   FILE *stream; /* for tree file */
   struct tree tree_record; /* record structure */

   /* set file name */
   strcpy(&dest_file [0],"ch11_1.dat");

   /* open file containing mailing list */
   if ((stream = fopen(dest_file,"r+b")) == NULL) {
      putch(7); /* beep */
      gotoxy(10,24);
      printf("Unable to open file\n");
      exit(1);
   }

   for (;;) {
      /* get key of record to delete */
      clrscr();
      gotoxy(10,5);
      printf("Name to delete? ");
      get_info(26,5,key,KEY_LEN - 1);

      /* default */
      found = false;

      /* check for valid key */
      if (strlen(key) == 0) {
         putch(7);
         gotoxy(10,20);
```

```c
            printf("No name entered\n");
            pause();
            break;
      }

      /* search and delete record if found */
      delete_ratree(key,&found,stream); /* do it! */

      /* tell the operator what's happening */
      gotoxy(10,10);
      if (found == true)
         printf("%s successfully deleted\n",key);
      else
         printf("%s not found\n",key);
      /* more? */
      gotoxy(10,16);
      printf("Another? ");
      answer = getch();
      if (answer == 'N' || answer == 'n')
         break;
   } /* end for */
   fclose(stream);
}


void print(void)
/* print the file */
{
   char dest_file [13]; /* for file name */
   FILE *stream; /* for tree file */
   struct tree tree_record; /* record structure */
   int answer; /* reply to prompt */

   /* set file name */
   strcpy(&dest_file [0],"ch11_1.dat");

   /* open file containing mailing list */
   if ((stream = fopen(dest_file,"r+b")) == NULL) {
      putch(7); /* beep */
      gotoxy(10,24);
      printf("Unable to open file\n");
      exit(1);
   }
```

```
      /* wait till printer is ready */
      for (;;) {
         clrscr();

         gotoxy(10,16);
         printf("Printer ready? ");
         answer = getch();
         if (answer == 'Y' || answer == 'y')
            break;
      } /* end for */

      /* print file's contents */
      read_ratree(&tree_record,stream);

      fclose(stream);
   }


void load_radtree(struct tree *dup_tree,FILE *stream)
/* create and load items into random access binary tree */
{
   long first_empty, /* first vacant tree location */
        del_len, /* number of deleted nodes */
        delete, /* delete value in record */
        counter,
        var_size = (long) sizeof(struct tree), /* for
                                              fseek() */
        locator; /* tree node indicator */
        size_t size = sizeof(struct tree); /* for fseek and
                                       fwrite functions */

        int left = 1, /* current travel direction */
            right = 2, /* current travel direction */
            direction; /* last direction traveled */
      struct tree tree_record; /* for record data */
      for (;;) {
         /* get number of records in tree */
         if ((fseek(stream,0L,SEEK_SET)) != 0)
            complain();
         fread(&tree_record,size,1,stream);
         /* lpointer in record 0 used to hold total record
            count */
```

```
if (tree_record.lpointer == 0L) {
   /* empty tree */

   /* update record count */
   tree_record.lpointer++; /* record count */
   if ((fseek(stream,0L,SEEK_SET)) !- 0)
      complain();
   fwrite(&tree_record,size,1,stream);

   /* to get delete value, if any */
   if ((fseek(stream,1L * var_size,SEEK_SET)) != 0)
      complain();
   fread(&tree_record,size,1,stream);

   /* first record */
   dup_tree->lpointer = 0L;
   dup_tree->rpointer = 0L;
   /* save original delete node, if any */
   dup_tree->delete = tree_record.delete;

   /* save data in record one */
   if ((fseek(stream,1L * var_size,SEEK_SET)) != 0)
      complain();
   fwrite(dup_tree,size,1,stream);

   break; /* leave function */
}

/* number of deleted nodes*/
1f ((fseek(stream,0L,SEEK_SET)) != 0)
   complain();
/* get deleted record count */
fread(&tree_record,size,1,stream);
del_len = tree_record.delete;

if (del_len > 0L) {
   /* reuse a deleted node */
   del_len--; /* don't use this node next time */
   /* new delete count */
   tree_record.delete = del_len;
   /* save new delete count */
   if ((fseek(stream,0L,SEEK_SET)) != 0)
      complain();
```

```
            fwrite(&tree_record,size,1,stream);
            /* get most recent deleted node */
            if ((fseek(stream,(del_len + 1) *
                                     var_size,SEEK_SET)) != 0)
               complain();
            fread(&tree_record,size,1,stream);
            /* use it for current record */
            first_empty = tree_record.delete;
        }
        else {
            /* no nodes in deleted list */
            /* (total count) next unused node */
            tree_record.lpointer++;
            /* first empty record */
            first_empty = tree_record.lpointer;
            /* save new record count */
            if ((fseek(stream,0L,SEEK_SET)) != 0)
               complain();
            fwrite(&tree_record,size,1,stream);
        }

        locator = 1L; /* first record (tree root) */

        /* find highest value less than num */
        do {
            counter = locator; /* current array row */
            /* which direction? */
            if ((fseek(stream,counter * var_size,
                                        SEEK_SET)) != 0)
               complain();
            fread(&tree_record,size,1,stream);
            if (strcmp(dup_tree->key,tree_record.key) < 0) {
               /* smaller */
               /* left pointer */
               locator = tree_record.lpointer;
               direction = left;
            }
            else {
               /* larger than or equal to */
               /* right pointer */
               locator = tree_record.rpointer;
               direction = right;
            }
```

```
        }
        while (locator != 0);

        /* set the tree pointer */
        if ((fseek(stream,counter * var_size,SEEK_SET)) != 0)
           complain();
        fread(&tree_record,size,1,stream);
        /* point to record to be used */
        if (direction == left)
           tree_record.lpointer = first_empty;
        else
           tree_record.rpointer = first_empty;

        /* save new pointer info */
        if ((fseek(stream,counter * var_size,SEEK_SET)) != 0)
          complain();
        fwrite(&tree_record,size,1,stream);

        /* to get deleted value, if any */
        if ((fseek(stream,first_empty * var_size,
                                      SEEK_SET)) != 0)
           complain();
        fread(&tree_record,size,1,stream);

        /* save new record */
        dup_tree->lpointer = 0L;
        dup_tree->rpointer = 0L;
        /* save original delete node, if present */
        dup_tree->delete = tree_record.delete;

        /* save new data */
        if ((fseek(stream,first_empty * var_size,
                                      SEEK_SET)) != 0)
           complain();
        fwrite(dup_tree,size,1,stream);

        break; /* leave function */
    }
}

void read_ratree(struct tree *tree_record,FILE *stream)
/* read the binary tree and display contents in ascending
   order from already opened file */
```

```
{
    /* to keep track of position within tree */
    long counter,
        var_size = (long) sizeof(struct tree),
        locator, /* tree pointer */
        bcount; /* back_count array position */
    size_t size = sizeof(struct tree);
    int back_handle; /* previous location */
    char back_file [13]; /* visited nodes file name */
    FILE *back_stream; /* keeps track of visited nodes */

    /* set visited nodes file name */
    strcpy(&back_file [0],"ch11_1b.dat");

    /* open file to contain visited nodeslist */
    if ((back_stream = fopen(back_file,"w+b")) == NULL) {
        putch(7); /* beep */
        gotoxy(10,24);
        printf("Unable to open file\n");
        exit(1);
    }

    /* record number */
    counter = 1L;
    /* back counter position */
    bcount = 0L;
    /* value to test for completion */
    if ((fseek(back_stream,0L,SEEK_SET)) != 0)
        complain();
    fwrite(0L,(size_t) sizeof(long),1,back_stream);
    /* next record */
    locator = 1L;

    /* do it */
    for (;;) {
        /* back down through tree to get lowest value,
           keeping track of nodes visited in back_list file */
        while (locator > 0L) {
            /* read next lower item */
            if ((fseek(stream,counter * var_size,
                                    SEEK_SET)) != 0)
                complain();
            fread(tree_record,size,1,stream);
```

```
            /* save next back list item */
            bcount++;
            if ((fseek(back_stream,bcount *
                        (long) sizeof(long),SEEK_SET)) != 0)
                complain();
            fwrite(&counter,(size_t) sizeof(long),1,
                                            back_stream);

            /* left pointer */
            /* next lower item */
            locator = tree_record->lpointer;
            counter = locator;
        }
        /* lowest value */

        /* get latest node visited */
        if ((fseek(back_stream,bcount *
                        (long) sizeof(long),SEEK_SET)) != 0)
            complain();
        fread(&counter,(size_t) sizeof(long),1,back_stream);

        /* remove latest node from list */
        bcount--;
        if (counter == 0L)
            /* end of list */
            break; /* leave function */

        /* print structure */
        if ((fseek(stream,counter * var_size,SEEK_SET)) != 0)
            complain();
        fread(tree_record,size,1,stream);
        fprintf(stdprn,"%s\n\r",tree_record->name);
        fprintf(stdprn,"%s\n\r",tree_record->address);
        fprintf(stdprn,"%s\n\r",tree_record->city);
        fprintf(stdprn,"%s\n\r",tree_record->state);
        fprintf(stdprn,"%s\n\r",tree_record->zip);
        fprintf(stdprn,"\n\r");

        /* look for next node */
        locator = tree_record->rpointer;
        counter = locator;
    }
    fclose(back_stream);
```

```
      remove(back_file);
}


void complain(void)
/* fseek failed */
{
   putch(7); /* beep */
   gotoxy(10,24);
   printf("Unable to position file\n");
   exit(1);
}
void complain(void); /* bug fix */


void delete_ratree(char key [],int *found,FILE *stream)
/* delete a node from the tree and store the node location
   in a file */
{
   int true = 1, /* boolean */
       false = 0;
   size_t size = sizeof(struct tree);
   long temp_lpointer, /* temporary pointer variables */
        temp_rpointer,
        delete, /* temporary delete value holder */
        back_pointer, /* a previous position in the tree */
        locator, /* another tree position */
        old_locator, /* another previous position */
        counter, /* another tree position */
        var_size = (long) sizeof(struct tree),
        del_len, /* length of deleted node file */
        save_place; /* deleted node number */
   struct tree tree_record, /* record structure */
               dup_tree, /* transfer structure */
               empty_tree; /* blank structure */

   /* initialize blank structure */
   blank_tree(&empty_tree);

   /* default */
   *found = false;
   back_pointer = 0L;
```

```
for (;;) {
    /* get record count from record zero */
    if ((fseek(stream,0L,SEEK_SET)) != 0)
        complain();
    fread(&tree_record,size,1,stream);

    if (tree_record.lpointer == 0L) /* node 0 */
        /* empty tree */
        break;

    /* is it in root node? */
    if ((fseek(stream,1L * var_size,SEEK_SET)) != 0)
        complain();
    fread(&tree_record,size,1,stream);
    /* save deleted node count for possible later use */
    delete = tree_record.delete;

    if (strcmp(tree_record.key,key) == 0) { /* node 1 */
        /* special case of deletion of root node */
        *found = true;
        if (tree_record.lpointer == 0L ||
                        tree_record.rpointer == 0L) {
            /* node 1 */
            /* at least one pointer null, select other */
            if (tree_record.lpointer == 0L) /* node 1 */
                locator = tree_record.rpointer; /* node 1 */
            else
                locator = tree_record.lpointer; /* node 1 */
            if (locator == 0L) {
                /* both pointers null */
                /* save old delete value, if any */
                /* set tree to blanks */
                blank_tree(&empty_tree); /* null structure */
                /* save original deleted node, if any */
                empty_tree.delete = delete;
                /* save blank record */
                if ((fseek(stream,1L * var_size,
                                        SEEK_SET)) != 0)
                    complain();
                fwrite(&empty_tree,size,1,stream);
```

```
                    /* get record 0 for record count change */
                    if ((fseek(stream,0L,SEEK_SET)) != 0)
                        complain();
                    fread(&tree_record,size,1,stream);

                    /* save record count */
                    tree_record.lpointer = 0L; /* node 0 */
                    if ((fseek(stream,0L,SEEK_SET)) != 0)
                        complain();
                    fwrite(&tree_record,size,1,stream);
                    break;
                }
            }

            else {
                /* both pointers in use */
                locator = tree_record.rpointer; /* node 1 */

                /* find first free lpointer in right half of
                    tree */
                do {
                    /* will be previous record node when search
                        is completed */
                    back_pointer = locator;
                    if ((fseek(stream,locator * var_size,
                                           SEEK_SET)) != 0)
                        complain();
                    fread(&tree_record,size,1,stream);
                    /* node locator */
                    locator = tree_record.lpointer;
                }
                while (locator != 0L);

                /* add left half of tree to that pointer */
                if ((fseek(stream,1L * var_size,SEEK_SET)) != 0)
                    complain();
                fread(&tree_record,size,1,stream);

                /* save pointers in record to be deleted */
                temp_lpointer = tree_record.lpointer;
                temp_rpointer = tree_record.rpointer;
```

```
         /* get record previous to record soon to be
            deleted */
         if ((fseek(stream,back_pointer * var_size,
                                      SEEK_SET)) != 0)
            complain();
         fread(&tree_record,size,1,stream);

         /* change previous node's pointer to record to
            be deleted */
         tree_record.lpointer = temp_lpointer;

         /* save with new pointer to record following
            record to be deleted */
         if ((fseek(stream,back_pointer * var_size,
                                      SEEK_SET)) != 0)
            complain();
         fwrite(&tree_record,size,1,stream);

         /* get pointer to first node in right half of
            tree */
         locator = temp_rpointer; /* node 1 */
      }

   /* move that node to root node */
   /* start by getting record to be moved */
   if ((fseek(stream,locator * var_size,
                                   SEEK_SET)) != 0)
      complain();
   fread(&tree_record,size,1,stream);

   /* make a copy of record */
   dup_tree = tree_record;

   /* save original delete values */
   blank_tree(&empty_tree);
   empty_tree.delete = tree_record.delete;
   dup_tree.delete = delete;

   /* delete moved node by replacing it with a blank
      record */
   if ((fseek(stream,locator * var_size,
                                   SEEK_SET)) != 0)
```

```
         complain();
      fwrite(&empty_tree,size,1,stream);

      /* save old first right node record in root node */
      if ((fseek(stream,1L * var_size,SEEK_SET)) != 0)
         complain();
      fwrite(&dup_tree,size,1,stream);

      /* add deleted node to deleted node list */

      /* number of deleted nodes*/
      if ((fseek(stream,0L,SEEK_SET)) != 0)
         complain();
      fread(&tree_record,size,1,stream);
      del_len = tree_record.delete;

      /* update node counts */
      del_len++;
      tree_record.delete = del_len;
      if ((fseek(stream,0L,SEEK_SET)) != 0)
         complain();
      fwrite(&tree_record,size,1,stream);

      /* store added deleted node position */
      /* get next available record to store a deleted
         node value */
      if ((fseek(stream,del_len * var_size,
                                    SEEK_SET)) != 0)
         complain();
      fread(&tree_record,size,1,stream);
      /* deleted node value */
      tree_record.delete = locator;
      /* store deleted node value */
      if ((fseek(stream,del_len * var_size,
                                    SEEK_SET)) != 0)
         complain();
      fwrite(&tree_record,size,1,stream);

      break;
   }
```

```
/* not root node */
/* next tree node */
counter = 1L;
/* tree node */
locator = 1L;

/* find the value to be deleted from the tree
   or a null tree pointer */
do {
    counter = locator; /* previous node */
    if ((fseek(stream,counter * var_size,
                                SEEK_SET)) != 0)
        complain();
    /* get record to test */
    fread(&tree_record,size,1,stream);

    /* what to do */
    /* lower than searched-for value */
    if (strcmp(key,tree_record.key) < 0) {
        /* left pointer */
        /* will be previous node when record to be
           deleted is found */
        back_pointer = locator;
        locator = tree_record.lpointer;
    }
    else {
        /* equal to or greater than searched-for
           value */
        if (strcmp(key,tree_record.key) > 0) {
            /* right pointer */
            back_pointer = locator;
            locator = tree_record.rpointer;
        }
        else {
            *found = true;
            break;
        }
    }
}
while (locator != 0L);
```

```
/* no luck */
if (*found == false)
   /* record not found */
   break; /* leave function */

/* record to be deleted was found */
if (tree_record.rpointer == 0L) { /* rpointer free */
   /* delete record */
   /* set fields to blank */
   blank_tree(&empty_tree);
   /* retain original delete value, if any */
   empty_tree.delete = tree_record.delete;
   /* node that record to be deleted points to */
   /* counter node */
   temp_lpointer = tree_record.lpointer;
   /* overwrite record to be deleted with blank
      record */
   if ((fseek(stream,counter * var_size,
                             SEEK_SET)) != 0)
      complain();
   fwrite(&empty_tree,size,1,stream);

   /* remember deleted node */
   save_place = counter;

   /* move tree pointer to previous record*/
   if ((fseek(stream,back_pointer * var_size,
                             SEEK_SET)) != 0)
      complain();
   fread(&tree_record,size,1,stream);

   /* which previous record pointer indicates deleted
      record? */
   /* back_pointer node */
   if (tree_record.lpointer == counter)
      /* from counter node to previous node */
      tree_record.lpointer = temp_lpointer;
   else
      /* counter node */
      tree_record.rpointer = temp_lpointer;
```

```
        /* bypass deleted record node */
        if ((fseek(stream,back_pointer * var_size,
                                    SEEK_SET)) != 0)
            complain();
        fwrite(&tree_record,size,1,stream);
    }
    else {
        /* get record to be deleted */
        if ((fseek(stream,counter * var_size,
                                    SEEK_SET)) != 0)
            complain();
        fread(&tree_record,size,1,stream);
        if (tree_record.lpointer == 0L) {
            /* counter node lpointer free */
            /* delete record */
            blank_tree(&empty_tree);
            /* retain original delete value */
            empty_tree.delete = tree_record.delete;
            /* save other pointer from deleted record */
            /* counter node */
            temp_rpointer = tree_record.rpointer;
            /* replace deleted record with blank record */
            if ((fseek(stream,counter * var_size,
                                    SEEK_SET)) != 0)
                complain();
            fwrite(&empty_tree,size,1,stream);

            /* remember deleted node */
            save_place = counter;

            /* move tree pointer */
            if ((fseek(stream,back_pointer * var_size,
                                    SEEK_SET)) != 0)
                complain();
            fread(&tree_record,size,1,stream);
            /* change previous record's pointer to that
               saved from deleted record */
            /* back_pointer node */
            if (tree_record.lpointer == counter)
```

```
                  /* counter node */
                  tree_record.lpointer = temp_rpointer;
               else
                  tree_record.rpointer = temp_rpointer;
               /* save previous record with new pointer */
               if ((fseek(stream,back_pointer * var_size,
                                            SEEK_SET)) != 0)
                  complain();
               fwrite(&tree_record,size,1,stream);
            }
            else {
               /* neither pointer free */
               /* get previous record */
               if ((fseek(stream,back_pointer * var_size,
                                            SEEK_SET)) != 0)
                  complain();
               fread(&tree_record,size,1,stream);
               /* find pointer to deleted record */
               /* back_pointer node */
               if (tree_record.rpointer == counter) {
                  /* move tree pointer back one node */
                  if ((fseek(stream,counter * var_size,
                                         SEEK_SET)) != 0)
                     complain();
                  fread(&tree_record,size,1,stream);
                  /* save pointer to deleted record */
                  temp_rpointer = tree_record.rpointer;
                  /* read previous record */
                  if ((fseek(stream,back_pointer * var_size,
                                            SEEK_SET)) != 0)
                     complain();
                  fread(&tree_record,size,1,stream);
                  /* point to record deleted record used to
                     point to */
                  tree_record.rpointer = temp_rpointer;
                  /* save previous record with new pointer */
                  if ((fseek(stream,back_pointer * var_size,
                                            SEEK_SET)) != 0)
                     complain();
                  fwrite(&tree_record,size,1,stream);
```

```
/* save deleted record's other pointer */
if ((fseek(stream,counter * var_size,
                          SEEK_SET)) != 0)
   complain();
fread(&tree_record,size,1,stream);
/* save other pointer */
locator = tree_record.rpointer;

/* find a null lpointer */
do {
   old_locator = locator;
   if ((fseek(stream,locator * var_size,
                          SEEK_SET)) != 0)
      complain();
   fread(&tree_record,size,1,stream);
   /* locator node */
   locator = tree_record.lpointer;
}
while (locator != 0L);

/* move tree pointer from deleted record */
if ((fseek(stream,counter * var_size,
                          SEEK_SET)) != 0)
   complain();
fread(&tree_record,size,1,stream);
/* save pointer to be deleted */
temp_lpointer = tree_record.lpointer;
/* get record with null pointer just found */
if ((fseek(stream,old_locator * var_size,
                          SEEK_SET)) != 0)
   complain();
fread(&tree_record,size,1,stream);
/* put deleted record's pointer in it */
tree_record.lpointer = temp_lpointer;
/* save */
if ((fseek(stream,old_locator * var_size,
                          SEEK_SET)) != 0)
   complain();
fwrite(&tree_record,size,1,stream);
```

```
                    /* delete just saved pointer from deleted
                       record */
                    if ((fseek(stream,counter * var_size,
                                           SEEK_SET)) != 0)
                       complain();
                    fread(&tree_record,size,1,stream);

                    /* overwrite deleted record with blank
                       record */
                    blank_tree(&empty_tree);
                    /* retain original delete value */
                    empty_tree.delete = tree_record.delete;
                    if ((fseek(stream,counter * var_size,
                                           SEEK_SET)) != 0)
                       complain();
                    fwrite(&empty_tree,size,1,stream);

                    /* remember deleted node */
                    save_place = counter;
                 }
                 else {
                    /* previous record's lpointer points to
                       deleted record */
                    /* move pointer back one node */
                    /* get deleted record */
                    if ((fseek(stream,counter * var_size,
                                           SEEK_SET)) != 0)
                       complain();
                    fread(&tree_record,size,1,stream);
                    /* save lpointer which will be moved to
                       another record */
                    temp_lpointer = tree_record.lpointer;
                    if ((fseek(stream,back_pointer * var_size,
                                           SEEK_SET)) != 0)
                       complain();
                    fread(&tree_record,size,1,stream);
                    /* put saved lpointer in previous record */
                    tree_record.lpointer = temp_lpointer;
                    /* save previous record with new lpointer */
```

```
if ((fseek(stream,back_pointer * var_size,
                           SEEK_SET)) != 0)
   complain();
fwrite(&tree_record,size,1,stream);

/* save tree pointer */
if ((fseek(stream,counter * var_size,
                           SEEK_SET)) != 0)
   complain();
fread(&tree_record,size,1,stream);
/* get other pointer from deleted record */
locator = tree_record.lpointer;

/* find first free rpointer */
do {
   old_locator = locator;
   if ((fseek(stream,locator * var_size,
                           SEEK_SET)) != 0)
      complain();
   fread(&tree_record,size,1,stream);
   /* locator node */
   locator = tree_record.rpointer;
}
while (locator != 0L);

/* get unsaved pointer from deleted record */
if ((fseek(stream,counter * var_size,
                           SEEK_SET)) != 0)
   complain();
fread(&tree_record,size,1,stream);
/* save it in temporary variable */
temp_rpointer = tree_record.rpointer;
/* put the pointer in record */
if ((fseek(stream,old_locator * var_size,
                           SEEK_SET)) != 0)
   complain();
fread(&tree_record,size,1,stream);
tree_record.rpointer = temp_rpointer;
```

```
                    if ((fseek(stream,old_locator * var_size,
                                        SEEK_SET)) != 0)
                      complain();
                    fwrite(&tree_record,size,1,stream);

                    /* delete pointer from deleted record */
                    if ((fseek(stream,counter * var_size,
                                        SEEK_SET)) != 0)
                      complain();
                    fread(&tree_record,size,1,stream);

                    /* blank out deleted record */
                    blank_tree(&empty_tree);
                    /* retain original delete value */
                    empty_tree.delete = tree_record.delete;
                    if ((fseek(stream,counter * var_size,
                                        SEEK_SET)) != 0)
                      complain();
                    fwrite(&empty_tree,size,1,stream);

                    /* remember deleted node */
                    save_place = counter;
                  }
              }
          }
          /* add deleted node to deleted list */

          /* number of deleted nodes*/
          if ((fseek(stream,0L,SEEK_SET)) != 0)
            complain();
          fread(&tree_record,size,1,stream);
          del_len = tree_record.delete;
          /* update node count */
          del_len++;
          tree_record.delete = del_len;
          if ((fseek(stream,0L,SEEK_SET)) != 0)
            complain();
          fwrite(&tree_record,size,1,stream);

          /* store deleted node */
          if ((fseek(stream,del_len * var_size,SEEK_SET)) != 0)
            complain();
```

```
        fread(&tree_record,size,1,stream);
        tree_record.delete = save_place;
        if ((fseek(stream,del_len * var_size,SEEK_SET)) != 0)
           complain();
        fwrite(&tree_record,size,1,stream);
        break;
   } /* end for(;;) */
} /* end function */


void pause(void)
/* wait for keypress */
{
   printf("Press any key to continue\n");
   getch();
}
void clrscr(void)
/* clear the screen */
{
   union REGS regs;

   regs.h.ah = 6;                     /* bios function */
   regs.h.al = 0;                     /* clear entire screen */
   regs.h.bh = 7;                     /* normal attribute */
   regs.h.ch = 0;                     /* upper row position */
   regs.h.cl = 0;                     /* upper-left column
                                          position */
   regs.h.dh = 24;                    /* lowest row */
   regs.h.dl = 79;                    /* rightmost column */
   int86(0x10,&regs,&regs);           /* bios interrupt number */
} /* end function clear screen */


void gotoxy(int x,int y)
/* position cursor */
{

   union REGS regs;


   regs.h.ah = 2;                     /* bios function */
   regs.h.dh = (char) y;              /* row */
```

```
        regs.h.dl = (char) x;        /* column */
        regs.h.bh = 0;               /* video page number */
        int86(0x10,&regs,&regs);     /* bios interrupt number */
} /* end function gotoxy */


void blank_tree(struct tree *empty_tree)
/* set structure to zeros or null strings */
{
    empty_tree->key [0] = '\0';
    empty_tree->name [0] = '\0';
    empty_tree->address [0] = '\0';
    empty_tree->city [0] = '\0';
    empty_tree->state [0] = '\0';
    empty_tree->zip [0] = '\0';
    empty_tree->lpointer = 0L;
    empty_tree->rpointer = 0L;
    empty_tree->delete = 0L;
}
```

If you key in this program, watch out for subprograms that are almost but not quite the same as their counterparts in preceding chapters.

The file is opened and closed for each menu choice. This is to be sure that the file's buffers are flushed to the disk. C's flush functions only flush C's buffers, not DOS's. I've heard that you can use the dup function to open a second file handle for the open file; then closing the duplicate will flush DOS's buffers. It seemed just as simple and fast to close and reopen the database file itself and not use the additional file handle, frequently in short supply in database programs.

USING AN INSERTION SORT INDEX

This next example differs from the previous in that the record structure is divided into three instead of two groups. One group uses the field delete to hold the deleted record numbers. The total of these is contained in the delete field in record zero. The next group contains the fields key and record_num. (The total number

of keys is stored in the record_num field in record zero.) The key
is the search key for the record and the record_num field contains
the record number of the record in this same file. Thus, in this
case the key and its associated name and address are not usually
in the same record. Therefore, this file actually contains three files:
the name and address file, the index file, and the list of deleted
record numbers. This was done because such files are frequently
used in database programs. These programs frequently need more
files than there are file handles available. By combining three files
into one like this, the number of file handles required is reduced
significantly.

```c
/* Chapter 11, Example 2, QuickC, 4/25/88
   Mailing list database using random access
   and index using insertion sort */

#include <stdio.h>
#include <stdlib.h>
#include <conio.h>
#include <io.h>
#include <string.h>
#include <bios.h>

#define KEY_LEN 25
#define NAME_LEN 25
#define ADR_LEN 25
#define CITY_LEN 15
#define STATE_LEN 3
#define ZIP_LEN 6

/* structure to contain list elements */
struct list {
    long record_num;
    long delete;
    char key [KEY_LEN];
    char name [NAME_LEN];
    char address [ADR_LEN];
    char city [CITY_LEN];
    char state [STATE_LEN];
    char zip [ZIP_LEN];
};
```

```c
/* function prototypes */
void complain(void);
void pause(void);
void add(char dest_file []);
void change(char dest_file []);
void delete(char dest_file []);
void print(char dest_file []);
void get_info(int col,int row,char entry [],int length);
void find_index(char key [],long *position,int *found,
                FILE *stream);
void replace_index(char key [],long record_num,
                   long position,FILE *stream);
void delete_index(long position,FILE *stream);
void empty_record(long *record_num,FILE *stream);
void gotoxy(int x,int y);
void clrscr(void);
void main(void);


void main()
{
   size_t size = sizeof(struct list); /* for fread and
                                         fwrite functions */
   int choice; /* menu choice */
   char dest_file [13]; /* for data (list) file name */
   FILE *stream; /* for list file */
   struct list list; /* record structure */

   /* set name of data file */
   strcpy(&dest_file [0],"ch11_2.dat");

   /* see if file exists */
   if (access(dest_file,0) != 0) {
      /* create file to contain list */
      if ((stream = fopen(dest_file,"wb")) == NULL) {
         putch(7); /* beep */
         gotoxy(10,24);
         printf("Unable to open file\n");
         exit(1);
      }
```

```
        /* initialize structure */
        list.key [0] = '\0';
        list.name [0] = '\0';
        list.address [0] = '\0';
        list.city [0] = '\0';
        list.state [0] = '\0';
        list.zip [0] = '\0';

        /* number of deleted nodes to start */
        list.delete = 0L;

        /* number of items in list to start */
        list.record_num = 0L; /* use record_num in record 0 to
                                  contain total of records */
        if ((fseek(stream,0L,SEEK_SET)) != 0)
            complain();
        fwrite(&list,size,1,stream); /* store record zero */

        fclose(stream);
    }

    printf("\n");
    /* menu */
    for (;;) {
        clrscr();
        gotoxy(20,10);
        printf("Menu");
        gotoxy(10,12);
        printf("Add a name");
        gotoxy(10,13);
        printf("Change a name");
        gotoxy(10,14);
        printf("Delete a name");
        gotoxy(10,15);
        printf("Print names");
        gotoxy(10,17);
        printf("End program");
        gotoxy(10,19);
        printf("Your choice by first letter ");
        choice = getche();
```

```
        switch (choice) {
        case 'A':
        case 'a':
           add(dest_file);
           break;

        case 'C':
        case 'c':
           change(dest_file);
           break;

        case 'D':
        case 'd':
           delete(dest_file);
           break;

        case 'P':
        case 'p':
           print(dest_file);
           break;

        case 'E':
        case 'e':
           break;

        default:
           putch(7);
           break;
        }
        if (choice == 'E' || choice == 'e')
        break;
   } /* end for */
} /* end main */


void add(char dest_file [])
/* add a record */
{
   char key [KEY_LEN],
       name [NAME_LEN],
       address [ADR_LEN],
```

```
            city [CITY_LEN],
            state [STATE_LEN],
            zip [ZIP_LEN];
    FILE *stream; /* for list file */
    struct list list; /* record structure */
    size_t size = sizeof(struct list); /* for fread and
                                          fwrite functions */

    int answer,
        found, /* used when searching for index key */
        false = 0;
    long var_size = (long) sizeof(struct list), /* for
                                                   fseek */

        position, /* position of key in index file */
        record_num; /* record number */

    /* open file containing mailing list */
    if ((stream = fopen(dest_file,"r+b")) == NULL) {
        putch(7); /* beep */
        gotoxy(10,24);
        printf("Unable to open file\n");
        exit(1);
    }

    /* get data */
    for (;;) {
        clrscr();
        gotoxy(10,10);
        printf("Name? ");
        name [0] = '\0';
        get_info(16,10,name,NAME_LEN - 1);

        gotoxy(10,11);
        printf("Address? ");
        address [0] = '\0';
        get_info(19,11,address,ADR_LEN - 1);

        gotoxy(10,12);
        printf("City? ");
        city [0] = '\0';
        get_info(16,12,city,CITY_LEN - 1);
```

```
gotoxy(10,13);
printf("State? ");
state [0] = '\0';
get_info(17,13,state,STATE_LEN - 1);

gotoxy(10,14);
printf("Zip? ");
zip [0] = '\0';
get_info(15,14,zip,ZIP_LEN - 1);

/* see if a name was entered */
if (strlen(name) == 0) {
   putch(7);
   gotoxy(10,20);
   printf("No name entered\n");
   pause();
   break;
}

/* save record */
strcpy(key,name);
found = false;

/* get a record number for storing name, etc. */
empty_record(&record_num,stream);

/* find a place for the new key in the index file */
find_index(key,&position,&found,stream);

/* put the new key in the index file */
replace_index(key,record_num,position,stream);

/* get the list structure at the record number
   position */
if ((fseek(stream,record_num * var_size,
                              SEEK_SET)) != 0)
   complain();
fread(&list,size,1,stream);

/* fill the structure with the name, etc. */
strcpy(list.name,name);
strcpy(list.address,address);
```

```
          strcpy(list.city,city);
          strcpy(list.state,state);
          strcpy(list.zip,zip);

          /* save the structure */
          if ((fseek(stream,record_num * var_size,
                                        SEEK_SET)) != 0)
              complain();
          fwrite(&list,size,1,stream);

          gotoxy(10,16);
          printf("Another? ");
          answer = getch();
          if (answer == 'N' || answer == 'n')
              break;
      } /* end for */
      fclose(stream);
}

void get_info(int col,int row,char entry [],int length)
/* get the operator's data input */
{
    int counter,
        ch;

    gotoxy(col,row); /* start the input here */

    /* get the data from the operator */
    for (counter = 0;counter < length;counter++) {
        ch = getche(); /* get character and echo */
        if (ch == 13) /* carriage return */
            break;
        if (ch == 8) { /* backspace */
            col --;
            gotoxy(col,row);
            putch(32);
            col--;
            counter -= 2;
        }
        else {
            /* store character */
            entry [counter] = (char) ch;
        }
```

```
            /* next character */
            col++;
            gotoxy(col,row);
        }
        putch(7); /* tell operator field is completed */
        entry [counter] = '\0';
    }


    void change(char dest_file [])
    /* change a record's contents */
    {
        long var_size = (long) sizeof(struct list), /* for
                                                    fseek */
                record_num, /* record number */
                position; /* record node */
        size_t size = sizeof(struct list); /* for fread and
                                            fwrite functions */
        int true = -1,
            false = 0,
            found, /* for key search */
            answer;
        char old_key [KEY_LEN],
            key [KEY_LEN], /* data variables */
            name [NAME_LEN],
            address [ADR_LEN],
            city [CITY_LEN],
            state [STATE_LEN],
            zip [ZIP_LEN];
        FILE *stream; /* for list file */
        struct list list; /* data record structure */


        /* open file containing mailing list */
        if ((stream = fopen(dest_file,"r+b")) == NULL) {
            putch(7); /* beep */
            gotoxy(10,24);
            printf("Unable to open file\n");
            exit(1);
        }
```

```
/* show old data, get new data */
for (;;) {
  /* start with blank fields */
  old_key [0] = '\0';
  name [0] = '\0';
  address [0] = '\0';
  city [0] = '\0';
  state [0] = '\0';
  zip [0] = '\0';

  clrscr();
  gotoxy(10,1);
  printf("Name to change? ");
  get_info(26,1,old_key,KEY_LEN -1);

  if (strlen(old_key) == 0) {
     putch(7);
     gotoxy(10,20);
     printf("No name entered\n");
     pause();
     break;
  }

  /* look for record */
  found = false;
  find_index(old_key,&position,&found,stream);

  /* get changed data */
  if (found == true) {
     if ((fseek(stream,position * var_size,
                               SEEK_SET)) != 0)
        complain();
     fread(&list,size,1,stream);
     if ((fseek(stream,list.record_num * var_size,
                               SEEK_SET)) != 0)
        complain();
     fread(&list,size,1,stream);

     gotoxy(10,2);
     printf("Name is %s\n",list.name);
```

```
gotoxy(10,3);
printf("New name? Press return to skip\n");
get_info(10,4,name,NAME_LEN - 1);
if (strlen(name) == 0)
   strcpy(name,list.name);

gotoxy(10,5);
printf("Address is %s\n",list.address);
gotoxy(10,6);
printf("New address? Press return to skip\n");
get_info(10,7,address,ADR_LEN - 1);
if (strlen(address) == 0)
   strcpy(address,list.address);

gotoxy(10,8);
printf("City is %s\n",list.city);
gotoxy(10,9);
printf("New city? Press return to skip\n");
get_info(10,10,city,CITY_LEN - 1);
if (strlen(city) == 0)
   strcpy(city,list.city);

gotoxy(10,11);
printf("State is %s\n",list.state);
gotoxy(10,12);
printf("New state? Press return to skip\n");
get_info(10,13,state,STATE_LEN - 1);
if (strlen(state) == 0)
   strcpy(state,list.state);

gotoxy(10,14);
printf("Zip is %s\n",list.zip);
gotoxy(10,15);
printf("New zip? Press return to skip\n");
get_info(10,16,zip,ZIP_LEN - 1);
if (strlen(zip) == 0)
   strcpy(zip,list.zip);

strcpy(key,name);

/* delete the old version */
delete_index(position,stream);
```

```
                    /* replace with new version */
                    /* to remove deleted record just added from list */
                    empty_record(&record_num,stream);

                    /* find a place for the new index */
                    find_index(key,&position,&found,stream);

                    /* store the new index */
                    replace_index(key,record_num,position,stream);

                    /* store the name, etc. */
                    if ((fseek(stream,record_num * var_size,
                                              SEEK_SET)) != 0)
                       complain();
                    fread(&list,size,1,stream);

                    strcpy(list.name,name);
                    strcpy(list.address,address);
                    strcpy(list.city,city);
                    strcpy(list.state,state);
                    strcpy(list.zip,zip);

                    if ((fseek(stream,record_num * var_size,
                                              SEEK_SET)) != 0)
                       complain();
                    fwrite(&list,size,1,stream);

                }
                else {
                   gotoxy(10,18);
                   printf("Name not found\n");
                }
                gotoxy(10,20);
                printf("Another? ");
                answer = getch();
                if (answer == 'N' || answer == 'n')
                   break;
        } /* end for */
        fclose(stream);
    }
```

```c
void delete(char dest_file [])
/* delete a record */
{
    int true = -1,
        false = 0,
        found, /* record found? */
        answer; /* reply to prompt */
    char key [KEY_LEN];
    FILE *stream; /* for list file */
    struct list list; /* record structure */
    long position; /* index entry position */

    /* open file containing mailing list */
    if ((stream = fopen(dest_file,"r+b")) == NULL) {
        putch(7); /* beep */
        gotoxy(10,24);
        printf("Unable to open file\n");
        exit(1);
    }

    for (;;) {
        clrscr();
        gotoxy(10,5);
        printf("Name to delete? ");
        key [0] = '\0';
        get_info(26,5,key,KEY_LEN - 1);

        /* default */
        found = false;

        /* is it a valid name? */
        if (strlen(key) == 0) {
            putch(7);
            gotoxy(10,20);
            printf("No name entered\n");
            pause();
            break;
        }

        /* find name in index */
        find_index(key,&position,&found,stream);
```

```
      /* report what happened */
      gotoxy(10,10);
      if (found == true) {
         delete_index(position,stream);
         printf("%s successfully deleted\n",key);
      }
      else
         printf("%s not found\n",key);

      gotoxy(10,16);
      printf("Another? ");
      answer = getch();
      if (answer == 'N' || answer == 'n')
         break;
   } /* end for */
   fclose(stream);
}

void print(char dest_file [])
/* print the file */
{
   int answer; /* reply to prompt */
   FILE *stream; /* for list file */
   struct list list; /* record structure */
   size_t size = sizeof(struct list); /* for fread and
                                          fwrite functions */
   long var_size = (long) sizeof(struct list), /* for
                                                   fseek */
       count,
       record_total; /* number of records in file */

   /* open file containing mailing list */
   if ((stream = fopen(dest_file,"r+b")) == NULL) {
      putch(7); /* beep */
      gotoxy(10,24);
      printf("Unable to open file\n");
      exit(1);
   }

   /* be sure printer is ready */
   for (;;) {
      clrscr();
```

```
        gotoxy(10,16);
        printf("Printer ready? ");
        answer = getch();
        if (answer == 'Y' || answer == 'y')
           break;
    } /* end for */

    /* get number of records in file */
    rewind(stream);
    fread(&list,size,1,stream);
    record_total = list.record_num;

    /* display all the records */
    for (count = 1L;count <= record_total;count++) {
       /* get record number from index */
       if ((fseek(stream,count * var_size,SEEK_SET)) != 0)
          complain();
       fread(&list,size,1,stream);

       /* get record */
       if ((fseek(stream,list.record_num * var_size,
                                      SEEK_SET)) != 0)
          complain();
       fread(&list,size,1,stream);

       /* print record */
       fprintf(stdprn,"%s\n\r",list.name);
       fprintf(stdprn,"%s\n\r",list.address);
       fprintf(stdprn,"%s\n\r",list.city);
       fprintf(stdprn,"%s\n\r",list.state);
       fprintf(stdprn,"%s\n\r",list.zip);
       fprintf(stdprn,"\n\r");
    }

    fclose(stream);
}

void complain(void)
/* fseek failed */
{
    putch(7); /* beep */
    gotoxy(10,24);
    printf("Unable to position file\n");
```

```
      exit(1);
   }
void complain(void); /* bug fix */



void pause(void)
/* wait for keypress */
{
   printf("Press any key to continue\n");
   getch();
}



void find_index(char key [],long *position,int *found,
                FILE *stream)
/* find location of a value or the largest value preceding
   it */
{
   size_t size = sizeof(struct list);
   int true = -1,
       false = 0;
   long var_size = (long) sizeof(struct list),
        try, /* test this value for a match */
        lowlimit = 1L, /* low end of active file area */
        highlimit; /* high end of active file area */
   struct list list; /* record structure */
   char test_key [KEY_LEN]; /* record key for comparison */

   rewind(stream);
   /* number of values presently in file */
   fread(&list,size,1,stream);
   highlimit = list.record_num;
   *found = false;

   for (;;) {
      if (highlimit == 0L) {
         *position = 0L;
         /* empty list */
         break;
      }
      for (;;) {
         /* center of remainder of list */
         try = (lowlimit + highlimit) / 2L;
```

```
                    if ((fseek(stream,try * var_size,SEEK_SET)) != 0)
                        complain();
                    fread(&list,size,1,stream);
                    strcpy(test_key,list.key);

                    if (strcmp(key,test_key) > 0) {
                        /* take high half of remainder */
                        lowlimit = try + 1L;
                    }
                    else {
                        if (strcmp(key,test_key) == 0L) {
                            /* success! */
                            *found = true;
                            *position = try;
                            break;
                        }
                        else {
                            /* key < test_key */
                            /* take low half of remainder */
                            highlimit = try - 1L;
                        }
                    }
                    /* no more remainder */
                    if (lowlimit > highlimit)
                        break;
                }
                if (*found == false) {
                    /* highest value in array preceding num */
                    *position = highlimit;
                }
                break;
            }
} /* end find_index function */


void replace_index(char key [],long record_num,
                   long position,FILE *stream)
/* move all the items in list above num up one notch */
{
    long var_size = (long) sizeof(struct list), /* for
                                                    fseek */
```

```
        temp_num,
        highlimit, /* last record in file */
        counter;
size_t size = sizeof(struct list);
struct list list; /* record structure */
char temp_key [KEY_LEN];

/* get number of records from record zero */
rewind(stream);
fread(&list,size,1,stream);
highlimit = list.record_num;

/* move all records above found item up one notch
   starting at end of file and working back to the found
   value */
for (counter = highlimit;counter >=
                              (position + 1L);counter--) {
   /* get a record */
  if ((fseek(stream,counter * var_size,SEEK_SET)) != 0)
      complain();
   fread(&list,size,1,stream);
   /* temporary save */
   strcpy(temp_key,list.key);
   temp_num = list.record_num;

   /* get following record */
   if ((fseek(stream,(counter + 1L) * var_size,
                                    SEEK_SET)) != 0)
      complain();
   fread(&list,size,1,stream);
   /* put previous record's value in this record's
      structure */
   strcpy(list.key,temp_key);
   list.record_num = temp_num;

   /* save record with new value */
   if ((fseek(stream,(counter + 1L) * var_size,
                                    SEEK_SET)) != 0)
      complain();
   fwrite(&list,size,1,stream);
}
```

```
                     /* plug new value into gap created */
                     if ((fseek(stream,(position + 1L) * var_size,
                                                     SEEK_SET)) != 0)
                        complain();
                     fread(&list,size,1,stream);
                     /* save index data */
                     strcpy(list.key,key);
                     list.record_num = record_num;

                     /* save record */
                     if ((fseek(stream,(position + 1L) * var_size,
                                                     SEEK_SET)) != 0)
                        complain();
                     fwrite(&list,size,1,stream);

                     /* increment file total */
                     highlimit++;
                     rewind(stream);
                     fread(&list,size,1,stream);
                     list.record_num = highlimit;
                     rewind(stream);
                     fwrite(&list,size,1,stream);
                  }


         void delete_index(long position,FILE *stream)
         /* store deleted node */
         {
             long var_size = (long) sizeof(struct list), /* for
                                                             fseek */
                  highlimit, /* number of records in file */
                  temp_num, /* temporary variables */
                  save_num,
                  del_len, /* number of deleted records in file */
                  counter;
             size_t size = sizeof(struct list); /* for fread and
                                                     fwrite functions */
             struct list list;
             char temp_key [KEY_LEN]; /* temporary variable */

             /* get number of records and deleted records in file */
             rewind(stream);
```

```
fread(&list,size,1,stream);
highlimit = list.record_num;
del_len = list.delete;

/* get record to be deleted */
if ((fseek(stream,position * var_size,SEEK_SET)) != 0)
    complain();
fread(&list,size,1,stream);

/* save the record number it points to so record can be
   deleted later */
save_num = list.record_num;

/* move all the records down one notch, beginning at the
   record following the one to be deleted */
for (counter = position;counter < highlimit;counter++) {
    if ((fseek(stream,(counter + 1L) * var_size,
                                        SEEK_SET)) != 0)
        complain();
    fread(&list,size,1,stream);
    /* save values to be moved */
    strcpy(temp_key,list.key);
    temp_num = list.record_num;
    /* get record to receive new values */
    if ((fseek(stream,counter * var_size,SEEK_SET)) != 0)
        complain();
    fread(&list,size,1,stream);
    /* store values from following record */
    strcpy(list.key,temp_key);
    list.record_num = temp_num;
    /* save record with new values */
    if ((fseek(stream,counter * var_size,SEEK_SET)) != 0)
        complain();
    fwrite(&list,size,1,stream);
}

/* add deleted record number to list */
rewind(stream);
fread(&list,size,1,stream);
del_len = list.delete;
/* increment total */
del_len++;
```

```
                  /* save deleted record number */
                  if ((fseek(stream,del_len * var_size,SEEK_SET)) != 0)
                     complain();
                  fread(&list,size,1,stream);
                  list.delete = save_num;
                  if ((fseek(stream,del_len * var_size,SEEK_SET)) != 0)
                     complain();
                  fwrite(&list,size,1,stream);

                  /* decrement array total and store deleted size */
                  highlimit--;
                  rewind(stream);
                  fread(&list,size,1,stream);
                  list.record_num = highlimit;
                  list.delete = del_len;
                  rewind(stream);
                  fwrite(&list,size,1,stream);
               }


         void empty_record(long *record_num,FILE *stream)
         /* get the next empty record from */
         {
             long var_size = (long) sizeof(struct list), /* for
                                                             fseek */
                  highlimit, /* number of records in file */
                  del_len; /* number of deleted records */
             size_t size = sizeof(struct list); /* for fread and
                                                    fwrite functions */
             struct list list; /* record structure */

             /* check delete file */
             rewind(stream);
             fread(&list,size,1,stream);
             highlimit = list.record_num;
             del_len = list.delete;

             if (del_len > 0L) {
                 /* there's a deleted record number we can reuse */
                 if ((fseek(stream,del_len * var_size,SEEK_SET)) != 0)
                    complain();
                 fread(&list,size,1,stream);
```

```
            /* get deleted record number */
            *record_num = list.delete;
            /* one less deleted record */
            del_len--;
            /* get record zero */
            rewind(stream);
            fread(&list,size,1,stream);
            /* store new deleted record total */
            list.delete = del_len;
            /* save new total */
            rewind(stream);
            fwrite(&list,size,1,stream);
        }
        else
            /* no deleted records available, append the new record
                to the end of the data file */
            *record_num = highlimit + 1L;
}


void clrscr(void)
/* clear the screen */
{
    union REGS regs;

    regs.h.ah = 6;                      /* bios function */
    regs.h.al = 0;                      /* clear entire screen */
    regs.h.bh = 7;                      /* normal attribute */
    regs.h.ch = 0;                      /* upper row position */
    regs.h.cl = 0;                      /* upper-left column
                                            position */
    regs.h.dh = 24;                     /* lowest row */
    regs.h.dl = 79;                     /* rightmost column */
    int86(0x10,&regs,&regs);            /* bios interrupt number */
} /* end function clear screen */



void gotoxy(int x,int y)
/* position cursor */
{

    union REGS regs;
```

```
        regs.h.ah = 2;              /* bios function */
        regs.h.dh = (char) y;       /* row */
        regs.h.dl = (char) x;       /* column */
        regs.h.bh = 0;              /* video page number */
        int86(0x10,&regs,&regs);    /* bios interrupt number */
} /* end function gotoxy */
```

This version of a mailing list is shorter and simpler but is also slower when the files get very long. (It takes time to move an average of half the index entries every time a record is added or deleted.)

DATE INDEXES

It is a simple matter to use numbers or strings in indexes. However, dates are a special case of strings. If you enter

```
10/28/34
10/28/35
11/28/34
```

and index on them, the index will be arranged in that same order because the string "10/28/35" precedes "11/28/34." But if you rearrange the date format to read

```
34/10/28
35/10/28
34/11/28
```

they will be arranged in the correct order,

```
34/10/28
34/11/28
35/10/28
```

You could also use some version of a "Julian date," which is the date coded as some large number rather than a string. One such system arranges the date as a 5-digit numeric value with the first two digits representing the last two digits of the year and the next three digits the day of the year. Thus, 87010 would be January 10, 1987, and 86032 would be February 1, 1986.

If they are to be useful, Julian dates should also provide the number of days between two dates by simple subtraction.

12

Graphs

This chapter includes three graphics examples: **a bar graph, a line graph, and a pie chart.**

BAR GRAPH

The first example shows a bar graph display that will **adjust itself,** within reason, to the data entered. **Try changing the values in** graph_data [ ]. It counts the number of bars required and scales the vertical height of the bars. Unfortunately, **the minimum size** of the vertical scale is 100 (SCALE_STEP), **and it increases in** steps of 100. The scale is divided into ten (NUM_STEPS) segments. You might wish to make this automatic **vertical scaling more versatile. Try it with my values first to see how it works.**

The example also illustrates the **use of text on the graphics** screen.

```
/* Chapter 12, Example 1, QuickC, 4/28/88
   A program to draw a bar graph with automatic sizing */

   /* set up program list including ch12_1.c and
      graphics.lib */

#include <stdio.h>
#include <stdlib.h>
#include <math.h>
#include <graph.h>
#include <conio.h>

#define SCALE_STEP 100 /* size of vertical scale step */
#define NUM_STEPS 10 /* number of vertical scale steps */
#define FUDGE_FACTOR 2 /* to make scale numbers print in
                          correct position */
#define SCREEN_ROWS 25 /* text rows on screen */

/* values to graph */
int graph_data [] = {100,200,400,300,50,250,125,50};
 /* fill mask for bar pattern */
unsigned char fill_mask [] = {0x44,0x88,0x11,0x22,0x44,0x88,
                              0x11,0x22};
```

```
/* function prototypes */
void main(void);
int set_mode(void);
void pause(void);


void main()
{

    int graphdriver, /* select highest resolution */
        counter,
        left_base, /* distance left side of graph is from
                       left side of screen */
        right_base, /* distance right side of graph is from
                       right side of screen*/
        base_hite, /* distance bottom of graph is above
                       bottom of screen */
        bar_count, /* number of values to graph */
        h_offset, /* distance from top or bottom of screen */
        v_offset, /* distance from left or right side of
                       screen */
        v_size, /* maximum value in data */
        v_scale, /* rounded-up maximum value in vertical
                     scale */
        v_pos, /* vertical position to display a vertical
                   scale number */
        scale_value, /* vertical scale value to display */
        scale_segment, /* distance between displayed vertical
                           scale value in pixels */
        scale_print, /* vertical position to print vertical
                         scale value in pixels */
        text_offset, /* to print at x,y rather than directly
                         above x,y */
        left, /* position value for left edge of bar to
                  display */
        right, /* position value for right edge of bar to
                   display */
        top, /* position value for top of bar to be
                 displayed */
        bottom, /* position value for bottom of bar to be
                    displayed */
```

```
        total_width, /* available width in pixels for entire
                        graph */
        space_width, /* width of space between bars */
        bar_width; /* width of a bar */
   float h_div; /* temp value for calculating pixels */
   char text [7]; /* for displaying scale values */
   struct videoconfig vc; /* graphics data */

   graphdriver = set_mode(); /* find graphics type */
   if (graphdriver == 0) {
      putch(7);
      printf("No graphics card\n");
      printf("Press a key to continue\n");
      getch();
      exit(1);
   }

   /* choose color */
   if (graphdriver == _HRESBW) { /* cga */
      _setbkcolor(15L); /* white lines */
      _settextcolor(15); /* white text */
   }
   else { /* ega/vga */
      _setcolor(14); /* yellow lines */
      _setbkcolor(1L); /* blue background */
      _settextcolor(14); /* yellow text */
   }

   _getvideoconfig(&vc); /* get info about graphics mode */
   _setfillmask(fill_mask); /* use this to fill bars */

   /* see variable declarations for desriptions */
   h_offset = (int) (vc.numxpixels * .05); /* adjust for
                                              aspect ratio */
   v_offset = (int) (vc.numypixels * .075); /* adjust for
                                              aspect ratio */
   base_hite = vc.numypixels - v_offset;
   left_base = h_offset;
   right_base = vc.numxpixels - h_offset;
   bar_count = sizeof(graph_data) / sizeof(int);
```

```
/* draw base line */
_moveto(left_base,base_hite);
_lineto(right_base,base_hite);

/* calculate bar width and spacing */
total_width = right_base - left_base;
h_div = (float) total_width / bar_count;
bar_width = (int) (h_div * .6);
h_div = (((float) total_width - bar_width *
                       bar_count) / (bar_count - 1));
space_width = (int) h_div / 2; /* set space between bars
                               to half of bar width */

/* calculate vertical scaling */
/* Note, this scaling works in increments of 100,
   up to 32700. You must modify for smaller or larger
   ranges. */

/* find largest data value */
v_size = 0;
for (counter = 0;counter < bar_count;counter++) {
   if (v_size < graph_data [counter])
      v_size = graph_data [counter];
}

/* calculate maximum vertical scale value in steps of
   SCALE_STEP */
v_scale = 0;
for (;;) {
   if (v_size < v_scale)
      break;
   else
   v_scale += SCALE_STEP;
}

/* get ready to print vertical scale */
/* scale step size */
scale_value = v_scale / NUM_STEPS;
/* convert vertical scale to pixels */
scale_segment = (int) ((vc.numypixels - v_offset) /
                               (NUM_STEPS + 1));
```

```
        /* so scale value appears in proper position */
        text_offset = (int) (scale_segment * .6);
        /* start number display above base line */
        v_pos = v_offset;

        /* show vertical scale values at display's left edge */
        /* first value, minimum */
        scale_print = scale_value;
        while (scale_print <= v_scale) {
           /* convert numeric value to ASCII */
           itoa(scale_print,text,10);
           /* where vertical scale value will display */
           _settextposition((vc.numypixels - v_offset +
                          text_offset - v_pos + scale_segment) *
                          SCREEN_ROWS / vc.numypixels -
                          FUDGE_FACTOR,1);
           _outtext(text); /* display number */
           v_pos += scale_segment; /* move up the screen */
           scale_print += scale_value; /* move up the screen */
        }

        /* display bars */
        for (counter = 0;counter < bar_count;counter++) {
           left = (counter * (bar_width + space_width)) +
                                              left_base;
           top = vc.numypixels - v_offset -
                      (graph_data [counter] * scale_segment /
                      scale_value);
           right = left + bar_width;
           bottom = base_hite;
           /* display a bar */
           _rectangle(_GFILLINTERIOR,left,top,right,bottom);
        }
        pause(); /* let operator see graph */
        _setvideomode(_DEFAULTMODE); /* end of demo */
}


int set_mode(void)
/* get video mode */
{
    if (_setvideomode(_HRES16COLOR))
        return(_HRES16COLOR); /* 16 color hi_res */
```

```
        if (_setvideomode(_HRESBW))
            return(_HRESBW); /* two color hi-res */
        return(0); /* no video card */
    }
    void pause(void)
    {
        _settextposition(25,1);
        _outtext("Press a key to continue");

        while (kbhit() == 0);
    }
```

LINE GRAPH

This next example is similar to the first; they share a lot of the code. Instead of bars, this example draws a line graph.

```
/* Chapter 12, Example 2, QuickC, 4/28/88
   A program to draw a line graph with automatic sizing */

    /* set up program list including ch12_2.c and
        graphics.lib */

#include <stdio.h>
#include <stdlib.h>
#include <math.h>
#include <graph.h>
#include <conio.h>

#define SCALE_STEP 100 /* size of vertical scale steps */
#define NUM_STEPS 10 /* number of steps in vertical scale */
#define FUDGE_FACTOR 2 /* to make scale numbers print in
                            correct position */
#define SCREEN_ROWS 25 /* text rows on screen */

/* values to graph */
int graph_data [] = {100,200,400,300,50,250,125,50};

/* function prototypes */
void main(void);
```

```
int set_mode(void);
void pause(void);


void main()
{

    int graphdriver, /* select highest resolution */
        counter,
        left_base, /* distance left side of graph is from
                        left side of screen */
        right_base, /* distance right side of graph is from
                        right side of screen*/
        base_hite, /* distance bottom of graph is above
                        bottom of screen */
        point_count, /* number of values to graph */
        h_offset, /* distance from top or bottom of screen */
        v_offset, /* distance from left or right side of
                        screen */
        v_size, /* maximum value in data */
        v_scale, /* rounded-up maximum value in vertical
                        scale */
        v_pos, /* vertical position to display a vertical
                        scale number */
        scale_value, /* vertical scale value to display */
        scale_segment, /* distance between displayed vertical
                            scale value in pixels */
        scale_print, /* vertical position to print vertical
                            scale value in pixels */
        text_offset, /* to print at x,y rather than directly
                            above x,y */
        horizontal, /* horizontal position value for point to
                        display */
        vertical, /* vertical position value for point to be
                        displayed */
        total_width; /* available width in pixels for entire
                        graph */
    float h_div; /* horizontal distance in pixels between
                        points */
    char text [7]; /* for displaying scale values */
    struct videoconfig vc; /* graphics display data */
```

```
graphdriver = set_mode(); /* find graphics type */
if (graphdriver == 0) {
   putch(7);
   printf("No graphics card\n");
   printf("Press a key to continue\n");
   getch();
   exit(1);
}

/* choose color */
if (graphdriver == _HRESBW) { /* cga */
   _setbkcolor(15L); /* white lines */
   _settextcolor(15); /* white text */
}
else { /* ega/vga */
   _setcolor(14); /* yellow lines */
   _setbkcolor(1L); /* blue background */
   _settextcolor(14); /* yellow text */
}

_getvideoconfig(&vc); /* get info about graphics mode */

/* see variable declarations for descriptions */
h_offset = (int) (vc.numxpixels * .05); /* adjust for
                                           aspect ratio */
v_offset = (int) (vc.numypixels * .075); /* adjust for
                                            aspect ratio */
base_hite = vc.numypixels - v_offset;
left_base = h_offset;
right_base = vc.numxpixels - h_offset;
point_count = sizeof(graph_data) / sizeof(int);


/* draw base line */
_moveto(left_base,base_hite);
_lineto(right_base,base_hite);

/* calculate horizontal scaling */
total_width = right_base - left_base;
h_div = (float) (total_width / point_count);
```

```
/* calculate vertical scaling */
/* Note, this scaling works in increments of 100,
   up to 32700. You must modify for smaller or larger
   ranges. */
v_size = 0;

/* find largest data value */
for (counter = 0;counter < point_count;counter++) {
   if (v_size < graph_data [counter])
      v_size = graph_data [counter];
}
/* calculate maximum vertical scale value in steps of
   SCALE_STEP */
v_scale = 0;
for (;;) {
   if (v_size < v_scale)
      break;
   else
   v_scale += SCALE_STEP;
}

/* get ready to print vertical scale */
/* vertical scale divisions */
scale_value = v_scale / NUM_STEPS;
scale_segment = (int) ((vc.numypixels - v_offset) /
                                      (NUM_STEPS + 1));
text_offset = (int) (scale_segment * .6);
/* start number display above base line */
v_pos = v_offset;

/* display vertical scale */
scale_print = scale_value; /* minimum value */
while (scale_print <= v_scale) {
   /* convert numeric value to ASCII */
   itoa(scale_print,text,10);
   /* set position to display current scale value */
   _settextposition(((vc.numypixels - v_offset +
                  text_offset - v_pos + scale_segment) *
                  SCREEN_ROWS / vc.numypixels -
                  FUDGE_FACTOR,1);
   _outtext(text); /* display number */
```

```
            v_pos += scale_segment; /* move up the screen */
            scale_print += scale_value; /* move up the screen */
      }

      /* display lines */
      /* first graph position */
      horizontal = left_base;
      /* vertical position */
      vertical = vc.numypixels - v_offset - (graph_data [0] *
                                 scale_segment / scale_value);
      /* starting position */
      _moveto(horizontal,vertical);
      /* mark the point */
      _ellipse( GBORDER,horizontal - 2,vertical - 1,
                                 horizontal + 2,vertical + 1);
      /* draw the remaining lines and points */
      for (counter = 1;counter < point_count;counter++) {
         /* horizontal position of next line ending */
         horizontal = (int) (counter * h_div) + left_base;
         /* vertical position of end of line */
         vertical = vc.numypixels - v_offset -
                                 (graph_data [counter] *
                                 scale_segment / scale_value);
         /* draw the line */
         _lineto(horizontal,vertical); /* display point */
         /* mark the point */
         _ellipse( GBORDER,horizontal - 2,vertical - 1,
                                 horizontal + 2,vertical + 1);
      }
      pause(); /* let operator see graph */
      _setvideomode( DEFAULTMODE); /* end of demo */
}

int set_mode(void)
/* get video mode */
{
   if (_setvideomode( HRES16COLOR))
      return( HRES16COLOR); /* 16 color hi-res */
   if (_setvideomode( HRESBW))
      return( HRESBW); /* two color hi-res */
   return(0); /* no video card */
}
```

```
void pause(void)
{
   _settextposition(25,1);
   _outtext("Press a key to continue");

      while (kbhit() == 0);
}
```

PIE CHART

The final graphics example displays a pie chart.

```
/* Chapter 12, Example 3, QuickC, 4/29/88
   A program to draw a pie chart */

   /* set up program list including ch12_3.c and
      graphics.lib */

#include <stdio.h>
#include <stdlib.h>
#include <math.h>
#include <graph.h>
#include <conio.h>

#define SCREEN_HEIGHT 3 /* normal monitor screen size */
#define SCREEN_WIDTH 4  /* ratio for aspect ratio */
#define CIRCLE_SIZE 300  /* in pixels */

/* values to graph */
int graph_data [] = {100,200,400,300,50,250,125,50};

/* function prototypes */
void main(void);
int set_mode(void);
void pause(void);


void main()
{
```

```
int graphdriver, /* select highest resolution */
    counter,
    temp, /* used as temp variable when summing graph
            value */
    h_start, /* first radius horizontal position */
    v_start, /* first radius vertical position */
    h_location, /* first side of wedge horizontal
                  position */
    v_location, /* first side of wedge vertical
                  position */
    current_size, /* running total of data graphed so
                    far */
    space_used, /* distance around framing square used so
                  far */
    next_location, /* used to determine next_h_position &
                     next_v_position */
    next_h_location, /* second side of wedge horizontal
                       position */
    next_v_location, /* second side of wedge vertical
                       position */
    left, /* distance left side of graph is from left
            side of screen */
    right, /* distance right side of graph is from left
             side of screen*/
    top, /* distance top of graph is below top of
           screen */
    bottom, /* distance bottom of graph is below top nf
              screen */
    wedge_count, /* number of values to graph */
    h_center, /* distance from top or bottom of screen */
    v_center; /* distance from left or right side of
                 screen */
float arc_value, /* graph data value conversion factor */
      aspect_ratio; /* amount vertical lines must be
                      shrunk to match horizontal sizes */
struct videoconfig vc; /* graphics format info */

graphdriver = set_mode(); /* find graphics type */
if (graphdriver == 0) {
    putch(7);
    printf("No graphics card");
    printf("Press a key to continue");
```

```
        getch();
        exit(1);
    }

    /* choose color */
    if (graphdriver == _HRESBW) { /* cga */
        _setbkcolor(15L); /* white lines */
        _settextcolor(15); /* white text */
    }
    else { /* ega/vga */
        _setcolor(14); /* yellow lines */
        _setbkcolor(1L); /* blue background */
        _settextcolor(14); /* yellow text */
    }

    /* get info about chosen graphics mode */
    _getvideoconfig(&vc);

    /* see variable declarations for descriptions */
    aspect_ratio = (float) (SCREEN_WIDTH * vc.numypixels) /
                   (float) (SCREEN_HEIGHT * vc.numxpixels);
    h_center= (int) (vc.numxpixels / 2);
    /* add vertical offset because of aspect ratio */
    v_center = (int) ((vc.numypixels / 2) +
                          (vc.numypixels * aspect_ratio));
    top = v_center - CIRCLE_SIZE / 2;
    left = h_center - CIRCLE_SIZE / 2;
    bottom = v_center + CIRCLE_SIZE / 2;
    right = h_center + CIRCLE_SIZE / 2;
    wedge_count = sizeof(graph_data) / sizeof(int);

    /* value/arc pixel ratio */
    temp = 0;
    /* total graph values */
    for (counter = 0;counter < wedge_count;counter++)
        temp += graph_data [counter];
    /* graph value to pixel conversion factor */
    arc_value = ((float) (CIRCLE_SIZE * 4) / temp);

    /* display graph */
    /* see desriptions of variables given earlier */
    h_start = h_center;
```

```
v_start = top;
h_location = h_start;
v_location = v_start;
current_size = 0;
space_used = 0;
/* draw all but the last pie slice */
/* the last value should equal the pie space remaining */
for (counter = 0;counter < (wedge_count - 1);counter++) {
   /* convert graph data to pixels and add to previous
      position */
   next_location = (int) (graph_data [counter] *
                                 arc_value) + current_size;
   /* keep track of framing square perimeter used */
   current_size = next_location;
   /* desired next horizontal position */
   next_location = h_start + current_size;
   /* current vertical position */
   next_v_location = v_start;
   /* tentative next_h_position if next if not true */
   next_h_location = next_location;
   if (next_location > right) {
      /* ran out of room on top of framing square,
         need to turn corner */
      /* amount of perimeter used so far */
      space_used = (right - h_center);
      /* current horizontal position */
      next_h_location = right;
      /* desired next vertical position */
      next_location = current_size - space_used;
      /* tentative next_v_position if next if not true */
      next_v_location = top + next_location;
      if (next_location > (bottom - top)) {
         /* ran out of room on right side of framing
            square, need to turn corner */
         /* current vertical position */
         next_v_location = bottom;
         /* amount of perimeter used so far */
         space_used += (bottom - top);
         /* desired next horizontal position */
         next_location = current_size - space_used;
         /* tentative next_h_position if next if not
            true */
```

```
                next_h_location = right - next_location;
                if (next_location > (right - left)) {
                    /* ran out of room on bottom of framing
                       square, need to turn corner */
                    /* current horizontal position */
                    next_h_location = left;
                    /* amount of perimeter used so far */
                    space_used += (right - left);
                    /* desired next vertical position */
                    next_location = current_size - space_used;
                    /* tentative next_v_position if next if not
                       true */
                    next_v_location = bottom - next_location;
                    if (next_location > (bottom - top)) {
                        /* ran out of room on left side of framing
                           square, need to turn corner */
                        /* current vertical position */
                        next_v_location = top;
                        /* amount of perimeter used so far */
                        space_used += (bottom - top);
                        /* desired next horizontal position */
                        next_location = current_size - space_used;
                        /* next horizontal position */
                        next_h_location = left + next_location;
                    }
                }
            }
        }
        /* draw the pie */
        _pie(_GBORDER,left,(int) (top * aspect_ratio),
                right,(int) (bottom * aspect_ratio),
                h_location,(int) (v_location * aspect_ratio),
                next_h_location,(int) (next_v_location *
                aspect_ratio));
        /* save new locations */
        h_location = next_h_location;
        v_location = next_v_location;
    }
    pause(); /* let operator see graph */
    _setvideomode(_DEFAULTMODE); /* end of demo */
}
```

```
int set_mode(void)
/* get video mode */
{
    if (_setvideomode(_HRES16COLOR))
        return(_HRES16COLOR); /* 16 color hi-res */
    if (_setvideomode(_HRESBW))
        return(_HRESBW); /* two color hi-res */
    return(0); /* no video card */
}



void pause(void)
{
    _settextposition(25,1);
    _outtext("Press a key to continue");

    /* loop while waiting for a keypress */
    while (kbhit() == 0);
}
```

Because the trigonometry functions are not available in the standard QC library, I used a different method of calculating the pie segment endpoints. I converted the complete circle size (360 degrees) to pixels around the framing square by dividing the perimeter of the square by 360. I then used this pixel value multiplied by the graph values to position the endpoints. As I ran out of room along each edge, I turned the corners around the perimeter. This method seems to give an accurate representation of the values.

It would have been nice if the developers had used the more natural degree or radian value to size the pie slices. That would have made this program a great deal easier to write.

A

Programs Where Functions Appear

FUNCTION LIST

FUNCTION LIST

Chapter 10, Example 4
Chapter 11, Example 1
Chapter 11, Example 2
Chapter 12, Example 1
Chapter 12, Example 2
Chapter 12, Example 3

fclose( )
Chapter 3, Example 1
Chapter 3, Example 3
Chapter 4, Example 1
Chapter 4, Example 2
Chapter 5, Example 2
Chapter 6, Example 2
Chapter 7, Example 1
Chapter 7, Example 2
Chapter 7, Example 3
Chapter 8, Example 6
Chapter 8, Example 8
Chapter 9, Example 2
Chapter 9, Example 4
Chapter 11, Example 1
Chapter 11, Example 2

filelength( )
Chapter 3, Example 1
Chapter 4, Example 2
Chapter 7, Example 2

fileno( )
Chapter 3, Example 1
Chapter 4, Example 2
Chapter 7, Example 2
Chapter 10, Example 2

fopen( )
Chapter 3, Example 1
Chapter 3, Example 3
Chapter 4, Example 1
Chapter 4, Example 2
Chapter 5, Example 2

fseek( )
Chapter 4, Example 1
Chapter 4, Example 2
Chapter 5, Example 2
Chapter 7, Example 3
Chapter 8, Example 6
Chapter 8, Example 8
Chapter 9, Example 2
Chapter 9, Example 4
Chapter 10, Example 2
Chapter 11, Example 1
Chapter 11, Example 2

fwrite( )
Chapter 3, Example 3
Chapter 4, Example 1
Chapter 5, Example 2
Chapter 6, Example 2
Chapter 7, Example 1
Chapter 7, Example 2
Chapter 7, Example 3
Chapter 8, Example 6
Chapter 8, Example 8
Chapter 9, Example 2
Chapter 9, Example 4
Chapter 10, Example 2
Chapter 11, Example 1
Chapter 11, Example 2

getch( )
Chapter 2, Example 4
Chapter 2, Example 5
Chapter 3, Example 1
Chapter 4, Example 2
Chapter 9, Example 3
Chapter 9, Example 4
Chapter 11, Example 1
Chapter 11, Example 2
Chapter 12, Example 1
Chapter 12, Example 2
Chapter 12, Example 3

_pie( )
Chapter 12, Example 3
′
printf( )
Chapter 1, Example 1
Chapter 1, Example 2
Chapter 1, Example 3
Chapter 1, Example 4
Chapter 1, Example 5
Chapter 2, Example 1
Chapter 2, Example 2
Chapter 2, Example 3
Chapter 2, Example 4
Chapter 2, Example 5
Chapter 3, Example 1
Chapter 3, Example 2
Chapter 3, Example 3
Chapter 4, Example 1
Chapter 4, Example 2
Chapter 5, Example 1
Chapter 5, Example 2
Chapter 5, Example 3
Chapter 5, Example 4
Chapter 5, Example 5
Chapter 5, Example 6
Chapter 5, Example 7
Chapter 6, Example 1
Chapter 6, Example 2
Chapter 6, Example 3
Chapter 7, Example 1
Chapter 7, Example 2
Chapter 7, Example 3
Chapter 8, Example 1
Chapter 8, Example 2
Chapter 8, Example 3
Chapter 8, Example 4
Chapter 8, Example 5
Chapter 8, Example 6
Chapter 8, Example 7
Chapter 8, Example 8
Chapter 8, Example 9
Chapter 9, Example 1

Chapter 9, Example 2
Chapter 9, Example 3
Chapter 9, Example 4
Chapter 9, Example 5
Chapter 10, Example 1
Chapter 10, Example 2
Chapter 10, Example 3
Chapter 10, Example 4
Chapter 11, Example 1
Chapter 11, Example 2
Chapter 12, Example 1
Chapter 12, Example 2
Chapter 12, Example 3

putch( )
Chapter 1, Example 1
Chapter 1, Example 2
Chapter 1, Example 3
Chapter 1, Example 4
Chapter 1, Example 5
Chapter 2, Example 1
Chapter 2, Example 2
Chapter 2, Example 3
Chapter 2, Example 4
Chapter 2, Example 5
Chapter 3, Example 1
Chapter 3, Example 2
Chapter 3, Example 3
Chapter 4, Example 1
Chapter 4, Example 2
Chapter 5, Example 2
Chapter 6, Example 2
Chapter 7, Example 1
Chapter 7, Example 2
Chapter 7, Example 3
Chapter 8, Example 6
Chapter 8, Example 8
Chapter 8, Example 9
Chapter 9, Example 2
Chapter 9, Example 3
Chapter 9, Example 4
Chapter 9, Example 5

Chapter 1, Example 4
Chapter 1, Example 5
Chapter 2, Example 1
Chapter 2, Example 2
Chapter 2, Example 3
Chapter 2, Example 4
Chapter 2, Example 5
Chapter 3, Example 1
Chapter 3, Example 2
Chapter 3, Example 3
Chapter 4, Example 1
Chapter 4, Example 2
Chapter 5, Example 7
Chapter 7, Example 1
Chapter 7, Example 2
Chapter 7, Example 3
Chapter 8, Example 6
Chapter 8, Example 8
Chapter 9, Example 2
Chapter 9, Example 4
Chapter 10, Example 1
Chapter 10, Example 2
Chapter 10, Example 3
Chapter 10, Example 4
Chapter 11, Example 1
Chapter 11, Example 2

strlen( )
Chapter 1, Example 1
Chapter 1, Example 2
Chapter 1, Example 3
Chapter 1, Example 4
Chapter 1, Example 5
Chapter 2, Example 1
Chapter 2, Example 2
Chapter 2, Example 3
Chapter 2, Example 4
Chapter 2, Example 5
Chapter 3, Example 2
Chapter 3, Example 3
Chapter 4, Example 1
Chapter 10, Example 1

INDEX

NOTES

NOTES

NOTES

NOTES

NOTES

NOTES